Memoirs of Sarah Duchess of Marlborough, and of the Court of Queen Anne
Volume 1

Memoirs of Sarah Duchess of Marlborough, and of the Court of Queen Anne
Volume 1

A. T. Thomson

*Memoirs of Sarah Duchess of Marlborough,
and of the Court of Queen Anne
Volume 1*
by A. T. Thomson

First published under the title
*Memoirs of Sarah Duchess of Marlborough,
and of the Court of Queen Anne
Volume 1*

Leonaur is an imprint
of Oakpast Ltd

Copyright in this form © 2010 Oakpast Ltd

ISBN: 978-0-85706-140-9(hardcover)
ISBN: 978-0-85706-139-3 (softcover)

http://www.leonaur.com

Publisher's Notes

In the interests of authenticity, the spellings, grammar and place names used have been retained from the original editions.

The opinions of the authors represent a view of events in which she was a participant related from her own perspective,
as such the text is relevant as an historical document.

The views expressed in this book are not necessarily those of the publisher.

Contents

Introduction	7
Her Parentage	19
Court of Charles II	37
State of Manners and Morals	55
Surrender of the Crown to William	75
State of the British Court	89
Attachment of Marlborough to his wife	102
Disgrace of Lord Marlborough	112
Release of Marlborough from Prison	140
Appointment of Marlborough	157
Illness and Deathbed of William	173
Efforts of Lady Marlborough	182
Dissatisfaction of the Countess of Marlborough	204
Dangers Which Beset Marlborough	215
Death of the Marquis of Blandford	234
Costume and Manners	245
Appendix	257

Introduction

Had the subject of this *Memoir* lived in the present day, copious accounts of the part which she performed in public life would have instantly been given to the world. Her domestic habits, and her merits and demerits of every description, would have been amply discussed. With her personal qualities we should, from a thousand channels, have been familiarised. Every peculiarity of her resolute and singular character would have been unveiled to the inspection of an inquisitive and amused public: nor would there have been wanting those who would have eagerly grasped at such an opportunity of commenting upon the politics, manners, and events of the day, as that which the biography of the Duchess of Marlborough affords.

It is, nevertheless, a fact, that ninety-six years have elapsed since the death of this celebrated woman, (*since original production*), and, as yet, no complete account of her singular career, no memoirs of her as a private individual, of any length, or of any importance in other respects, have appeared; and it is remarkable, that both the Duke and Duchess of Marlborough, two persons who acquired in their lifetime as great a share of celebrity as any British subjects ever enjoyed, incurred a risk of not being commemorated, after their decease, by any connected and adequate work.

The biography of John Duke of Marlborough, undertaken by three individuals, was completed only by Lediard, who had served under the hero of Blenheim, and who may be supposed to have felt a sort of personal interest in his illustrious career. The coldness of those to whom the task was deputed, recommended as it was to their zealous attention by the promise of a considerable sum to forward its completion, proves how feebly the public called for such a production. It was not until the Duchess was on her deathbed that she began to arrange the voluminous materials of the life of her husband. It was not until two years before her death that she published her own *Vindication*, which she entitled *An Account of the Conduct of the Dowager Duchess of Marlborough, from her first coming to Court, to the year 1610.*

This book, published in 1742, after provoking several replies, fell into a partial oblivion. The animadversions and discussions to which it gave rise, and the contemptuous opinion pronounced upon it by Horace Walpole, whose fiat in the fashionable world was decisive, have therefore remained unanswered. Garbled as it was, it is yet a work replete with ability, carrying a conviction of the sincerity of its authoress, and unfolding the motives by which she was actuated, with force and clearness. The following extract will afford the reader an opportunity to form a judgement of the *Vindication* by the Preface to the Duchess's narrative. The just and noble sentiments which she expresses upon the acquisition of a good name, and likewise upon posthumous reputation, must prepossess the mind strongly in favour of that which is to follow these sound and well-expressed motives of action.

> I have been often told that there is a sort of philosophy, by which people have brought themselves to be indifferent, not only whether they be at all remembered after death, but whether, in case their names should survive them, they be mentioned with praise or infamy. If this be really a point of wisdom, it is infinitely beyond my reach; and I shall own further, that it seems to me too refined and sublimed to be attained by anybody who has not first got rid of the prejudices of common sense and common honesty, will not pretend to say that the passion for fame may not sometimes be excessive, and deservedly the subject of ridicule.
>
> But surely, my lord, there never was a single instance of a person of true honour, who was willing to be spoken of, either during life or after it, as a betrayer of his country or his friend; and I am persuaded that your lordship must have observed, that all those who, at this day, declare themselves wholly careless about what the world, or the circle of their acquaintance, will say of them when they are dead, are quite as unconcerned to *deserve* a good character while they live.
>
> For my own part, I frankly confess to you, and to the world, that whatever vanity or weakness the ambition of a good name may be thought, either by philosophers or by ministers of state, to imply, I have ever felt some degree of that ambition from the moment I could distinguish between good and evil. My chief

aim (if I have any acquaintance with my own heart) has been, both in public and private life, to deserve approbation: but I have never been without an earnest desire to *have* it, too, both living and dead, from the wise and virtuous.

My lord, this passion has led me to take more pains than you would easily imagine. It has sometimes carried me beyond the sphere to which the men have thought proper, and, perhaps, generally speaking, with good reason, to confine our sex. I have been a kind of author. About forty years ago, having understood that the wife of the late Bishop Burnet, a lady whom I greatly esteemed, had received unfavourable impressions of me, on account of the unhappy differences between Queen Mary and her sister, I wrote a faithful narrative of that affair purely to satisfy that one person.

And when, after my dismissal from Queen Anne's service, I perceived how industriously malice was employed in inventing calumnies to load me with, I drew up an account of my conduct in the several offices I had filled under Her Majesty. This piece I intended to publish immediately, but was dissuaded from it by a person (of great eminence at this day) whom I thought my friend. I have since imagined that he had, by instinct, an aversion to *accounting*. It was said, as a reason for deferring the publication of my Account, that prejudice and passion were grown too violent and stormy for the voice of reason to be heard, but that those would, after some time, subside, and that the truth then brought to light would unavoidably prevail. I followed the advice with the less reluctance, as being conscious of the power of an easy vindication, whenever my patience should be pushed to extremity.

After this I set myself another task, to which I was partly urged by the injustice, and I may say ingratitude, of the Whigs. It was to give an account of my conduct with regard to parties, and of the successful artifice of Mr. Harley and Mrs. Masham, in taking advantage of the Queen's passion for what she called *the church,* to undermine me in her affections. In this undertaking I had the assistance of a friend to whom I furnished materials. Some parts of the work were of my own composition, being such passages as nobody but myself could relate with exactness. This was not originally intended to be published until after my death.

But, my lord, as I am now drawing near my end, and very soon there will remain nothing of me but a *name*, I am desirous, under the little capacity which age and infirmities have left me for other enjoyments, to have the satisfaction, before I die, of seeing that *name* (which, from the station I have held in the great world, must unavoidably survive me,) in possession of what was only designed it for a legacy.

From this desire I have caused the several pieces above mentioned to be connected together, and thrown into the form into which I now venture to address them to your lordship. They may possibly be of some use towards correcting the folly and injustice of those who, in order to judge of the conduct of others, begin with forming to themselves characters of them, upon slight and idle reports, and then make such characters the rule by which they admit or reject whatever they afterwards hear concerning them.

If any such happy effect as this might reasonably be hoped from the perusal of these papers, I should be far from making any apology for offering them to your lordship; I would not call it *troubling* your lordship with them. No, my lord, you will not esteem it a *trouble* to read them, even though you should judge them useless for the purpose I have mentioned. The friendship you favour me with will make you find a particular satisfaction in this justification of my injured character to the world. And I imagine that there is no honest mind, how much so ever it may chance to be prejudiced against me, but will feel something of the same pleasure in being undeceived.

The original letters, of which, either in whole or in part, the copies will be here found, I have directed to be preserved in my family as incontestable vouchers of the truth of what I am going to relate.

The works which this *Account* very soon elicited, in reply to its able strictures upon persons and things, are enumerated in those chapters of this work which relate particularly to the scurrilous attacks from which the Duke and Duchess perpetually suffered. The latter, indeed, lived too short a period after her *Account of her Conduct* appeared, to refute the misstatements which were circulated in various pamphlets, and by other works of ephemeral celebrity. It was, perhaps, for the best, that an opportunity of acrimonious retaliation was not afforded to one who was apt, to use her own expression, to "tumble out her mind" in a manner not always either very decorous, nor very gratifying to her hearers. Those who recommended the Duchess to postpone her work were doubtless well acquainted with her peculiarities, and dreaded the violence of that explosion which must ensue. It was, probably, the wish of her friends and relations, as it is said to have been their expectation, that the Vindication should be posthumous.

The Duchess of Marlborough, in addition to her own powerful efforts, had the good fortune also to be defended by the pen of the celebrated Henry Fielding. It must, however, be acknowledged, that possibly the defence of the great novelist was not disinterested. Fielding wrote, as it is well known, many fugitive political tracts, for which he was accused of venality, and it was generally understood that they were remunerated by the party whom he espoused. It is extremely probable that a man disposed to make his talents profitable may not have been ashamed to vindicate the conduct of the wealthy and powerful Duchess, for a consideration; and there were circumstances in the family of Fielding which confirm the supposition. His father, Edward Fielding, served under the Duke of Marlborough; and his sister Sarah, the accomplished friend of Bishop Hoadly, had, through that medium, ample opportunities of introducing her brother to the Duchess.

The work which Fielding published in 1742, was entitled *A Full Vindication of the Dowager Duchess of Marlborough, both with regard to the Account lately published by her Grace, and to her Character in general; against the base and malicious invectives contained in a late scurrilous pamphlet, entitled 'Remarks on the Account,' &c. In a Letter to the noble Author of those Remarks.*

The Duchess had been dead nearly two years, when an anonymous biography, concise and meagre, entitled *The Life of Sarah Duchess of Marlborough*, was published in 1745. This small volume, for into one small volume in those days was the long life of the departed Duchess compressed, has every appearance of being written by a person amicable to the Duchess, although not in her confidence; no original letters are introduced, and the anecdotes of the Duchess, which are given, though favourable, are not so voluminous as those which one might glean in an hour, in the present day, from newspapers. The Life was, in all probability, according to the custom of the Duchess, ordered and paid for by her; perhaps the task was remunerated whilst she was alive; but, from the coldness with which it is written, it was probably completed after her death.

This little book has hitherto constituted the sole biography of Sarah Duchess of Marlborough. Her own Vindication commences and ends with her court life, and its title-page distinctly states it to be *An Account of the Conduct of the Dowager Duchess of Marlborough, from her first coming to Court to the year 1710. In a letter from herself to my Lord* ——. The name of this favoured nobleman, Earl Cholmondeley, has been supplied by Sir John Dalrymple in his manuscript notes on the work entitled the *Opinions of the Duchess of Marlborough*.

With such scanty materials for a foundation, those who are disposed to read the work of which this Introduction forms a portion, might naturally dread that many of its details must be gleaned from report, supported by questionable authority. Fortunately, however, the Duchess, among other precise and valuable habits, had a custom, not only of preserving every letter that she had received, but of describing its contents in her own peculiar terms on each epistle.

During her residence abroad with the Duke, after their reverse of favour, she composed, also, an elaborate justification of herself, in the form of a letter to Mr. Hutchinson; a narrative which supplies ample materials for compiling that period of her life to which it relates. She likewise prepared other statements, which, with her letter to Mr. Hutchinson, she was persuaded, as she says, by her friends, not to publish, until a very long time after the events to which they related were almost forgotten by the world. These she framed afterwards into the Account of her Conduct, leaving out, as Horace Walpole declared upon report, and as subsequent investigations have manifested, the most pungent, and of course the most interesting, portion of her communications.

A great portion of the Duchesses narrative having been delivered in conversation to Hooke, the historian whom she employed to make the book intelligible, the most characteristic portion of the Account, which was suppressed by the prudence of Hooke, is of course wholly lost. In the materials which the Duchess collected to form the volume, many minute particulars which were not deemed worthy of insertion in the Account, are, however, preserved; and it has been the good fortune of the authoress of these *Memoirs* to supply, in some instances, the garbled passages from the Duchess's papers, and to restore to the Vindication the Duchesses own language; those expressive and happy phrases which, as the reader will perceive, described her own sentiments, and portrayed the characters of others, in a manner that no dispassionate historian could imitate.

Of such papers as were deemed fit for publication by the Marlborough and Spencer families. Archdeacon Coxe, in compiling his elaborate *Life of John Duke of Marlborough*, had the free use, with the privilege of making copies. In the able work of this indefatigable historian he availed himself, in some measure, of most of these valuable materials; but in the progress of his heavy task, he never forgot that he was compiling a biography of the Duke, not the Duchess, of Marlborough; that he was dealing with the enterprises, the treaties, the opinions, and the projects, of men, and not with the intrigues, the foibles, the feelings, and the quarrels of women. He has, therefore, but rarely, and incidentally, referred to the Duchess of Marlborough: hastening from the subject, as if he indeed feared that her formidable spirit might be recalled by the expressions of disapproval which he cautiously bestows upon her, by the hints which he gives of her temper, and the conclusion to which he fails not to lead the reader, that she was the source of all the Duke's disappointments and reverses.

This determination on the part of the Archdeacon, and the manifest prejudice which he had imbibed against the Duchess of Marlborough, may readily be traced, by those who are induced to examine the manuscripts which were placed in the Museum by the executors of Dr. Coxe. These papers, which formed, in part, the materials for the Life of the great General, and also for the Duchess's "*Account*," are extremely interesting, and afford a satisfactory basis for a memoir. They contain, amongst other documents, many private letters, from which a selection has been already published, with great success, under the title of *Private Correspondence of the Duchess of Marlborough*. They comprise also, not only a mass of papers relating to the Duke's continental and political affairs, but a discussion upon the reasons for the dismissal of Lord Godolphin, the mode in which it was effected by Queen Anne, some curious correspondence relative to the building of Blenheim, the letters of Lord Coningsby to the Duchess, and her grace's long and reiterated remonstrances with the Treasury upon various topics, passages of which develop more of her character than long pages of description could unfold.

These documents arrived at the manuscript office of the British Museum in a state of the greatest confusion, rendering it almost surprising that they had been preserved at all. By the industry and judgement of Mr. Holmes, they have been carefully arranged, in a manner well adapted to lighten the task of examining manuscripts, always, be the writing ever so legible, more or less laborious. To them, many of the details, and much of the interest, which the second volume of this work may perhaps be found to possess, are to be attributed. An author may augur somewhat confidently of interesting and pleasing a reading public, when he can make his principal characters speak for themselves.

Without the aid of these manuscripts, the *Memoirs* of the Duchess would not have had the character of originality to which, in some degree, it is presumed, they may aspire. It is curious that in many instances the Authoress has found it desirable to extract from these documents the very passages which Dr. Coxe had most carefully rejected. In the few memorials of the Duchess to which he has referred in his work, he has passed his pen across all lively observations, as irrelevant, all detail, however illustrative of her character, as unnecessary. Everything that could cheer the reader during the recital of vexatious politics, and after the enumeration of battles, was discarded, or discussed briefly.

Such are some of the sources from which information for these *Memoirs* has been gleaned. The published works which have been consulted, were selected without any reference to their political bias. The merits of those famous questions which agitated this country in the reigns of James the Second, William, and Anne, have been so fully and ably treated in the histories of Dalrymple, Macpherson, Cunningham, Somerville, Swift, and by many other writers, that it would be presumptuous, inadequate to the task as the Authoress considers herself, to revive such discussions. The aim of this work is chiefly to develop private history, connecting it, by general remarks, with the leading events of the day. From a sense of her own incompetency, the Authoress has, therefore, abstained as much as possible from political discussions; conceiving also, that to the generality of readers, it is a relief to escape from subjects which provoke controversy, and to retire into the private sphere of life, where the contemplation of character, and the investigation of motives, become chiefly interesting.

These *Memoirs*, although they aspire not to the dignity of history, must, however, necessarily embrace various themes, and comprise descriptions of public men. The Authoress has endeavoured, in all that she has had to perform, to regard justice and moderation as her guides; to draw her portraits from the most approved sources, discarding all considerations of party, until the outlines were traced, and the colours filled in. The ferment of political strife which impeded important business, and disgraced society in the reign of Anne, subsiding during the reign of her successor and his son, is revived amongst us; and the similarity of those great topics which then came before parliament, to those which have, of late years, engaged our legislators, cannot but be obvious to such persons as are conversant with our annals.

It is singular that a degree of uncertainty prevails both with respect to the birthplace of the Duchess of Marlborough, and with regard to the place of her grace's decease. Neither is there any record in the possession of her descendants which supplies us with an account of her last moments. Regarding this important point, the Authoress applied both to his Grace the Duke of Marlborough and to Earl Spencer for information. To her inquiries, a prompt, but unsatisfactory reply was returned by the Duke of Marlborough; namely, that he had, in compliance with the Authoress's request, examined such documents as he possessed, relating to the Duchess of Marlborough; but that the search had been fruitless, as far as any account whatsoever of her death was concerned.

His Grace expressed also uncertainty respecting the spot where his celebrated ancestor breathed her last, but stated that he believed it to have been at Holywell. To Earl Spencer a similar application was made. His lordship answered, almost in the same terms as the Duke of Marlborough, that every paper relative to the Duchess which was fit for publication had been published, and that there was nothing in such as were not deemed proper for publication, relating in any way to her last hours.

It appears singular that there should have been no record preserved, among her numerous grandchildren and relatives, of the decline and death of one who had played so conspicuous a part in life as the Duchess of Marlborough. Perhaps this deficiency may be accounted for by the dissensions which divided the Duchess from her grandchildren, more particularly Charles Duke of Marlborough, her grandson, and from his Duchess, the daughter of her enemy, Lord Trevor. On the other hand, her favourite and heir, the honourable John Spencer, was one of those reckless beings who are not likely to dwell with much attention upon the deathbed of an aged relative. With respect to the belief entertained by the present Duke, though not, as his grace expresses it, with any certainty, that the Duchess died at Holywell, the Authoress has only to offer the opposing testimony of the work before alluded to, namely, the *Life of Sarah Duchess of Marlborough,* which states that she died at the Friary, St. James's, Marlborough-house.

There is much presumptive evidence in favour of this statement. Almost to her latest hour, as may be seen in the Coxe Manuscripts, the

Duchess was in correspondence with Mr. Scrope, secretary to Mr. Pelham, who, in one of his letters, begs the honour of an interview, and names an evening. This occurred about four days before the Duchess's demise. Now it is not probable that a man in an official station could undertake a journey to St. Albans in those days, when even the passengers by the mail-coach to Windsor rested at Staines, and dined upon the road. It seems, therefore, probable that her Grace's earliest biographer was right, and that the worn-out frame and restless spirit of this wonderful woman ceased to exist in the great metropolis.

It is incumbent upon the Authoress to express to his Grace the present Duke of Marlborough her thanks for his prompt and polite replies to the inquiries with which she ventured to trouble his Grace. To the right honourable Earl Spencer she has to make similar acknowledgments. To several of her literary friends she also owes obligations.

It seems scarcely necessary, where anything curious is to be elicited, or any kind action to be performed, to mention the name of William Upcott. That name occurs many times in the course of this work. To Mr. Upcott the Authoress owes, besides several valuable suggestions, two interesting manuscript letters, now for the first time published in the Appendix of the second volume. The first of these completes the correspondence,—on the part of the Duchess, angry and characteristic,—between her Grace and the Duke of Newcastle; part of which is to be found in the *Private Correspondence.*

The second letter, likewise in the Duchess's handwriting, a copy of which Mr. Upcott has allowed the Authoress to make from his valuable collection of autographs, relates to an action with which the Duchess was threatened in 1712. The Authoress is also indebted to Mr. Upcott for a facsimile of the Duchess's handwriting, for various anecdotes selected from the newspapers of the day, those perishable but important records; and for a perusal of several scarce tracts and books, of which ample use has been made in these volumes. She cannot, indeed, recall to mind the urbanity, liberality, and intelligence of that gentleman, without rejoicing that she has been favoured with his aid, in the performance of a task of no inconsiderable difficulty.

It is with the greatest pleasure and gratitude that the Authoress acknowledges her obligations to Mr. Holmes. Upon her application to him at the Museum, he entered with a kind and lively interest into her researches, and facilitated them in every way. To his aid, and to his intimate knowledge of the manuscripts, she owes that selection of materials which he pointed out as most remarkable.

The Authoress has expressed, in a note in the first volume of these Memoirs, her acknowledgments to the Rev. Henry Nicholson, Rector of St. Alban's Abbey, for the important information which she derived from him, regarding the birth- place of the Duchess. Had it not been for the assistance of that gentleman, directed to the subject by the local inquiries of friends, she must have followed Dr. Coxe in erroneously stating that the Duchess was born at Sandridge.[1]

The Authoress has great pleasure in acknowledging her obligations to another gentleman of great classical and literary attainments, the Rev. I. S. Brewer, to whom she owes so many useful suggestions, that she only regrets she had not the benefit of referring to his superior knowledge at an earlier period of the work than that at which it was first obtained.

The Authoress cannot close this introduction to the latest of four historical and biographical works, without thus publicly expressing her thanks to Mr. Keats, of the British Museum, for his indefatigable attentions to her; and for the assistance which she has on many occasions de rived from his endeavours to aid her researches.

Hinde Street, London,
April 27, 1839.

---

1. It is the impression of her descendant. Earl Spencer, that the Duchess was born at Holywell: and the facts which are stated in chapter 1 of the first volume, and for which the Authoress is indebted to the kindness of Mr. Nicholson, abundantly prove that conviction to be just.

THE FACSIMILE OF A LETTER OF THE DUCHESS OF MARLBOROUGH

CHAPTER 1
FROM 1660 TO 1678

Her Parentage

The period which preceded the birth of the distinguished individual whose singular course is traced out in these *Memoirs*, was one of apparent luxury and security, but of actual and imminent peril to the national welfare. Charles the Second, in the decline of what could scarcely be deemed his days of prosperity, had not, indeed, experienced the bitterness of grief, which, in the fatal events that succeeded the rebellion of Monmouth, reduced the afflicted monarch to a state of depression which hurried him to an unhonoured grave. That painful scene, which in its effects upon the health and happiness of Charles recalled to remembrance the anguish of the royal mourner for Absalom, had not been as yet enacted: Monmouth was to appearance still loyal, at least, still trusted; and the ascendancy of the Roman Catholic persuasion over our Established worship was, at that time, problematical.

The opinions of reflective men, hushed by the wise determination not to anticipate the effect of probable events, which might accomplish all that they secretly desired, were resolving, nevertheless, into those famous schools of politics, which it were wrong to denominate factions, and which were afterwards divided into the three parties interwoven with all modern history, denominated Jacobites, Tories, and Whigs.

It is true it was not until some years afterwards that these celebrated appellations affixed to each combination certain characters, which have ever since, with little variation, retained the stamp which each originally bore; but the names only were wanting. Public opinion, in those worthy to assert its importance, had actually arranged itself under three different banners; although it required some signal manifestations on the part of government, to draw forth the forces marshalled under these, from the state of inaction in which for the present they remained. Amongst the middle, or moderate party,—who, not contending, like the Jacobites, for the indefeasible and divine right inherent in one family under every circumstance, asserted generally the principles of arbitrary government,—a great portion of the gentry, landed proprietors, numbers of whom had fought and bled for the Royal cause, and yet, who were, from the same high spirit and loyal dispositions, equally ready to defend their country from oppression should occasion require, might at this period be enumerated. This respectable portion of the community were, for the greater part, of the Protestant faith; and, therefore, whilst dreading the notion of republicanism, they were attached to the reigning monarchs, and averse to the succession of James, or to the Yorkist Party, as it was called—a name which, by a singular coincidence, had already proved fatal to the peace of England.

Upon the virtue and strength of the Tories, as they might then be called,—though eventually they merged, as the abettors of the Revolution, into the bolder faction, with whom from necessity they were joined,—much of what has since been preserved to us, depended. Notwithstanding the practice which obtained among those who had sufficient influence, of sending their sons into the army, and their daughters to court, it is from the royalist families that many of those who promoted the Revolution, and who even suffered for their premature exertions in the cause of liberty, have sprung. Individuals who would have shuddered at the name of Revolution, whilst yet their restored monarch ruled the country,—with a facility which, when we consider his character and example, is incomprehensible,—became, in after times, impatient to distinguish themselves in a resistance to the unsettled mandates of a court, and in their eagerness to promote the dominion of just and fixed laws. Amongst this class was the family of Churchill; and, if we consider the Duchess as its chief representative, that of Jennings. The origin, principles, and circumstances of the latter family we are now about to discuss.

Sarah Duchess of Marlborough, the subject of this *Memoir*, a gentlewoman by birth, and a favourite of fortune, affords, in the narrative of her chequered life, an instance that integrity, unless accompanied by moderation, cannot protect from the assaults of slander, nor personal and hereditary advantages insure happiness.

This celebrated woman, the beautiful and intellectual offspring of wealthy and well-descended parents; the wife of the most distinguished, and also of the most domestic and affectionate of men; blessed as a parent beyond the lot of most mothers; the favourite of her sovereign, and endowed with superabundant temporal means; lived, nevertheless, in turbulence and discontent, and died, unloved, unregretted, and calumniated.

Her original condition in life was fixed by Providence in a station, neither too high to enjoy the quiet privileges of domestic comfort, nor too low to aspire to distinction; and it was rather her misfortune than her privilege, that she was singled out, in early life, to receive the favours of the great. She was the daughter of a country gentleman in good circumstances. Her family had, for many generations, possessed an estate at Sandridge in Hertfordshire, near St. Albans, at which place, it has been stated, the father of the Duchess could muster a tenantry sufficient to influence considerably the election of members for the adjacent borough of St. Albans.[1]

The family of Jennings had been held in high estimation by the House of Stuart, and were distinguished among the adherents to the Royal cause. The Duchess, whatever might be her subsequent opinions of rulers and princes, sprang from a race devoted to the hereditary monarchy. Her grandfather, Sir John Jennings, received the order of the Bath, in company with his unfortunate young patron, Charles the First, then Prince of Wales; and the partiality of the Stuart family, when restored, was successively manifested by proofs of favour to the owners of Sandridge.[2]

These details refute the reports which prevailed, during the sunshine of prosperity which the Duchess enjoyed, that her parents were of mean origin. It was also stated, by the scandalous writers of the day, that her mother was a woman of abandoned character, rejected from society, and of the lowest extraction.

Among the various proofs which might be adduced in contradiction of this aspersion, the most convincing is the correspondence which Mrs. Jennings maintained, with families of respectability in her own neighbourhood. A letter is still extant, between Sarah Duchess of Marlborough and the daughter-in-law of Sir John Wittewronge of Rothamsted Park, near St. Albans, in which this calumniated lady is referred to by Mrs. Wittewronge, addressing the Duchess, as "your

---
1. *Life of Sarah Duchess of Marlborough, 1745*, p. 61.
2. Collins's *Baronage*, Art. Churchill.

noble mother."[3] This, and the still stronger testimony which will be presently adduced, disprove the insinuations of party writers, who required but a slender foundation of surmise upon which to ground their injurious attacks.

Those who thus wrote were perhaps aware, that they could scarcely wound a person of the Duchess's disposition more deeply than by an aspersion of this description. Yet, in her celebrated Vindication, written in old age, the Duchess, with calmness, refutes in these terms those who sought to defame her origin:

> Though I am very little concerned about pedigree or families, I know not why I should not tell you, that his (her father's) was reckoned a good one; and that he had in Somersetshire, Kent, and St. Albans, about four thousand pounds a year.[4]

The mother of the Duchess belonged, in fact, to a family in some degree superior to that of her husband. She was Frances Thornhurst, daughter of Sir Giffard Thornhurst of Agnes Court in Kent, and heiress to her father's property. Thus, on both sides, the Duchess might regard her origin with complacency; and the expression of the antiquary Collins, when he describes her relatives "as a considerable family," is justified.[5]

This point, of little importance had it not been obscured by malignity, is readily ascertained: but of the dispositions, principles, and attainments of the parents who nurtured one who played so conspicuous a part, we have no authentic record. It is a singular fact, that until a diligent inquiry was made, with a view to the compilation of these *Memoirs*, a degree of obscurity existed, even with regard to the birthplace of the Duchess. Archdeacon Coxe explicitly declares that she was born at Sandridge; but, on examining the parish registers of that place, no mention of that fact, nor indeed of the birth of any of the Jennings family, is to be found in them; nor are there in the church, as it now stands, any monuments inscribed with that name. Neither does there appear to have been any house on the estate at Sandridge,

---

3. The letter, now amongst the papers of John Bennet Lawes, Esq., the descendant of Sir John Wittewronge, Bart., is too much mutilated to be copied or inserted in the appendix. The Duchess, from the vicinity of Sandridge to Rothamsted Park, was probably early acquainted with the family of Wittewronge. She bought some land from Sir John Wittewronge.—See her Grace's will.
4. A Letter from the Duchess. *Private Correspondence of the Duke of Marlborough. Colburn, 1837,* vol. 2. p. 112.
5. For a more detailed account of the Jennings or Jennyns family, see Appendix 1.

of nearly sufficient importance to have been the residence of the Jennings family.[6]

It appears, however, from indisputable testimony, that Sarah Jennings was born on the twenty-ninth day of May,[7] in the year 1660, at Holywell, a suburb of St. Albans, and in a small house, very near the site of the spacious mansion afterwards erected there by her husband, John Duke of Marlborough.

It is to be regretted that a reference to the registers of the Abbey of St. Albans will not assist in establishing this point: in the fire which broke out in that noble building in 1743, a portion of those valuable memorials was burnt. But tradition, corroborated by probability, has satisfied the minds of those most qualified to judge, that at Holywell, the future "viceroy," as she was sarcastically denominated, first saw the light.[8]

---

6. Sandridge is a straggling and by no means picturesque village, in the vicinity of St. Albans. The property once belonging to the Jennings family descended to the favourite grandson of the Duchess, Lord John Spencer, (commonly called "Jack Spencer,") and was sold by the present Lord Spencer to John Kinder, Esq., who has built a handsome house on the estate.

The manor of Sandridge, at the time of the dissolution, formed part of the possessions of the Abbot of St. Albans, and is thus described in the Domesday Survey. "It answered for ten hides. There is land to thirteen ploughs. The Abbot himself holds Sandridge. Three hides are in the demesne, and there are two ploughs here, and a third may be made. Twenty-six villanes here have ten ploughs Meadow for two ploughs. Pasture for the cattle. Pasturage for three hundred hogs. The whole value is 18*l*. When received 12*l*. And the same in King Edward's time."—*Clutterbuck's Hist. of Hertfordshire*, p. 216.

Upon the dissolution, this manor came to the crown, and was granted by charter, *anno* 32 Henry VIII., to Ralph Rowlat, whose sister married Ralph Jennings, the grandfather of Richard Jennings.

7. With the day of her birth I have been assisted by the kindness of a friend. Coxe mentions merely the year.

8. I am enabled, by the kindness and intelligence of the Rev. Henry Nicholson, rector of the Abbey of St. Alban's, to give the corroborating evidence to this fact. A member of the highly respectable family of a former rector of St. Albans distinctly recollects that it used to be the boast of her aunt, an old lady of eighty, not many years deceased, that she had herself been removed, when ill of the smallpox, to the very room in the house where Sarah Duchess of Marlborough was born. This was a small building since pulled down, and its site is now occupied by a summer-house, between what is called Holywell-street and Sopwell-lane in St. Alban's, and within the space afterwards occupied by the pleasure-grounds of the great house at Holywell. Holywell is said by tradition to have been so called, because in it was a well, marked in an old map of St. Albans, where the nuns of Sopwell need to dip their crusts, too hard to be eaten without such a process.

This celebrated woman was one of five children, all of whom, excepting Frances Duchess of Tyrconnel, she survived. Her brothers Ralph and John died young; and one of her sisters, Barbara, who married a gentleman of St. Albans, named Griffiths, died in London in 1678, in the twenty-seventh year of her age.[9]

By the early demise of these relatives, the Duchess acquired that hereditary property which became afterwards her home. At a very early age, however, she must have left Holywell, to enter upon the duties of a courtier. She was preceded in the service of Anne Hyde, Duchess of York, by her eldest sister Frances, the celebrated *La Belle* Jennings, who graced the halls in which the dissolute Charles and James held carousal, and who followed the destinies of the exiled James to a foreign land.

Resembling in some respects her sister, Frances Jennings was equally celebrated for her talents and for her beauty. Her personal charms were, however, of a softer and more alluring character than those of the imperious Sarah. Her bright yet delicate complexion, her luxuriant flaxen hair, and her attractive but not elevated features, might have been liable to the charge of insipidity, but that a vivacity of manner and play of countenance were combined with youthful loveliness, in riveting the attention on a face not to be forgotten. Like her sister, Frances possessed shrewdness, decision, penetration, and, their frequent attendant in woman, a love of interfering. Proud rather than principled, and a coquette, this lovely, aspiring woman had no sooner entered upon her duties of a maid of honour, than her youth and innocence were assailed by every art which could be devised, among men whose professed occupation was what they termed gallantry.

Frances united to her other attractions remarkable powers of conversation; her raillery was admirable, her imagination vivid. It was not long before her fascinations attracted the notice of that devotee and reprobate, James Duke of York, whose Duchess she served. But James, in directing his attention to a Jennings, encountered all the secret contempt that a woman could feel, and received all the avowed disdain which she dared to show. To his compliments, the indignant and persecuted maid of honour turned a deaf ear; and the written expressions of the Duke's regard were torn to pieces, and scattered to the winds. Nor was it long before Frances Jennings found, in a sincere and honest attachment, an additional safeguard against temptation.

Sarah, at twelve years of age, was introduced into the same danger-

---

9. Clutterbuck's *History of Hertfordshire*, p. 57.

ous atmosphere. Fortunately for both sisters, in Anne Duchess of York they found a mistress whom they could respect, and in whose protection they felt security; for she possessed—the one great error in her career set apart—a sensible and well-conditioned mind.

Her court was then the chief resort of the gay and the great. It was the Duchess's foible (in such circumstances one of injurious effect) to pride herself upon the superior beauty of her court, and on its consequent distinction in the world of fashion, in comparison with that of the Queen, the homely Katharine of Braganza. But she had virtue and delicacy sufficient to appreciate the prudence and good conduct of those around her, and to set an example of propriety and dignity, in her own demeanour, becoming her high station.

United to a husband who, in the midst of depravity, "had," says Burnet, "a real sense of sin, and was ashamed of it,"[10] Anne, had she lived, might have possessed, as a Protestant, and as a woman of understanding, a salutary influence over the mind of her husband;— an influence which prudent women are found to retain, even when the affections of the heart are alienated on both sides. But her death, which happened in 1671, deprived England of a queen-consort who professed the national faith; and, in her, James lost a faithful and sensible wife, and the court a guide and pattern which might have checked the awful demoralization that prevailed.

Anne was succeeded by the unfortunate Maria Beatrix d'Esté, Princess of Modena, called, from her early calamities, "the Queen of Tears."[11] Into the service of this lovely child, for such she then was, Sarah Jennings, in consequence of the partiality entertained by the Stuarts for her family, who had been always Royalists, was, shortly after the death of her first patroness, preferred.

In the young Duchess of York Sarah found a kind mistress, an affectionate and a liberal friend. Her subsequent desertion of this unhappy Princess is, we are of opinion, one of the worst features of a character abounding in faults; and proves that ambition, like the fabled Upas tree, blights all the verdure of kindly affections which spring up within the human heart.

Maria Beatrix, the beloved, adopted daughter of Louis XIV., encountered, in her marriage with James, a fate still more calamitous than that which the ungainly Katharine of Braganza, or the lofty but neglected Anne Hyde, bore in unappreciated submission. Beautiful

---

10. Bishop Burnett's *Hist. of His Own Times*, vol. v. p. 53.
11. *Granger*, Art. M. B.

beyond the common standard, and joyous as youth and innocence usually are, this unhappy woman came, in all the unconsciousness of childhood, to incur the miseries of suspicion and obloquy, and to experience subsequent reverse, even poverty. She was hurried over to England, when little more than fourteen years of age, to become the bride of James, then no longer young, in whom bigotry was strangely united to looseness of morals, which habitual and prompt repentance could not restrain. In his phlegmatic deportment, in spite of the natural grace of all the Stuarts, vice failed to attract, yet ceased not to disgust; nor can we be surprised that repeated and fruitless negotiations were necessary to procure him a wife, after remaining a widower for more than two years.[12]

In November, 1673, the ill-fated Princess of Modena landed at Dover. The match, which had been accelerated by the promise of a portion to Maria, his adopted daughter, from the King of France, was universally unpopular in England. It had been, however, already concluded, the Earl of Peterborough having, in September, married the Princess by proxy, in Italy. He had conducted the bride to Paris, when Parliament met, and the Commons voted an address to the King, to prevent the marriage of his brother and the Princess, on the plea of her religion. The hopes of a dowry prevailed, at a time when Charles was so impoverished as to entertain an idea of recalling the ambassadors from foreign courts, from the want of means to support them; and the Princess was married to the Duke, at Dover, on the same evening that she landed, to prevent further obstacles, the ceremony being performed according to the rites of the Church of England.[13]

The Duke and the Duchess proceeded to Whitehall, where no very cordial welcome awaited their arrival. The Duchess was refused the use of the private chapel, which had been stipulated by the marriage articles, and the Duke was advised by his friends to withdraw from the country.[14]

Such was the reception of Maria D'Esté, the mother of the Pretender, and, as such, the innocent cause of many national disasters. In her service, and favoured by her kindness, Sarah Jennings passed many years; nor can the subsequent desertion of this lovely and unfortunate Princess, which the then influential Countess of Marlborough justified to herself, be viewed in any other light than as an act of the cold-

---

12. Macpherson's *Hist, of Great Britain*, vol. 1. p. 174.
13. Macpherson, p. 177.
14. *Life of James II.*, edited by Macpherson, vol. 1 p. 73.

est ingratitude. During the twelve years that Mary enjoyed a comparatively private station as Duchess of York, she passed her time, and engaged those around her, in innocent amusements and revels, which have been always peculiarly agreeable in their rulers to the English people. Young and light-hearted as she then was, Mary was herself the fairest flower of the court, over which she presided with the gay grace of her country. "She was," says Macpherson, "of exquisite beauty. Her complexion was very fair, her hair black, her eyes full of sweetness and fire. She was tall in her person, and admirably shaped; dignified in her manner, and graceful in her deportment."[15]

By the sweetness and propriety of her conduct, she, in her hours of sunshine, made herself universally beloved, notwithstanding her religion; and amid the storms of her subsequent career she showed a spirit and heroism which deserved a better cause, and a clinging attachment to James which merited a worthier object.

There is no reason to conclude that at first Sarah Jennings lived constantly in the household of the Duchess. "I was often at court," is an expression which occurs in a passage of her Vindication. She seems, indeed, to have remained in the proximity of the Duchess, chiefly for the purpose of being a sort of playmate, rather than attendant, of the Princess Anne, the stepdaughter of her royal mistress, whose favour she ultimately succeeded in obtaining, and for whose dawning greatness she relinquished her adherence to the falling fortunes of the Duchess. It is probably to this intimacy with the juvenile branches of the court that Sarah, in part, owed that correctness of conduct, which not even the malice of her enemies could successfully impugn; and soon a sincere and well-founded attachment, the great safeguard to wandering affections, ended in an engagement which gave to the beautiful Miss Jennings an efficient and devoted protector.

In the year 1673, John Churchill, afterwards Duke of Marlborough, was appointed to be a gentleman of the bedchamber to the Duke of York,—probably on occasion of the Duke's marriage. Churchill was at this time a colonel in the army, and already his fame stood high as an officer of enterprise; whilst, at the court, there were few of the young gallants of the day who could cope with this gifted man, in the dignity and symmetry of his person, in the graces of his manner, or in the charm which good-breeding, and a species of benevolence in small and everyday matters, confer upon the deportment.

The illustrious name of Churchill requires, however, some com-

---
15. *Hist. Brit.*, vol. 1. p. 178.

ment, before the disturbed course of his lovesuit to his future wife, the solace and torment of his later days, can be unfolded.

Roger de Courselle, or Courcil, one of the Barons of Poitou, who followed William the Conqueror to England, and settled first in Somersetshire, and afterwards in Devonshire, under the anglicised name of Churchill, was the direct progenitor of Colonel Churchill. It is worthy of remark, that at different periods the ancestors of our great warrior have been noted for valour. In the reign of Stephen, Sir Bartholomew Churchill lost his life defending Bristol Castle, in the cause of the king; and in the disturbed times of Edward the Fourth, William, a lineal descendant of Sir Bartholomew, fought under the banners of the Courtenays in Devonshire, for his sovereign. Successive proofs of loyalty were given by the Churchill family; and Sir Winston, the father of the hero of Blenheim, left the University of Oxford, whilst a youth, to enlist in the army of Charles the First, in which he served with distinction, as a captain of horse, in several battles.[16]

It was the inevitable consequence of the political turmoil in which the family of Colonel Churchill bore a part, that his patrimony should have suffered. His youth was passed in privacy and restraint; and perhaps to that circumstance may be traced that love of order in his affairs, and that close regulation of his expenditure, which in his prosperous days procured for him the opprobrium of penuriousness. During the civil wars, his father had married a daughter of Sir John Drake, of Ashe in Dorsetshire, where Sir Winston was thankful, after the execution of Charles the First, to retire, his estates being sequestrated by Parliament, and a fine of upwards of four thousand pounds imposed upon him for his adherence to the Royal cause.

In the safe seclusion of Ashe, John Churchill was nurtured; and, although upon the restoration of Charles the Second the family estate was recovered, his father was honoured with knight- hood, and employed by government, his valiant son never derived any pecuniary advantage from the paternal property.[17] Sir Winston ultimately was reduced to circumstances of difficulty, in which he died, bequeathing his estate to his widow, with a request that she would leave it to his third son, Charles. To his family connexion, not solely to fortune or to his own merits, was John indebted for his elevation to distinction.

---

16. See Archdeacon Coxe's *Life of John Duke of Marlborough*, vol. 1 Introduction, p. 45; also Lediard's *Life of Marlborough*. For a further account of the Churchill name and lineage, see Appendix 2.
17. See Coxe, p. 47 and 49.

His condition therefore, in some respects, resembled that of his early and late affection, as far as worldly and external circumstances are concerned.

The family of Churchill, like that of Jennings, was ancient; and young Churchill possessed, in the power of referring to a long line of ancestry, an incentive, to an ardent mind peculiarly attractive, to aim at distinction, not only for self-gratification, but with the hope of restoring to former honour those whose fortunes and fame had been crushed, but not obliterated. Colonel Churchill, even from his childhood, had been connected with a court, and destined to share a courtier's duties and rewards. From his boyhood he was honoured with the notice of Royalty, the Duke of York being his first patron.

To the influence of James he owed his rapid promotion in the army; and, as in all similar cases, several causes, such as were incidental to the Stuart family, and probably from their known looseness of principle, were assigned for his success. But to the good-nature and discernment of James the Second, the first opportunity afforded to Marlborough of becoming great must be attributed. Observing the enthusiasm of the high-minded boy, then his page, during the reviews of the regiments of Foot Guards, James inquired of the youth "what profession he would prefer?" Churchill, neither overpowered nor abashed by this trait of condescension, fell upon his knees, and owned a predilection for that of arms, venturing to beg "for a pair of colours in one of those fine regiments." His petition was granted, and at sixteen years of age Churchill entered the army.

This commencement of his fortune has been stated, but erroneously, to have been the result of James's passion for Arabella Churchill, the sister of the young officer, and afterwards the acknowledged mistress of the prince. But Arabella, who was younger than her brother, had not at that time attracted the notice of her brother's patron. In all probability her transient influence over the Duke—that influence which excited the sole pang of jealousy ever evinced by Anne Hyde—accelerated the rise to eminence which Churchill gained with unusual rapidity, and in consideration of which he appears, in compliance with the custom of the day, to have witnessed, without the burning blushes of shame, his sister's disgrace. Arabella, indolent, easy, not beautiful,[18] and unambitious, soon lost her royal lover's regard. She bore him, however, two sons, one, the celebrated James Fitz-James, Duke of Berwick; the other, Henry, Grand Prior of France; and two

---

18. See Grammont.

daughters, Lady Waldegrave and Mrs. Godfrey.

At the period of his appointment in the household of the Duke of York, Colonel Churchill was in his twenty-fourth year. Already had he distinguished himself at the siege of Tangier during his first campaign, and had served afterwards under the Duke of Monmouth, and nominally under Louis the Fourteenth; but, to the especial advantage of his military character, he had fought under the banners of Marshal Turenne. Already had he signalised himself in the attacks on Nimeguen, where his courage attracted the discerning eye of Turenne, who gave him the name of the "handsome Englishman;" and a station of importance having been abandoned by one of Turenne's officers. Captain Churchill was appointed to maintain it, which he effected, expelling the enemy.[19]

At the siege of Maestricht Churchill still further advanced his fame, and received the thanks of Louis the Fourteenth, and his fortunes seemed to his youthful mind advancing to their climax, when he was presented to Charles the Second by the Duke of Monmouth, with this warm-hearted asseveration, characteristic of that gallant nobleman. "To the bravery of this gallant officer," said the Duke, addressing his royal father, "I owe my life." The last reward of Churchill's valiant exertions had been an appointment to the command of the English troops auxiliary to France; a post which the Earl of Peterborough had resigned.[20] The fame of these various services had been extolled by friends at court, and by connexions, influential in various degrees, and for various reasons.

Recalled, at sundry times, to the duties of a court life, the hero who surpassed the generals under whom he served, surpassed also the courtiers with whom he came into frequent collision. He was endowed with personal beauty, height of stature, (being above the middle size,) activity, and sweetness of expression: in short, the perfection of the species, high intellect combined with perfect grace, was exhibited in this great, and, when chastened by the course of events, subsequently good man. His countenance was mild, thoughtful, commanding; his brow lofty, his features regular but flexible. His deportment was dignified, and, at the same time, winning. "No one," said

---

[19] This early exploit was the result of a wager of Turenne's. "I will bet a supper and a dozen of claret," said the general, "that my handsome Englishman will recover the post with half the number of men commanded by the officer who has lost it." The wager was accepted and won.—Lediard, vol. 1.

[20] Coxe; p. 9.

one who knew him personally, ever said a pert thing to the Duke of Marlborough."[21]

The same consummate judge even attributed the great success of the Duke "to the Graces, who protected and promoted him." "His manner," Lord Chesterfield declares, "was irresistible, either by man or woman."

Like most young men destined to the profession of arms, the education of Churchill was limited. Lord Chesterfield, indeed, declares that the great Marlborough was "eminently illiterate, wrote bad English, and spelt it worse;" and he goes so far as to assert, that "he had no share of what is commonly called parts; he had no brightness, nothing shining in his genius."

But with this opinion, however backed by high authority, it is impossible for those who trace the career of Marlborough to agree. That he was not a man of extensive intellectual cultivation, as far as the learning to be acquired from books was concerned—that he was not calculate to harangue in the senate with peculiar distinction, nor addicted deeply to the study of the closet—may readily be admitted. It may even be allowed that he was deficient in the science of orthography—in those days less carefully instilled in youth than in the present time.[22] But that he was absolutely illiterate, or even of mediocre parts moderately cultivated, his private letters sufficiently disprove. They are all admirably expressed; clear, emphatic, and in well-constructed sentences. His father was a man of letters, the author of an historical work,[23] and by Sir Winston was the education of Churchill superintended, until he was placed at St. Paul's school, London.[24]

To the "cool head and warm heart" of Marlborough, as King William the Third expressed it, he owed his early and progressive success. He was at once the object of affection and of confidence. His calmness, the suavity of his temper, until disease, most cruel in its effects on *that* broke down his self-command; his forbearance—his consideration for others—the gentleness with which he refused what he could not grant—the grace with which he conferred favours—these qualities, combined with indefatigable industry, hardihood, and

---

21. *Lord Chesterfield's Letters,* 136.
22. For a specimen of the errors, in this respect, imputed to the Duke, see Appendix, No. 1., in an extract from the newspapers of his time.
23. "*Divi Britannici*; being a Remark on all the Kings of this isle, from the year of the world 2855 unto the year of Grace 1660."—*General Biography,* Art. Churchill.
24. Coxe, p. 1, 2.

a judgement never prejudiced by passion, were the true sources of Churchill's greatness, the benignant spirits which made the gifts of fortune sweeter when they came.

It is uncertain at what time or in what manner the first tokens of ardent affection between Colonel Churchill and the youthful Sarah were exchanged. The authoress of the *Life of Zarah* has given a romantic description of their first meeting, in which, as in other ephemeral works, we may suppose there may be some foundation of truth, but no accuracy of detail. According to this account, the youthful fancy of Sarah was first attracted by the grace of her valiant lover in the dance—a recreation in which he particularly excelled. "Every step he took carried death in it,"[25] and the applause and admiration which Colonel Churchill obtained, sank deep into the heart of one whose ambition was perhaps as easily stimulated as her love. Yet that her affections were interested in the addresses of the brave Churchill, is manifest from her rejection of another suitor of higher rank, the Earl of Lindsay, afterwards Marquis of Ancaster, and of others, by whom she was considered as "the star and ornament of the court."[26]

The correspondence between these celebrated lovers during the anxious days of courtship was preserved by the survivor, with a care that marked the honour which she felt she had received in being beloved by such a man as Marlborough, They are said, by Archdeacon Coxe, to have displayed the most ardent tenderness on the part of Churchill, with alternations of regard and petulance on that of the lady. Her haughtiness, and the sensibility of her future husband, fully appear in these letters. Yet, notwithstanding the defects of character which they betrayed in the one party, the attachment on the side of the other increased in ardour, and continued sufficiently strong to overcome all obstacles. Amongst these, the scanty portion of Sarah, no less than the still greater deficiency of means on the part of her lover, formed the principal impediment. In order to show the different circumstances of each of the families with which they were connected, it is necessary to give some account of their various members, and of the fortunes which they had at this time begun to share.

The adherence of the Churchill family to the royal House of Stuart, and the adverse effect of that adherence upon the fortunes of Sir Winston Churchill, have been already mentioned. Sir Winston, a man of considerable learning and of approved bravery, had indeed so far

---

25. See *Life of Zarah*, p. 2.
26. *Life of Zarah*, p. 3.

retrieved his circumstances, and relieved his estate of its heavy burdens, as to be able, in 1661, to stand for the borough of Weymouth, and to sit in the first parliament called by Charles the Second. He was afterwards appointed a commissioner of the Court of Claims in Ireland, and constituted, on his return from that country, one of the comptrollers of the Board of Green Cloth,— an office from which he was removed, but to which he was restored. But these appointments appear to have been the sole compensation which he received for his active services; and he seems to have devoted the latter portion of his days to pursuits of literature rather than of ambition, being one of the first fellows of the Royal Society, and the author of an able and elegant historical work on the Kings of England, which composition he dedicated to Charles the Second.[27]

Sir Winston's means were encumbered, however, with seven sons and four daughters; and although seven of this numerous family died in infancy, yet still a sufficient number remained to entail anxiety upon the owner of an impoverished estate. George Churchill, the third surviving son, like his brother John, owed the first gleams of royal favour to family interest, but insured its continuance by his merit. He distinguished himself both by sea and land; was a faithful servant, for twenty years, as a gentleman of the bedchamber to George of Denmark, and attained, under King William, the post of one of the commissioners of the Admiralty.

Charles, the fourth son, was also bred to arms, and, at an early age, signalised himself at the time of the Revolution. To him the landed property of Sir Winston descended, on account of some pecuniary obligations which his father owed him, and which prove how circumscribed were still the means of the brave and estimable Sir Winston. Like his brothers, Charles held offices under the crown, and was appointed governor of the Tower of London by Queen Anne.[28] Thus, whilst, by merit and interest conjoined, the sons of Sir Winston Churchill attained independence, and perhaps wealth, it was natural for him to desire that his eldest surviving son should farther advance his fortunes by an advantageous marriage; nor was it inconsistent with the notions of the day, to look upon marriage solely as a negotiation in which the affections were not even consulted, or were at least regarded as of secondary import.

That such were the sentiments of Sir Winston and Lady Churchill,

---

27. Collins's *Baronage*, vol. 2 p. 131.
28. Collins's *Baronage*, Art. Churchill.

appears from the strenuous opposition which they made to their son's union with Miss Jennings: for at present her portion was inconsiderable, and her family interest not to be compared with that of the Churchills. It is true that the estate at Sandridge, to which the Duchess afterwards became co-heiress, was more productive than those lands which Sir Winston Churchill had saved from the grasp of the parliament; but still it was encumbered by a provision for her grandfather's numerous issue; nor was it until the death of her brothers, without children, that Sarah and her sister Frances shared the patrimonial property. Thus circumstanced, and precluded on both sides from the expectation of parental aid, the young soldier was obliged to depend upon his own powers of exertion, to find means to form an establishment for the lady to whom he made his ardent suit.

The young Duchess of York was, at this juncture, the counsellor and confidante of Sarah, and she appears to have offered her and Colonel Churchill some pecuniary assistance in this emergency.[29] Nor was her bounty the only source from which a future provision for the lovers was derived.

It is always an ungracious task to touch upon the errors of those who, by a subsequent career of honour, have left, as the final testament to posterity, an example of domestic virtue. The income which Colonel Churchill possessed,[30] is said to have been derived from a dishonourable source.[31] Amongst the causes of his rapid rise in the army, as well as of his success at court, his relationship to the celebrated Barbara Villiers, afterwards Duchess of Cleveland, has been naturally regarded as one of the most powerful explanations of the favours which he received. This infamous woman, described by Bishop Burnet as "a woman of great beauty, but enormously vicious and ravenous, foolish, but imperious,"[32] governed Charles the Second, as it is well known, by the exhibition of the most tempestuous passions, which she ascribed in his presence to jealousy of him, whilst her intrigues with other men were notorious.

She was second cousin to Churchill by his mother's side, being

---

29. Coxe, 1 13.
30. *Chesterfield's Letters*, p. 136.
31. Bishop Burnet alludes to this intrigue between Marlborough and the Duchess. "The Duchess of Cleveland, finding that she had lost the king, abandoned herself to great disorders; one of which, by the artifice of the Duke of Buckingham, was discovered by the king in person. *Hist. of his own Times*, vol. 1 p. 370.
32. Burnet, vol. 1. p. 129.

the daughter of Villiers Lord Grandison, who was killed at the battle of Edge Hill. Whilst Churchill was a youth, she imbibed for him too strong a partiality, in such a mind as hers, to appear even innocent, if it really were so. Her passion for him was as sudden as it was disgusting; and however it may have procured him some temporary assistance, it drew upon him the displeasure of the King, who at one time forbade him the court.[33] The advocates of Churchill have endeavoured to attach little importance to this disgraceful connexion, for which his youth and the temptations of the court alone furnish an apology; yet they cannot, whilst they excuse, entirely deny a fact which undoubtedly sullies the fair fame of Churchill.

Lord Chesterfield, in holding up the Duke of Marlborough as a model of good breeding and irresistible elegance and suavity, thus touches upon the fact of his being under pecuniary obligations to the imperious Duchess of Cleveland. "He had," says his lordship, "most undoubtedly an excellent, good, plain understanding, with sound judgement. But these alone would probably have raised him but something higher than they found him, which was page to King James the Second's queen. There the graces protected and promoted him; for while he was an ensign in the Guards, the Duchess of Cleveland, then favourite mistress of the King, struck by those very graces, gave him five thousand pounds; with which he immediately bought an annuity of five hundred pounds a year, of my grandfather Halifax, which was the foundation of his subsequent fortune."[34]

Upon this slender annuity, thus disreputably obtained, the hopes of Churchill and of the young object of his affections depended. Sarah appears to have been capricious and undecided in her conduct during the progress of their engagement, which lasted three years.[35] The cause of these variations of feeling has been assigned to the opposition made by Sir Winston and Lady Churchill to their son's forming a union so far below their expectations; but it may be referred to various other sources. The high-minded Sarah must have been often offended and wounded, in the nicest feelings, by the past irregularities of Churchill's life. Those irregularities were renounced, it is true, upon his engagement with her, and his honourable and well-toned mind was recalled to a sense of that beauty which attends purity of conduct, and its power to dignify characters even of a common stamp.

---

33. Grammont, vol. 2. p. 284.
34. *Chesterfield's Letters*, p. 136.
35. From 1675 to 1678. See Coxe, vol. 1, 15.

But the effects of his past conduct were found in the bitterness and jealousy of those by whom he had been hitherto flattered,[36] and by whom doubtless the defects of his moral character may have been grossly exaggerated. Sarah may have intended to prove the constancy of her accomplished lover, when, hearing that his parents destined him to become the husband of a young lady of superior fortune to her own, though of less beauty, she petulantly entreated him "to renounce an attachment which militated against his worldly prospects;" and adding many reproaches, pungent as her pen could write,—and in the vituperative style she had few equals,—she declared that she would accompany her sister Frances, then Countess of Hamilton, to Paris, thus finally to end their engagement. Her address to the honour, to the heart of Churchill, was not made in vain; he answered her by an appeal to her affection, and by earnest remonstrances against her cruelty, and a reconciliation was the result.[37]

Whilst these sentiments secretly occupied the heart of Churchill, and of her who loved him, perhaps, less for his excellencies than for the effect which they produced upon others, several events took place at the court of Charles, in which Colonel Churchill, during the intervals of his military service, participated,—his office of master of the robes to the Duke of York, an appointment granted him in 1673, retaining him near the court; whilst Sarah, in the course of her attendance on the Princess Anne, must have taken a considerable interest in the events which immediately concerned the royal family.

---

36. *Life of John Duke of Marlborough* , p. 39.
37. See Coxe, 14, 15.

Chapter 2
1677 to 1681

Court of Charles II

It was fortunate for the subject of this *Memoir* that her introduction into the great world took place under the auspices of a young and virtuous Princess, almost of the same age with herself. It is true, that to the charge of Katharine, the neglected wife of Charles the Second, no graver crime could be alleged than her subserviency to the King's pleasures; for in her own conduct she was irreproachable. When first she became Queen of England, she endeavoured, with such judgement as she possessed, to reform the manners of her adopted country, and to introduce propriety of demeanour into the court. Unhappily Katharine was not endowed with those graces which are likely to recommend virtue. She is described by a contemporary as "a little ungraceful woman, so short-legged, that when she stood upon her feet you would have thought she was on her knees, and yet so long-waisted, that when she sat down she appeared like a well-sized woman."[1]

Brought up in a monastery, the simple-minded Katharine vainly hoped to reform her dissolute husband, whose inconstancy at first grieved and shocked her virtuous notions. Unlike her rival, Anne Duchess of York, a shrewd and worldly woman, who strove to fill her saloons with the young and the fair, Katharine was surrounded by her countrywomen, old, stiff, ungainly, repulsive Portuguese ladies, of birth and pride, who soon became the subjects of infinite merriment to King Charles's court. These exemplary ladies came possessed with the notion that they should quickly bring the English to conform to their new customs; but Charles speedily undeceived them, and by his

---
1. *Continuation of Lord Clarendon's Life*, p. 167.

express order they were soon shipped off again for Portugal.[2]

The injured Queen was, at the time that Sarah and Colonel Churchill became acquainted, sinking fast into the obscurity which was alone redeemed from oblivion, after Charles's death, by her patronage of musical science, and by the concerts which she gave at Somerset House, whither she retired, to reside until she returned to Portugal.[3]

Charles, impoverished in circumstances, and governed at this time almost wholly by the Duchess of Portsmouth, who was under the influence of France, astonished both his subjects and the foreign courts, by the alliance which he selected for his niece, the Princess Mary, at this time in her fifteenth year. It was whilst Colonel Churchill and his future wife were in all the uncertainties of suspense, that the nuptials of William of Nassau with Mary were solemnised.

This young Princess is said to have owed the decision which gave her a husband to whom she was entirely subservient, to a sudden prepossession of her royal uncle in favour of the Prince. The King is reported to have said to Sir William Temple these characteristic words:—"I never yet was deceived in judging a man's honesty by his looks; and if I am not deceived in the Prince's face, he is the honestest man in the world, and I will trust him, and he shall have his wife; and you shall go immediately and tell my brother so, and thus it is a thing resolved on."[4]

This mode of deciding an union highly agreeable to the English, although unwelcome to the Duke of York, was adopted and carried instantly into effect, in order to avoid the importunities of the Duchess of Portsmouth, who was entirely an instrument in the interests of France. Louis the Fourteenth, when informed of the marriage being declared in council, could not help marking his resentment towards the Duke of York, through the English ambassador. Lord Darnley,—who justified James by saying that "he did not know of the King's decision until an hour before it was proclaimed, nor did the King himself above two hours previously." Upon which Louis uttered these prophetic words: that "James had given his daughter to his greatest enemy."[5]

In the ensuing year, 1678, the marriage of Sarah Jennings and

---

2. *Ibid.*, p. 148.
3. *Granger.*
4. Lediard, p. 32.
5. Echards *Hist. Revolution*, p. 113.

Colonel Churchill is presumed to have taken place.[6] Secret their union certainly was, for a letter addressed by Colonel Churchill to his wife, from Brussels, April 12, 1678, is directed to Miss Jennings; but the epistle was carefully preserved by his wife, who left, in her own handwriting, these words on the back: "I believe I was married when this was written, but it was not known to any but the Duchess" (of York.)

In the same year he writes to her, addressed to Mrs. Churchill, at Mintem, his father's seat, where probably the young bride had taken up her abode in the intervals of her attendance at court; or perhaps that attendance was discontinued, and not constantly resumed until a year or two afterwards. The ceremony took place in the presence of Mary Duchess of York, who bestowed presents of considerable value on the bride; and some months afterwards the marriage was avowed.[7]

Little of domestic comfort for several years seems to have been the portion of Colonel Churchill in his marriage. His first absence was on occasion of the Duke's retiring, first to Brussels, and afterwards to the Hague, accompanied by the Duchess of York, and by the Princess Anne; an event which took place in the beginning of the year 1678. But although at this time attached to the service of the Duke of York, and ignorant of the Duke's designs upon the religion and the liberties of England,[8] Colonel Churchill's interests with Charles appear not to have suffered; for he obtained in February a regiment of foot, and was shortly afterwards sent on a mission of importance to the Prince of Orange.

The following letter from him to his wife breathes sincere affection. It is dated Brussels, April 12th.

> I writ to you from Antwerp, which I hope you have received before now, for I should be glad you should hear from me by every post. I met with some difficulties in my business with the Prince of Orange, so that I was forced to write to England, which will cause me to be two or three days longer abroad than I should have been. But because I would lose no time, I despatch all other things in the meantime, for I do, with all my heart and soul, long to be with you, you being dearer to me than my own life. On Sunday morning I shall leave this place, so that on Monday night I shall be at Breda, where the Prince and Princess of Orange are; and from hence you shall be sure to

---

6. Coxe, vol. 1 p. 15.
7. Coxe.
8. Lediard.

hear from me again; till then, my soul's soul, farewell.[9]

Colonel Churchill had, however, the enjoyment of passing the summer of this year with his wife at Mintern, where he had the happiness of finding her reconciled to his parents; but this transient enjoyment of domestic quiet was not of long duration. The Colonel was obliged to repair to London, where he received instructions to join the allied troops in hostilities against France, and received a commission from the Duke of Monmouth, appointing him, as British commander-in-chief in the Netherlands, to the command of a brigade in Flanders. But, happily, being driven back by contrary winds to Margate, Colonel Churchill learned, in time to prevent his proceeding to the Continent, that the Prince of Orange had signed a treaty with the French, and that a general peace was the result.[10]

The dissolute rule of Charles was now drawing to a close; but its last years were disturbed by faction, and disgraced by acts of rigour, which were with justice imputed to the influence of the heir apparent. Colonel Churchill and his wife remained, however, attached to the service of the Duke and Duchess of York, and accompanied their royal highnesses to the Hague and to Brussels—a journey which was undertaken by James in compliance with a request addressed to him from his brother, that he would for a time absent himself from the British dominions.

This may probably be considered as the happiest epoch in the life of Churchill, and of the partner of his bright fortunes. Although confided in by James in all important points, notwithstanding the difference of their religious faith, Churchill took no share in political intrigues, and with a calm dignity retained his own opinions, unbiased by example, or by what might be deemed interest. "Though I have an aversion to popery," thus he explained his sentiments to a confidential friend, "yet I am no less averse to persecution for conscience sake. I deem it the highest act of injustice to set every one aside from his inheritance upon bare suppositions of intentional evils, when nothing that is actual appears to preclude him from the exercise of his just rights."[11]

On the other hand, Mrs. Churchill had at present no important part in life to act, no dreams of greatness to disturb her routine of duty

---

9. Coxe.
10. Coxe, vol. 1 p. 1.
11. Coxe, vol. 1, p. 18.

and service to a mistress who appears to have treated her with the utmost kindness. The Princess Anne, indeed, accompanied her father to the Continent, and shared with her stepmother the attentions and the society which afterwards became so essential to the future Queen of England. But Anne's importance was at present overshadowed, and her chances of future elevation were remote, even in her own anticipations.

During the course of the summer, James was recalled to England by the illness of his brother; but finding that Charles was likely to recover, he returned to Flanders, in order to bring over his family to the British Isles,[12] although he was not permitted by the King to remain in London. Colonel Churchill, meantime, was despatched to Paris upon diplomatic business, with an especial recommendation from James, who designated him in his letter "master of the wardrobe."[13] It was not, however, considered expedient by Charles or his advisers that the Duke of York should continue in England, and accordingly it was given out, by authority, that the Duke having represented to His Majesty that it would be more proper that he should remain in His Majesty's dominions than in those of any other Prince, the King had consented to his Royal Highness's removal to Scotland.

The Duke and Duchess of York, therefore, with a numerous suite, composed of many of the nobility and persons of distinction, departed for Edinburgh, leaving the Princess Anne, and Isabella, her half-sister, at St. James's. In this tedious journey, which, performed with much parade, lasted a month, Churchill and his wife accompanied the Duke and Duchess,[14]—Colonel Churchill, from the desire of escaping those contentions which then agitated public men, and occupied both Houses, concerning the succession,[15] prudently avoiding a seat in parliament, which he might readily have obtained.

It was for some years the occupation of Churchill, and of his wife, to follow the footsteps, and in some measure to share the anxieties, of the Duke and Duchess of York. During the present year, James returned to London; but he was again driven to Scotland by the efforts of the adverse party, and was again accompanied by Churchill.

After a year spent on the part of Churchill in many important missions, he had the happiness of hearing, on his return to Scotland

---

12. See Coxe, from *Lives of Marlborough and Eugene*, vol. 1. p. 15.
13. Dalrymple, Appendix, p. 239.
14. Lediard, p. 39, 40.
15. Coxe, vol. 1. p. 19.

after one of these embassies, that he had become a father. The infant Henrietta, afterwards Duchess of Marlborough, was born in London, whither Mrs. Churchill had accompanied the Duchess of York, July the tenth, 1681.[16]

The character of the Duchess of Marlborough as a mother remains yet to be developed; but the letters of Colonel Churchill to her, at this period, bespeak a sense of domestic happiness, and prove that she was still, as indeed she ever was, ardently beloved by his, the most affectionate, as it was the bravest heart.

> "I writ to you," he says in one of these unpremeditated epistles, "last night by the express, and since that I have no good news to send you. The yachts are not yet come, nor do we know when they will, for the wind is directly against them, so that you may believe I am not in a very good humour, since I desire nothing so much as being with you. The only comfort I had here was hearing from you, and now, if we should be stopped by contrary winds, and not hear from you, you may guess with what satisfaction I shall then pass my time; therefore, as you love me, you will pray for fair winds, that we may not stay here, nor be long at sea.
>
> "I hope all the red spots of our child will be gone against I see her, and her nose strait; so that I may fancy it to be like the mother, for she has your coloured hair. I would have her to be like you in all things else. Till next post-day farewell. By that time I hope we shall hear of the yachts, for till I do, I have no kind of patience."[17]

The constant services of Churchill were at length rewarded with an elevation to the peerage, an honour which he owed entirely to the recommendation of James in his favour. He was created Baron Churchill of Eyemouth in Scotland, and made also Colonel of the third troop of Guards.[18]

Weary, probably, of a courtier's life, it was now Lord Churchill's desire to withdraw Lady Churchill from the court, and to enjoy with her the privacy which their mutual affection might have rendered delightful. But so peaceful a lot was not to be the portion of this remarkable pair, who were destined to act a conspicuous part in the great sphere of public action.

---

16. Coxe.
17. Coxe.
18. Lediard.

It is not stated what were Lord Churchill's particular motives for thus wishing to withdraw from the greatness which was "thrust upon him," at a time when James, his patron, was restored to his royal brother's favour, and when his own influence was daily increasing. But we may look into the history of those fearful times for a solution of this inquiry.

The feelings, upright and humane, of Churchill, and even of his less sensitive wife, had doubtless been harrowed by the occurrences of the preceding year. The Rye House Plot, and its melancholy termination, must have saddened the heart even of the strictest adherent to James, and probably opened the eyes of Churchill to the real dispositions of that Prince, whose indifference to the value of human life gave the character of retribution to his subsequent misfortunes.

Russell sacrificed, and the unhappy Essex, impelled by a fear of his impending fate, forced to commit suicide, it is no wonder that Churchill was sickened by the events of those calamitous days, and that he longed to withdraw her who was dearest to him from a scene in which the events of tragedy were mingled with the heartless merriment of a festive court.

Whilst Lord Churchill was advancing his fortunes, the influence of his young wife over the pliant mind of the Princess Anne was equally advancing, though unseen, and establishing for Lady Churchill an ascendency which fixed her destiny in the public walks of life.

From childhood, Anne had been accustomed to the society of her future favourite. A slight difference of age, Lady Churchill being the elder of the two, aided, rather than impeded, the happy intimacy of girlhood. Anne was accustomed to depend for amusement upon her new friend; and as they grew up, and became severally absorbed in the cares of womanhood, Anne, as well as Sarah, found that hopes and disappointments, on the all-engrossing subject of wedlock, were the portion of the Princess as well as of the subject.

Anne, like others of her high rank, was spared the perplexity of choice. Already, at an early age, she had been addressed, in secret, with professions of attachment by the young Earl of Mulgrave, afterwards Marquis of Normanby, one of the most accomplished and amiable noblemen of his time. But these proposals were checked as soon as they were discovered, yet not before Anne had imbibed a partiality, or, in the cold words of the historian of her reign, an "esteem," for the young man, which continued in the form of a kindly regard, until party and politics broke the charm which the recollection of an early attachment had created.[19]

George the First, at that time possessing very slender hopes of becoming King of England, visited this country with the intention of marrying the Princess Anne, but left the British shores somewhat dishonourably, without justifying the hopes which he had excited.[20] At the period when he married his cousin, the ill-fated Dorothea, there was indeed a third daughter of James Duke of York living, the Princess Katharine, who died in 1671. Anne, therefore, was by no means an object of so much importance in the eyes of European princes as she became upon the failure of issue to Mary, and after the abdication of her father. Her uncle, Charles the Second, undertook, however, the disposal of her fate, as he had already decided that of her elder sister.

In selecting the husbands of his nieces, the profligate, well-bred monarch seems to have searched for qualities as opposite as possible to those displayed in the Stuart line; consigning Mary, at sixteen, to the sickly, reserved, grave, and even austere Prince of Orange; and choosing for Anne a worthy, staid individual, ten years older than herself, and exactly such a man as would have filled with propriety the situation of a country gentleman, and enjoyed the not arduous, but yet not unimportant duties which usually fall to the lot of that respectable class. Prince George of Denmark, recommended to the favour of Charles chiefly by his being of the Protestant faith,[21] had, four years previous to his marriage, visited England; and at the command of his brother, Christian the Fifth of Denmark, he returned to make an offer of marriage to the Princess Anne.[22]

It cannot for a moment be supposed that, even with the advantage of these renewed opportunities, there was any great attachment on either side. Never, however, in the annals of royal wedlock, were two characters more completely assimilated than that of Anne and her approved lover. The Prince was brave, good-natured, and not too wise; yet sufficiently sensible to be free from ambition, and to remain contented, in after times, with being the first royal consort that had not shared monarchical power.

His patrimony was small, but ample enough to render him comfortable until a settlement was made, and consisted in the revenues of some small islands belonging to the crown of Denmark, which

---

19. Boyer, p. 36
20. *Granger.*
21. Macpherson's *Hist. England*, p. 365.
22. Boyer.

yielded about ten thousand pounds a year.[23] He was inclined to those principles which had recently acquired the name of Toryism, but never took more than a subordinate part in politics; and was so unoffending, that he made not a personal enemy. Neither was the good Prince George without accomplishments. He had travelled much, was a linguist, somewhat of an antiquary, and patronized the arts. Report asserted that an asthmatic complaint, with which he was severely affected during the course of his life, and of which he ultimately died, had its origin in convivial habits, in which Anne, when Queen, has been declared not loath to join.[24] But that propensity, when not carried to excess, was never in England an unpopular quality; and Prince George was eminently qualified to endear himself to the English nation.

The Princess to whom he was affianced possessed a temper almost as replete with goodnature as his own. At the period of her marriage, the qualities which eventually formed the subject of so much vituperation and of so much praise, could not have been developed, even to the scrutinizing observation of her young companion, Mrs. Churchill, who afterwards portrayed her royal mistress with the distinctness of a powerful and sarcastic mind. The education of the Princess had been limited, and her capacity was inferior to that of her sister Mary; yet the characters of both these Princesses, represented differently by different parties, appear to have been possessed of considerable merit. If we set apart, first, her conduct to her father, and afterwards the undue jealousy evinced by Mary towards her sister, few individuals appear in so amiable a point of view as that of the Princess of Orange. Religious without bigotry, gentle yet firm, fond of domestic life, yet coming forward, when occasion called her) into the sphere of public duties with credit to herself and with benefit to the nation, Mary, as a queen and a wife, was a pattern not only to persons of her own elevated station, but to women of every sphere and in every age. This Princess was, at the time of her sister's marriage, in Holland, with her husband, William of Nassau.

Anne was a personage altogether of an inferior stamp. In many points she resembled strongly the other members of her family who have figured in history. Like Charles the First, she was pious, generous, and affectionate, but obstinate, and not devoid of duplicity when it suited her purpose. Her religion had not, however, the sublimated

---

23. *Granger*, vol. 1. p. 8.
24. *Ibid.*

character of that which consoled the unhappy Charles in adversity; but became, like all her other dispositions, a habit, an implicit faith, a formal observance, rather than a sentiment. Her nature was a strange compound of warm affections and of repelling coldness. As in all weak minds, her friendships were called into being by the gratification of her selfish inclinations; and hence, as the Duchess of Marlborough well describes them, "they were flames of extravagant passion, ending in indifference or aversion."[25]

With those defects which proceeded from deficient cultivation, Anne, however, as a lady of elevated rank, and afterwards as a ruler, possessed some admirable qualities. Her sense of duty supplied the place of strong sensibility. She was a kind mistress; as a wife, incomparable; though lavish to her favourites, (an hereditary trait,) not to be led by them into what she disapproved; just and economical, gracious in her manners, and desirous of popularity. Her nature was placid, her temperament phlegmatic; great designs and lofty sentiments were not to be expected from one of so gentle and easy a temper; but in propriety she equalled, if she could not excel, her reflective and discreet sister. In the early part of her life she was, like the Stuarts generally, extremely well bred, until unnecessary and indecorous familiarity with her inferiors broke down the effects of early habit.

In person Anne was comely, and of that ample conformation and stature well adapted for royalty. Her love of etiquette, and her exactness in trifles, were convenient and commendable qualities in the rules of a court, in the days of the good old school; and an attention to those forms which are much observed in the monarch of a people prone to free discussion, rendered her a favourite with the public. Her figure, before it became matronly, or in the words of the Duchess, (after their quarrel,) "exceeding gross and corpulent," was esteemed graceful; her face was agreeable, though, from a weakness in her eyes, her countenance had contracted somewhat of a scowl, described by the Duchess, whilst she admits that "there was something of majesty" in the Queen's look, "as mixed with a sullen and constant frown, that plainly betrayed a gloominess of soul and a cloudiness of disposition within."[26]

But this may have been the effect of years and of care, when the complexion also participated in the coarseness of the person, induced,

---

25. *Private Correspondence of the Duchess of Marlborough*, vol. 2 p. 116.
26. *Priv. Correspondence.*

as it was said, by the use of cordials, to which the Prince her husband incessantly invited his consort." [27] To complete the portrait of Anne, the beauty of her hands, and the sweetness of her voice in speaking and reading, must not be forgotten: they were universally allowed; whilst her graceful delivery in addressing the Houses of Parliament met with incessant applause.[28] It is remarkable that with such respect was Anne treated by her subjects, that the Peers, in her presence, waived the privilege of wearing hats in parliament, to show that they are hereditary legislators.[29] Such was the Princess Anne; and few contrasts could be more singular than herself, and the friend whom she selected for her confidante, and whom she made many sacrifices to conciliate.

The Duchess of Marlborough, according to Swift, was the victim of "three furies which reigned in her breast, the most mortal of all softer passions, which were—sordid avarice, disdainful pride, ungovernable rage."[30] The first of these demons may be the companion of middle age: rage and pride may have haunted the young and lovely maid of honour; but avarice is not the vice of youth. In all lesser points of disposition and feeling, the Princess and her favourite were dissimilar. The Princess was a lover of propriety and etiquette, even to an inspection of the ruffles and periwigs of her servants. Her sense of decorum was so nice, that, on her accession to the throne, she caused the bust of herself on the gold coin to be clothed as it was, according to ancient custom, on the silver. Nothing offended her, as Queen, so much as a breach of the customary observances; and Lord Bolingbroke having visited her one day in haste, in a Ramillie tie, she remarked "that she supposed his lordship would soon come to court in his nightcap."[31]

For the Duchess of Marlborough, in her old age, and probably still more in the days of her youth, to dwell on trifles, was a burden too heavy for one of so impetuous a nature. Though we are not authorised to conclude from the assertion of her enemy, "that she delighted in disputing the truth of the Christian religion, and held its doctrines to be both impossible and absurd,"[32] yet it is certain, from her own avowal, that she was a latitudinarian in matters of form, and detested and set at defiance those who made "the church" a word of excuse for

---

27. *Granger*, Art. Anne.
28. Boyer, p. 716.
29. *Ibid.*
30. *Four last Years of Queen Anne's Reign*, vol. 12. p. 11.
31. *Granger*.
32. *Four last Years*, p. 11

intolerance and action. The occupations in which these young friends delighted were also totally dissimilar. The Duchess, all her life, delighted in conversation, in which the Princess not only did not excel, but in which she took little pleasure.[33] Anne was an accomplished performer on the guitar; she loved the chase, and rode with the hounds until disabled by the gout. Her companion found the amusements of the court very tedious, and but little suited to her restless and energetic mind. But habit on the one hand, and interest on the other, soon reconcile differences.

From playing together as children, the Princess learned, first, to prefer her companion to any other child; next to endure, then to love, the plain-spoken, fearless girl, who, according to her own account, and to that of her friend Dr. Burnet, never flattered any one; then soon grew up a sentimental feeling, which they called friendship, and distinctions of rank were laid aside, and names of familiarity adopted in place of titles of honour.[34] When the Princess became the wife of George of Denmark, she made it her earnest request to her father that her friend should be appointed one of the ladies of the bedchamber—a wish with which James, an affectionate parent, readily complied. The Duchess of Marlborough, when arranging, in hours of sickness and in old age, the materials for her Vindication, thus simply relates the steps preparatory to her preferment.

> "The beginning of the Princess's favour for me," says the Duchess, "had a much earlier date than my entrance into her service. My promotion to this honour was chiefly owing to impressions she had before received to my advantage. We had used to play together when she was a child, and she had even then expressed a particular fondness for me. This inclination increased with our years. I was often at court, and the Princess always distinguished me by the pleasure she took to honour me, preferably to others, with her conversation and confidence. In all her parties for amusement I was sure, by her choice, to be one; and so desirous she became of having me near her, that upon her marriage with the Prince George of Denmark, 1683, it was at her own request to her father I was made one of the ladies of the bedchamber."[35]

---

33. *Conduct.*
34. *Conduct*, p. 11—15.
35. *Conduct*, p. 10.

Assisted by the force of early associations, the stronger mind quickly asserted an influence over the weaker intellect, an influence retained so long as prudence directed its workings. But the Duchess, in what appears to be an impartial statement of facts, declares that she owed this influence partly to a dislike which the Princess had imbibed against Lady Clarendon, her relation and first lady of the bedchamber, who, according to the Duchess, "looked like a mad woman, and talked like a scholar." And, indeed, she adds, "Her Highness's court was so oddly composed, that I think it would be making myself no great compliment if I should say, her choosing to spend more of her time with me than with any other of her servants did no discredit to her taste."

The writer of the foregoing paragraph might, however, have carried away the palm from women superior even to the Countess of Clarendon, whom she has been accused of misrepresenting. Beautiful according to the opinion of her contemporaries, her beauty indeed appears, in the portraits painted in her bloom of youth, to have been commanding as well as interesting. Her figure is asserted to have been peculiarly fine, and her countenance was set off by a profusion of fair hair, which she is said to have preserved, without its changing colour, even at an advanced age, by the use of honey-water.[36] Several years after she had become a grandmother, the freshness of her lovely complexion, and her unfaded attractions, caused her, even in the midst of four daughters, each distinguished for personal charms, to be deemed pre-eminent among those celebrated and high-bred belles.[37]

But the secret of that extraordinary influence which Sarah Duchess of Marlborough acquired over every being with whom she came into contact, originated not in her attributes of beauty and of grace. Mrs. Jennings, her mother, represented as she was by the infamous Mrs. Manley, the wretched authoress of the *New Atalantis*, as a sorceress and a depraved creature too vile to live, was also allowed by the same authority to have cultivated in her daughter every art that could charm.

That of conversation, in particular, the Duchess of Marlborough is said to have possessed. Shrewd, sarcastic, fearless, so beautiful that all she said was sure to be approved by the one sex; so much in fashion and in favour, that nothing she did could possibly be disapproved by the other; Sarah might readily, without any extraordinary cultivation

---

36. Lord Wharncliffe's edition of *Lady M. W. Montague's Works*, vol. 1.
37. *The Life of Colley Cibber*.

of intellect, figure greatly in repartee, dogmatize with the security of a youthful beauty, and gain, perhaps, in asserting her crude opinions, knowledge and experience from the replies which one so lively would know well how to elicit. It appears that at this time she had never even dreamed of politics, nor thought of cultivating that vigorous intellect so much applauded in after times by the great ones of the earth. Education had contributed little to extend the sphere of her inquiring mind. She knew no language but her own, and never had the industry nor the ambition to learn even French.

Bishop Burnet, who knew her intimately, thus describes his own and his wife's friend.

"The Duchess of Marlborough was," says he, "a woman of little knowledge, but of a clear apprehension and a true judgement."[38]

The account which the Duchess gives of the manner in which many hours of her day, in the season when the improvement of reason ought to be progressive, were dissipated, is, in few words, "that she never read nor employed her time in anything but playing cards, nor had she any ambition."[39] Well might she declare herself to be weary of a court life.

Such was the friend to whom the Princess was early bound by the ties of habit, and afterwards by something almost more ardent than common friendship; and exactly was she adapted, from independent, uncompromising spirit, half magnanimous and half insolent, to attain a complete dominion over every faculty of Anne's shallow mind. The Princess, inured to courts, and probably sickened by the mechanical homage which she could remember from her infancy, might have distrusted adulation in one not much older than herself, and who had been her playmate before the cruel distinctions of rank were recollected or regretted. "But a friend was what she most courted."[40]

"Kings and princes, for the most part," remarks the Duchess, "imagine they have a dignity peculiar to their birth and station, which ought to raise them above all connexions of friendship with an inferior. Their passion is to be admired and feared, to have subjects awfully obedient, and servants blindly obsequious to their pleasure. Friendship is an offensive word; it imports a kind of equality between the parties; it suggests nothing to the mind, of crowns or thrones; high titles, or immense revenues,

---

38. Burnet's *History of his own Times*, vol. 1,. p. 756.
39. *Conduct*, p. 11.
40. *Ibid* p. 20.

fountains of honour, or fountains of riches, prerogatives which the possessors would always have uppermost in the thoughts of those who approach them."[41]

Such were the notions of royalty which the Duchess entertained, and which Hook, the historian, whom she employed in her old age to write the famous Vindication of her career from which this quotation is borrowed, has well expressed in his own language. Yet the decided, dauntless way in which this clause against monarchs is struck off, is strongly characteristic of the Duchess, and must have met with her cordial approbation, if not solely suggested by herself.

"The Princess," she, however, proceeds to state, "had a different taste. A friend was what she most coveted; and, for the sake of friendship, (a relation which she did not disdain to have with *me*,) she was fond of that *equality* which she thought belonged to it. She grew uneasy to be treated by me with the form and ceremony due to her rank; nor could she bear from me the sound of words which implied in them distance and superiority. It was this turn of mind which made her one day propose to me, that whenever I should happen to be absent from her, we might in our letters write ourselves by feigned names, such as would import nothing of distinction between us. Morley and Freeman were the names her fancy hit upon, and she left me to choose by which of them I would be called. My frank, open temper led me to pitch upon Freeman, and so the Princess took the other; and from this time Mrs. Morley and Mrs. Freeman began to converse together as equals, made so by affection and friendship."[42]

This well-meant but dangerous experiment shows at least that Anne understood the nature of true friendship, which, like all other *perfect love, casteth out fear*; whilst it is also obvious that the kind-hearted Princess did not comprehend the character of the remarkable and highly gifted being for whose sake she thus broke through the trammels of etiquette. The friendly compact, unequal as it was, grew under the pressure of those trials which Anne had to encounter during the reign of her father and sister. When she found that James had complied with her earnest request that Lady Churchill might be placed in her service, she communicated the intelligence to her favourite, in

---

41. *Conduct*, p. 13.
42. *Conduct*, p. 15.

terms of joy and affection.

> The Duke came in just as you were gone, and made no difficulties, but has promised me that I shall have you, which I assure you is a great joy to me. I should say a great deal for your kindness in offering it, but I am not good at compliments. I will only say that I do take it extremely kind, and shall be ready at any time to do you all the service that lies in my power.[43]

This graceful mode of making the person on whom the favour was conferred, appear to give, not to receive, the benefit, was met by Lady Churchill, according to her own account, with a sincerity which was the surest test of regard, and the proof of real gratitude.

> I both obtained and held this place without the assistance of flattery—a charm which, in truth, her (the Princess's) inclination for me, together with my unwearied application to serve and amuse her, rendered needless; but which, had it been otherwise, my temper and turn of mind would never have suffered me to employ. "Young as I was when I first became this high favourite, I laid it down as a maxim, that flattery was falsehood to my trust, and ingratitude to my dearest friend.[44]

Well would it be for society if this maxim were universal!

> From this rule I never swerved; and though my temper and my notions in most things were widely different from those of the Princess, yet, during a long course of years, she was so far from being displeased with me for openly speaking my sentiments, that she sometimes professed a desire, and even added her command, that it should be always continued, promising never to be offended at it, but to love me the better for my frankness.[45]

Consistently with this injunction, we find the Princess thus affectionately addressing her future "viceroy."

> If you will not let me have the satisfaction of hearing from you again before I see you, let me beg of you not to call me your highness at every word, but to be as free with me as one friend ought to be with another; and you can never give me a greater proof of your friendship, than in telling me your mind freely in all things, which I do beg you to do, and if ever it were in my

---

43. Coxe, 27.
44. Conduct p.13.
45. Conduct p.12..

power to serve you, nobody would be more ready than myself. I am all impatience for Wednesday, till when, farewell.[46]

The marriage of Anne was followed immediately by the execution of Lord Russell, which, with the trial and condemnation of Algernon Sidney, took place during the same month, and within five days of each other; and the populace, who had viewed with smothered indignation the sufferings of these patriots, were ready to cheer their future Princess, the Defender of their Faith. Subsequent events brought all thinking and disinterested observers to regard with hope the consistent though quiet adherence of the Princess to those principles in which her uncle Charles had from policy caused her to be nurtured; his firmness in this respect showing both the laxity of his own faith, and the paramount influence which worldly considerations had over his wavering and probably sceptical mind.

The banishment of the Duke of Monmouth from court, the execution of Sidney, the sentence of fine upon Hampden, the surrender of their charters by the corporations, and lastly, the death of Charles the Second, succeeded each other in rapid and fearful array; and a critical period to all those connected with public affairs was now drawing near. But the thoughtless life and pernicious example of the monarch who had so grossly betrayed his trust, now drew to its close; and the retribution of what are called "the pleasant vices" became more painful to the beholder from the force of contrast.

In the midst of a plan for subverting the liberties of his people, by forming a military power, to be governed solely by Roman Catholic officers, and devoted to the crown, Charles fell into despondency. His usual vivacity forsook him; and, with it, his gaiety of spirits, his politeness, in him the result of innate good-nature, deserted him. The best bred man in Europe became rude and morose. He saw indeed that the popularity which he had in the early part of his reign enjoyed, was now no longer his; he reflected that he had no son to succeed him; that he was, as far as the crown was concerned, childless.

Monmouth, the child of shame, whom he had recklessly raised to honour and importance, had caballed against his father; yet that father loved him still. Monmouth had outraged the filial duties, but Charles could not eradicate from his own heart the parental affections. The unhappy King pined at the absence of his son. He perceived and

---

46. Coxe, 28.

dreaded the designs and principles of James, and was mortified at the court already paid to his successor. Upon some altercation between the brothers, Charles was one day heard to say, "Brother, I am too old to go to my travels a second time; perhaps you will."[47]

Broken-spirited, but not reclaimed, Charles sought to console himself in the dissolute conversation of those wretched women whose society had been the chief object of his life. But even the worst of men have an intuitive sense of what is due to domestic ties; and the mind is so constituted, that transient pleasure only, and not daily comfort, is to be found in those connexions which have the troubles, without the sanctity of marriage. The Duchess of Portsmouth, who is said really to have loved Charles, was unable to console him without sending for his son. Monmouth came, and was admitted to an interview with his father; but whilst measures were being concerted for sending James again into Scotland, Charles was struck with apoplexy. He died in two days afterwards, by his last act reconciling himself to the Church of Rome, and belying all his previous professions. "He was regretted," says Dalrymple, "more on account of the hatred which many bore to his successor, than of the love entertained to himself."[48]

---

47. Dalrymple, 1.
48. *Ibid.*

CHAPTER 3
1684 TO 1687

State of Manners and Morals

The new reign brought with it early demonstrations of royal confidence towards Lord Churchill, and consequently to his wife. Almost the first act of James was to despatch Churchill to Paris to notify his accession, and to establish more firmly the good faith which already subsisted between James and the French monarch.

Lady Churchill, meantime, continued to hold the same post near the person of Anne, who resided at her palace in the Cockpit, Westminster. The Duchess, in her *Conduct*, has given no insight into this period of her life. We may suppose it to have been passed in the quiescent round of duties more insipid than fatiguing, and in the still more irksome society of the domestic, good-natured, but uninteresting Princess.

The court amusements in those days were of a description perfectly in unison with the tastes and habits of the higher classes, to whom the satire of St. Evremond, upon a similar order of persons in France, might have been, without even a shadow of sarcasm, applied.

"You live in a country," says St. Evremond, writing to Mademoiselle de l'Enclos, "where people have wonderful opportunities of saving their souls: there, vice is almost as opposite to the mode as virtue; sinning passes for ill-breeding, and shocks decency and good manners, almost as *much* as religion."[1]

The sarcasm was just,—that not what is good or what is bad, but what was considered fashionable, or agreeable, was the rule for those who lived in the great world to observe. Gambling was the passion,

---
1. *Life of St. Evremond.* See *Notes to Grammont*, vol. 2, p. 351.

intrigue the amusement, of those days of fearful iniquity. The female sex, in all ages responsible for the tone given to morals and manners, were in a state of general depravity during the whole period of Lady Churchill's youth; and even those who were reputed most virtuous, and held up as patterns to their sex, overlooked, if they did not countenance, the open exhibition of vice within their very homes.

The Duchess of Buckingham, "a most virtuous and pious lady in a vicious age and court,"—"lived lovingly and decently with" her husband, the arch-profligate of the time; and though she knew his delinquencies, never noticed them, and had complaisance enough even to entertain his mistresses, and to lodge them in her own house.[2] Queen Katharine, the neglected and insulted wife of Charles the Second, deemed it her conjugal duty to fall down on her knees at his deathbed, and to entreat pardon for her offences. Whereupon the King vouchsafed to answer her, "that she had offended in nothing."[3] So humbled, so degraded, were the few virtuous female members of the debased English aristocracy; and so slight was that virtue which could bear, in the closest tie, the constant exhibition of vice! That a woman should forgive—that her best interests, her only chance of happiness, consist in a dignified endurance of the worst of evils, a vicious husband—no reasonable being can doubt; but that as a Christian, as a female, she cannot be excused in remaining within the contamination of vice, is not to be disputed.

Continental alliances, the exile of the restored Princes during the greater portion of their youth, and the consequent introduction of foreign amusements and foreign manners, to which we must add a yet tottering and unsettled national faith, may account, in a great measure, for this universal corruption. Nor can we suppose the lofty Lady Churchill to have escaped wholly from the pernicious influence of what she must have seen and heard. Masquerading was the rage; and not only in private, or in gay halls or banquet-rooms, but in the streets and alleys, the theatre, and other places of public resort, it was adopted as a diversion, to pass away hours tedious to uneducated minds.

In the reign of Charles, Frances Jennings, the elder sister of the Duchess, was flattered, rather than ashamed, at the publicity of her adventure in the theatre, disguised as an orange-girl, in the sight of the Duchess of York, her patroness, and of the whole court.[4] The frolic

---

2. Brian Fairfax's *Life of the Duke of Buckingham*, quoted in Grammont.
3. Macpherson, vol. 1. p. 384.
4. Grammont, 2 190.

was, indeed, fully borne out in its extravagance and assurance by precedent. "At this time," says Bishop Burnet, "the court fell into much extravagance in masquerading; both the King and the Queen and all the court went about masked, and came into houses unknown, and danced there with wild frolic In all this, people were so disguised, that, without being in the secret, none could know them. They were carried about in hackney chairs. Once the Queen's chairmen, not knowing who she was, went from her. So she was quite alone, and was much disturbed, and came to Whitehall in a hackney coach, some say in a cart."[5]

On another occasion. Queen Katharine thought it not unseemly to resort to a fair at Audley, in company with the Duchesses of Buckingham and Richmond, disguised like country lasses, all in red petticoats, waistcoats, *et cetera*; Sir Bernard Gascoigne riding before the Queen on "a cart jade," and the two Duchesses also on double horses, one with a stranger before her, the other with Mr. Roper. These ladies happened so to have overdressed their parts, as to excite the attention of the crowd; looking, as it is related, "more like antiques than country volk." The Queen, however, who made her way up to a booth, to buy "a pair of yellow stockings for her sweetheart," was discovered, as well as her attendant. Sir Bernard, "by their giberish," to be strangers. The result may easily be supposed; the assembled country people mounted their horses, and, all amazement and curiosity, pursued the royal party to the court gate.[6]

This adventure was, however, less remarkable in those days, from the practice which Charles the Second maintained, of pursuing his diversions almost continually in the midst of his people, walking about the town without guards, and with a single friend. Hyde Park, described by a contemporary as "a field near the town," and used as a course, was beginning to be fashionable, and was preferred to other places of resort by Charles, on account of its fine air, and extent of prospect. It was at this time the private property of a publican, and the entrance was guarded by porters with staves, by whom a sum of money was levied upon every horseman, coach, or cart that entered.[7] Here, to give a specimen of the manners of the day, Charles exhibited one of the first coaches made with glass windows, presented to him by the accomplished Grammont, and the source of a bitter contention

---

5. Burnet, vol. 1 p. 368.
6. See Notes to Grammont, vol. 1 p. 329.
7. *Ibid*. 261.

between Lady Castlemaine, and Miss Stewart, afterwards Duchess of Richmond, as to which of them should succeed the Queen, and the Duchess of York, in the distinction of driving in the new-fashioned vehicle.

Spring Gardens, the resort of the fashionable world after driving in Hyde Park, and the scene in which many of the plots of our old comedies are laid, were also much in vogue at this period. "Here," says an old writer, "were groves and warbling birds, alleys and thickets," and in the centre a place for selling refreshments, similar to the *cafés* in the Parc at Brussels, or in the Bois de Boulogne at Paris. And here, the enclosure opening into the broad walks of St. James's Park, were many idle hours wiled away by both sexes. These recreations, with water parties on the Thames, were the amusements in which the sober-minded Anne, and her high-bred and haughty attendant, Lady Churchill, might indulge without loss of dignity, or danger to reputation.

The Princess regulated her household concerns with the utmost order, and maintained a degree of economy which could not have been carried on had she mixed generally in the amusements of the court, or dipped into the dangerous diversions of games of chance.[8] According to the Duchess of Marlborough, she had a much less allowance for her privy purse than any previous sovereign had before received;[9] but she managed with so much prudence, as to pay out of that, and from the civil list, many pensions and other matters, which had never previously been discharged from the same source.

"She bought no jewels," says her friend, "nor made any foolish buildings during the whole of her reign;"—"and in the article of robes," continues the Duchess, "she was saving; for it will appear by all the records in the Exchequer, where the accounts were passed, that in nine years she spent only 32,050*l*., including the Coronation expenses."[10]

In the service of this staid Princess, Lady Churchill continued an inactive, but not an inattentive observer of all that was passing in the busy world, in which her turn to govern, and to shine with unrivalled splendour, had not yet arrived. Anne, meantime, was occupied with maternal cares. Her first living child, a daughter, died when a year old, in 1686;—another similar loss, nearly at the same age, succeeded.

---

8. See *Opinions of Sarah Duchess of Marlborough*. Edit. 1784, p. 4.
9. £20,000 a year.
10. *Ibid*. p. 6.

Some years afterwards, the birth of William, declared at his baptism to be Duke of Gloucester, an event which took place at Hampton Court in 1689, was regarded by the country, as well as by the royal parents of this cherished and promising child, as a boon which might completely establish the Protestant succession.

During the short but eventful reign of James, little is mentioned of Lord Churchill, or of his lady. Whatever were their sentiments, they engaged in no public discussion on the occurrences which agitated all men's minds, until the revolution was ripe for execution. From the King's first public attendance at mass, to his secret and hurried departure from his kingdom, all was confusion and mournful anticipation, and, by a succession of tragical events, the public mind was prepared for the last great result.

At length Queen Mary became the mother of a living son, and in the disputes to which the birth of the Prince of Wales gave rise, we find Lady Churchill's name mentioned in some correspondence relative to that affair. Party differences ran high upon this subject, and Lord Chesterfield is of opinion that the shameful fable of the Prince's supposititious birth effected more to secure the Protestant succession than any other event whatsoever. The concurring testimony of successive writers has now assigned to the unfortunate Pretender the legitimacy which, by the singular and audacious attempts of a faction, and the fabrication of a servant, was disputed. Happy would it have been for that individual if the calumnies of his enemies had had foundation, and the secure contentment of a private station had been his lot!

Lady Churchill appears, from some expressions of the Princess Anne, to have been a witness of the singular intrigues which, in behalf of Anne's interests, as well as to further those of the Protestant cause, were carried on, to throw discredit on the birth of the Prince. Various were the accounts of the part taken by Anne on this occasion. It is said, that upon some quarrel on the subject between her Highness and the Queen, touching the approaching confinement of the latter, Her Majesty, sitting at her toilet, threw her glove at the face of the Princess; upon which Anne, indignant, withdrew from court; and upon the pretext of her health, or perhaps in consequence of the command of the King, she repaired to Bath, in order to drink the waters at that fashionable place of resort.[11]

From this circumstance, the Princess was absent at the time of the

---

11. Boyer's *Life of Anne*, p. 3.

birth of the infant Prince; but her letters upon the subject, and the inferences which she draws from details gathered from hearsay, afford a curious specimen of the coarseness of court gossip, and the peculiar vulgarity and common-place character of Anne's mind.[12]

It is a proof of the consistent firmness of Lord Churchill in adhering to the mode of faith which he venerated, that no employment, nor any distinction but a colonelcy of a troop of horse-guards upon the quelling of Monmouth's insurrection, was assigned to him during the short reign of James, for he was not of that material which James wanted to turn to active purposes.

Whilst the King's designs were not developed, and the liberties of his country were not openly threatened. Lord Churchill remained inactive, if not neutral: but, after the declaration of Indulgences in 1686, he was roused into exertion by apprehensions from past events, perfectly justifiable. That he had also private intelligence of James's endeavours to gain the Princess over to his religious persuasion, appears from the statement given by the Duchess, in her concise account of affairs at this period.

> What were the designs of that unhappy Prince (James) everybody knows. They came soon to show themselves undisguised, and attempts were made to draw his daughter into them. The King, indeed, used no harshness with her; he only discovered his wishes, by putting into her hands some books and papers, which he hoped might induce her to a change of religion; and had she had any inclination that way, the chaplains were such divines as could have said but little in defence of their own religion "or to secure her against the pretences of popery, recommended to her by a father, and a King."[13]

Anne had been the object, since her father's accession, of the jealousy of the court, on account of her having borne children. In her heart a true Protestant, she had expressed herself to Lady Churchill, two years previously, in a manner which showed evidently that she was not disposed to be a convert, and which proved also her dependence upon her strong-minded friend. Her expressions relate to the introduction of four peers of the Roman Catholic persuasion into the privy council.

---

12. See letters from the Princess of Denmark to the Princess of Orange in Dalrymple's *Mem.* vol. 2. Appendix.
13. *Conduct*, p. 16.

"I was very much surprised," she writes, "when I heard of the four new privy counsellors, and am very sorry for it; for it will give great countenance to those sort of people, and methinks it has a very dismal prospect. Whatever changes there are in the world, I hope you will never forsake me, and I shall be happy."[14]

These sentiments, consistent with the character of a Princess who is said, by one who knew her best, "to have had no ambition,"[15] were participated by the Prince of Denmark, who, although a privy counsellor during the reign of his father-in-law, had always been treated with coldness by that sovereign. Upon the declaration of Indulgences by James in his own person, without the consent of parliament, Lord Churchill began overtures to the Prince of Orange, through Dykefelt his agent, and Russell and Sidney, the great instruments of the revolution. The resolution of the Princess Anne to "suffer all extremities, even to death itself, rather than be brought to change her religion," was transmitted through the same channel. The terms in which these assurances were conveyed, were worthy of the great mind from which they proceeded.

"In all things but this," writes Lord Churchill to the Prince of Orange, "the King may command me; and I call God to witness that, even with joy I should expose my life for his service, so sensible am I of his favours. I know the troubling you, sir, with this much of myself, I being of so little use, is very impertinent; but I think it may be a great ease to your Highness and the Princess to be satisfied that the Princess of Denmark is safe in the trusting of me; I being resolved, though I cannot live the life of a saint, if there be ever occasion for it, to show the resolution of a martyr."[16]

Happily, however, there proved to be no necessity for the performance of this brave determination; "the projects of that reign," as the Duchess well observes, "being effectually disappointed as soon as they were openly avowed."[17]

The birth of a son, and the ceremony which declared him to be Prince of Wales, accelerated, in a marked manner, the course of the

---

14. Coxe, 1, 33.
15. *Conduct.*
16. Coxe, 34.
17. *Conduct*, p. 16.

infatuated King's destruction. Nonconformists, and the High Church party, Whigs and Tories, now plainly foresaw a total subversion of government in Church and State, all hopes of a Protestant succession to the throne being annihilated. Those who had upheld the doctrine of passive obedience, perceived that they were authorised, by the measures which James adopted, to form schemes for the prevention of his further designs: otherwise there would be no difference between the constitution of Great Britain and that of an absolute monarchy.

The doctrines of passive obedience had, it was well understood, been so industriously spread throughout the laity, as well as among the clergy, from a dread of those excesses which the Presbyterians and Conformists had permitted and extenuated in the last revolution, that many conscientious persons for some time doubted whether they ought to refuse an unlimited obedience to the sovereign. But the dangers of a sinking state, and of a tottering church, opened the eyes even of the most scrupulous, and convinced them that much ought to be sacrificed, in order to restrain the royal prerogative, and to save their best interests, and the objects of their veneration, from destruction. [18]

Under these threatening clouds, an union of all parties began to be considered as the only safe, the only practicable, the only honourable project to guard the country from anarchy, by protecting the laws. Nor can those be censured, who from considerations of such importance, and from general views, divest themselves, in such an extremity, of private interests, even of private obligations, for the sake of ensuing peace, by obtaining justice, and with it, the protection of a moderate and constitutional ruler. It requires infinite moral courage to give up the long-maintained and often-repeated dogmas of a party; and we are bound to hope, and to believe, that when great evils require so great a sacrifice, the motive which impels the change must proceed from some source higher than mere personal advancement. But unhappily, the world generally judges otherwise.

Lord Churchill, and the gifted woman who probably in a great degree participated his irresolution, and influenced his counsels, have shared largely in the condemnation bestowed upon others who adopted the same course which they, on this great occasion, thought it wise and right to pursue. Those who accuse them of ingratitude, must, however, recollect that there is a higher degree of gratitude than any which can be due to an earthly power; and that there are duties which

---

18. Tindal, vol. 15. p. 150.

no obligations can annul; a disregard of which becomes treachery in its most extended sense.

The conduct of Lord Churchill, throughout the reign of James the Second, was a consistent endeavour to withdraw from all participation in honours which he could not receive from the King without degradation, and from schemes which he must have viewed with disgust. Even when James sent to require his presence at the birth of the Prince of Wales, he declined to attend, assigning some slight treason. His desertion of James, as it was called, was the work of some years, not the sudden impulse of a day; it was wrung from Churchill unwillingly, and by painful degrees, and not till after his reflective mind had been saddened by an unparalleled succession of injuries inflicted upon his unhappy country, until mournful presage knew not where to stop.

Brought up in notions of devoted loyalty to the Stuarts, his own family, that of his wife, his intimate friends, and his brothers, being all wedded to the same opinions and devoted to the same cause, the conduct of Churchill on this occasion astounded the King more, it is said, than that of any of the other men of character and influence of the time. It was easy for the enemies of Churchill, or of his party—for personal enemies he could scarcely have—to account for the measures taken with caution, but pursued with vigour and firmness, by this great man. Dean Swift, whose aspersions, unlike most ephemeral writings, ate into the heart of his victims like caustic, and when once engrafted on the memory even of the indifferent, can scarcely be erased, has thus in his own charitable way explained the matter.

In describing the character of Churchill he says:—

He was bred up in the height of what is called the Tory principle, and continued with a strong bias that way till the other party had bid higher for him than his friends could afford to give. [19]

In another singular production of the day, entitled *Oliver's Pocket Looking Glass*, he was compared to Judas, and even reproached for ingratitude towards James, on the score of his lavish generosity to the degraded Arabella Churchill, the sister of the Duke.[20] But Churchill adopted not the measures which he prudently but resolutely adhered to, without a respectful but manly remonstrance with James, which proved his real attachment to the royal person, and his desire to warn

---

19. *Four Last Years of Queen Anne*, p. 10.
20. See *Oliver's Pocket Looking Glass*, printed 1711, p. 25.

him, if possible, from continuing his infatuated course.[21]

The recapitulation of those events by which the liberties of the people, and the stability of the Church of England, were secured, belong to history. The fatal blow given to the King's power was struck by the union of the Tories and the Whigs. Whilst the majority of the laity and clergy laboured in conjunction to effect the important end in question, some there were who deemed that determined but calm resistance rebellion, and who formed the new party under the name of Jacobites.

After this explanation, it is obvious what path the subject of this *Memoir* was henceforth called to pursue; although in a secure and peaceful course, even in that popular career, she and Lord Churchill were not, from the difficulties of the times, enabled to continue.

1688. At length, after a delay of a month within his own territories, the Prince of Orange hastened to the sea-coast, in order to set sail for England. But he was prevented from embarking by continued southwest winds, which lasted for nearly three weeks, during which time the anxiety of the English, and of the inhabitants of London in particular, could only be equalled by the panic of James, and the miserable uncertainties of all who were connected with the royal family.

Meantime all ordinary occupations in the city of London were suspended; the usually busy citizens were employed in inquiring the news, and in looking at the steeples and weathercocks to ascertain which way the wind blew. The general eagerness for the arrival of William was only exceeded by the general apathy respecting James. Even prayers were offered for that usually unwelcome visitor, an east wind, or, as it was now christened, "the Protestant wind."[22] Many individuals were known to rise in the night, to gratify their curiosity on this point.

But this intense expectation pervaded the metropolis only. In the country there was an indifference more fatal to James than the utmost turbulence could have proved:

> "A state of apathy," says Dalrymple, "which to the wise appeared more dangerous to the King than all the zeal of those in London against him; for opposition leads to opposition of sentiment; but that Prince approaches to his ruin whose subjects are unconcerned about his fate." Meantime James, blinded by

---

21. Coxe, p. 34.
22. Dalrymple book 5 p. 215..

his danger, gave orders for the host to be elevated forty days for his protection: thus rashly offending the opinions of that people whom he vainly attempted to enslave."[23]

At length the Prince of Orange, after many interruptions and dangers, landed at Torbay, whilst the King, still confiding in the protection of those spiritual weapons upon which he placed reliance, remained inert. When a report that the armament of the Prince of Orange was shipwrecked was brought to him one day at dinner, he was heard with great devotion to say, "It is not to be wondered at, for the host has been exposed these several days." Even his adversary was not without some superstitious feelings; his great desire being to land on the fourth of November, because it was his birthday and his marriage-day, and it might therefore prove fortunate. But his English adherents were rejoiced that the landing could not be made effectual until the day after, which was the anniversary of the discovery of the gunpowder plot.

Notwithstanding a conditional promise from James, "upon the faith of a King," to call a free Parliament, disaffection to his cause grew rapidly, spreading among those upon whom the unhappy monarch had most fondly relied. He placed himself, however, at the head of his assembled troops, consisting of twenty-four thousand men, at Salisbury, resolving, as he declared, to show himself King of England.[24] He entrusted the command of a brigade to Lord Churchill, whom he appointed lieutenant-general. The memorable letter addressed by Churchill to his sovereign, relinquishing the command, did not guard him from certain strictures upon this passage of his life; with what measure of justice, it has been left to the biographers of that illustrious general to declare.[25]

Meantime the Princess Anne and Prince George were acting in concert with the popular party, whom they had long secretly favoured, although the exact mode and time of their proceedings appears not to have been fixed. During the six days that James remained at Salisbury, the unhappy monarch's mind was every hour fretted and depressed by the news of some fresh defection. The first sea-officer that went over to the Prince of Orange was the brother of Lord Churchill, Captain Churchill, who joined the Dutch fleet with his ship. Humbled and alarmed lest he should be delivered up even by his own troops, James retreated towards London. The night before he commenced his

23. Dalrymple book 5 p. 215.
24. Dalrymple, 228, book 5.
25. See Coxe, Lediard.

march, Prince George of Denmark and the young Duke of Ormond, who had lately received the order of the garter, supped with him.

The King was in deep dejection; the Prince and the Duke were also lost in thought, meditating their own private schemes. On the following morning intelligence was brought to James, that his two guests of the preceding evening had gone over in the night to the Prince of Orange. Prince George thought it his duty to leave a letter of excuses. This royal personage, long a cipher in the court, which he could be said neither to disturb nor to adorn, had been accustomed to say, when he heard of the desertion of any of James's friends, "*Est-il possible?*" an ingenious mode of avoiding any expected opinion on so awkward a subject. On being acquainted with the Prince's flight, James recalled to his attendants the notable phrase, by the sarcastic observation, "So *est-il possible* is gone too!" And with this sole exclamation he allowed his relative to pass from his remembrance.

Having left his troops quartered at different places, deserted indeed as he went along by most of his officers, but retaining the common soldiers, whose simple reasoning taught them to follow their sovereign, James re-entered his capital.

But here a severer blow than any which he had hitherto experienced, fell upon him: the Princess Anne had fled. At first, to aggravate the distress of James, a mystery was made of her flighty and it was insinuated that the King, by encouraging the Papists, had been instrumental in the death of his child. The Earl of Clarendon, her maternal uncle, and her nurse, ran up and down like distracted persons, declaring that the Papists had murdered the Princess. James, who had fondly loved his daughter, and who had always shown her the utmost tenderness,[26] burst into tears, and in the agonies of parental feeling exclaimed—"God help me, my own children have forsaken me!"

He had trusted, as it seemed, to the kindly and womanly nature of Anne; but her affection was considerably less than her prudence. Yet public opinion, adjudging to the Princess those softer qualities which become a wife and a daughter, were willing to exculpate her, at the expense of her advisers, for a feature in her character and conduct which offended the natural feelings. It was soon perceived that an ill-timed caution, not excusable fear, dictated her flight. By all good minds Anne has been, and she remains, condemned for this act.

It was doubtless the duty of the Princess to remain, to have received and consoled her father. However others might judge or counsel, she

---

26. Macpherson, 2, 479; *Clarendon's Diary*, Nov. 9, 1688.

was still his child; and the heart which could be cold towards a parent in such an extremity as that in which the degraded and unhappy monarch now found himself, must have been deficient in all that is high and generous, even if it could boast some amiable dispositions in the sunshine of life.

It was soon ascertained with whom, and where, Anne had fled; and the public, commonly right in matters of feeling, could not readily forgive her whom they fixed upon as the prime adviser of the Princess.

Upon learning that the Prince of Denmark had deserted the King, and that James was returning to London, the Princess, as Lady Churchill in her own Vindication declared, was "put into a great fright. She sent for me," continues the same writer, "told me her distress, and declared that rather than see her father she would jump out of the window. This was her very expression."[27]

Such was Anne's first outbreak of emotion, not for her father, but for herself; it was probable she was more afraid of her quick-tempered step mother than of her subdued and unhappy father. A rumour had indeed prevailed that the Queen had treated the Princess ill, and had even gone so far as to strike her.[28] Be that as it might, Anne addressed a letter to her stepmother, announcing that having heard of her husband's desertion of James, she felt too much afraid of the King's displeasure to remain, and to risk an interview. She stated her intention not to remove far away, in order that she might return in case of a happy reconciliation. She declared herself in a distressing condition, divided between duty to a husband, and affection to a father; and, after commenting upon the state of public affairs, she ended her epistle in these terms:—

> God grant a happy end to all these troubles, that the King's reign may be prosperous, and that I may shortly meet you again in peace and safety. Till then, let me beg of yon to continue the same favourable opinion that you hitherto had of
> Yours, &c.
> Anne.

The following account of the caution with which Anne concerted her flight, and the mode in which she put it into execution, is given by her who acted so conspicuous a part in the tragic-comic transaction.

---

27. *Conduct.*
28. Tindal, 15, p. 200.

A little before,[29] a note had been left with me, to tell me where I might find the Bishop of London, (who in that critical time absconded,) if her Royal Highness should have occasion for a friend. The Princess, on this alarm, sent me immediately for the Bishop. I acquainted him with her resolution to leave the court, and to put herself under his care. It was hereupon agreed that, when he had advised with his friends in the city, he should come about midnight in a hackney coach to the neighbourhood of the Cockpit, in order to convey the Princess to some place where she might be private and safe.

The Princess went to bed at the usual time, to avoid suspicion. I came to her soon after; and by the back-stairs which went down from her closet, her Royal Highness, my Lady Fitzharding, and I, with one servant, walked to the coach, where we found the Bishop and the Earl of Dorset. They conducted us that night to the Bishop's house in the city, and the next day to my Lord Dorset's, at Copt Hall. From thence we went to the Earl of Northampton's, and from thence to Nottingham, where the country gathered round the Princess; nor did she think herself safe until she saw herself surrounded by the Prince of Orange's friends.[30]

Inoffensive, and even popular from her strict adherence to Protestantism, Anne immediately met with defenders. A small body of volunteers mustered round her, and formed a guard, commanded by no less a person than Dr. Compton, Bishop of London, the resolute prelate who had opposed the court on various occasions, and especially in his refusal to suspend a Protestant clergyman for exposing papistical errors.[31] This zealous man, who had been a cornet of dragoons in his youth, now rode before the Princess and her suite, including Lady Churchill, carrying a drawn sword in his hand, and pistols on his saddle-bow.[32] In this chivalric guise the fugitive party reached Northampton, and travelled on to Nottingham; where the gallant Earl of Devonshire, the friend of Russell, had raised a band of volunteers to assist the cause of the revolution.

It happened that the famous Caius Gabriel Gibber, the sculptor, or, as it was called in those days, statuary, was at this time at Chatsworth,

---

29. Before the Princess had sent to declare her distress.
30. *Conduct*, p. 16.
31. Tindal, p. 75, vol. 15. See Appendix.
32. Dalrymple, b. 6. p. 230.

engaged by Lord Devonshire in the embellishment of that sumptuous place, and, in the words of Colley Gibber, in altering "from a Gothic to a Grecian magnificence." Colley Gibber himself was visiting at Chatsworth, in order to be under the restraint of his father's eye, until the period of his going to college should arrive; no unnecessary precaution, as it appeared by his after-life. Colley Gibber, in pursuance of his father's commands, travelled from London to Nottingham, and found the country in a state, if it may be so expressed, of peaceful commotion.

When he arrived at Nottingham, he found his father in arms there, among the Earl's volunteer company. Gaius, the sculptor, whose undying fame is preserved in the exquisite figures on Bethlehem Hospital, was aged, and averse to the thoughts of a winter campaign; and he persuaded his patron to allow him to retire to Chatsworth to finish his works, and to substitute his young son, more fit for the business of war, into his honours and regimentals.

The Earl consented, and Colley Gibber "jumped," as he expressed it, "into his father's saddle."

He had not been many days at Nottingham, before news of the Princess Anne's flight reached that city, accompanied by the report that two thousand of the king's dragoons were in pursuit to bring her back to London. On this alarm, the volunteers scrambled to arms, and advanced some miles on the London road, in order to meet the Princess and her cavalcade, Anne being attended only by the Lady Churchill and by the Lady Fitzharding. The party, thus guarded, entered Nottingham in safety, and were lodged and provided for by the care and at the charge of the Earl of Devonshire; and the same night all the noblemen and other persons of distinction in arms had the honour to sup at Her Highness's table. There being more guests in number than attendants out of liveries to be found, Gibber, being well known in the Earl of Devonshire's family, was desired by the *maître d'hotel* to assist at the table. It fell to the lot of the young officer of volunteers to attend upon Lady Churchill, and he has left the following interesting memorandum of that occasion.

> Being so near the table, you may naturally ask me what I might have heard to have passed in conversation at it, which I certainly should tell you, had I attended to above two words that were uttered there, and those were, '*some wine and water.*' These, as I remember, came distinguished to. my ear, because they came from the fair guest whom I took such pleasure to wait on. Ex-

cept at that single sound, all my senses were collected into my eyes, which, during the whole entertainment, wanted no better amusement than that of stealing now and then the delight of gazing on the fair object so near me. If so clear an emanation of beauty, such a commanding' grace of aspect, struck me into a regard that had something softer than the most profound respect in it, I cannot see why I may not, without offence, remember it, since beauty, like the sun, must sometimes lose its power to choose, and shine into equal warmth the peasant and the courtier.[33]

Such was the impression which Lady Churchill, most likely unconsciously, produced upon the imaginative Gibber, who, fifty years after this memorable scene, describes it in the foregoing glowing terms.

The Duchess, in more homely phrase, thus describes the share which she took in this event, in the narrative which her enemies feared would be posthumous;[34] so late in life was it before she could resolve to enter upon a review of those events of her youth, in which sweet and bitter recollections were mingled.

As the flight of the Princess to Nottingham has been by some ignorantly, not to say maliciously, imputed to my policy and premeditated contrivance, I thought it necessary to give this short but exact relation of it. It was a thing sudden and unconcerted; nor had I any share in it, further than obeying my mistress's orders in the particulars I have mentioned, though indeed I had, reason enough on my own account to get out of the way. Lord Churchill having likewise, at that time, left the King, and gone over to the other party.[35]

The assistance which Lady Churchill afforded the Princess on this occasion, was the first faction of her life in which she directly took a share in public affairs, and evinced the effects of that influence upon her gracious patroness, which afterwards became so conspicuous and remarkable. Her conduct was severely criticised, and "a deluge of scurrility, falsehood, and defamation,"[36] was drawn down upon her by this first manifestation of her importance in the political world.

In analysing her conduct in this transaction, we have first to. con-

---

33. *Life of Colley Cibber*, p. 48.
34. *The Other Side of the Question, in a Letter to Her Grace the Dowager Duchess of . . . . By a Woman of Quality*. Ed. London, 1742, p. 5.
35. *Conduct*, p. 19.
36. *Life of Sarah Duchess of Marlborough*, 1746, p.6.

sider the truth of her statements, and afterwards the cogency of those reasons which swayed her actions at so critical a period.

It is scarcely possible, in the first place, to suppose that no plan had been concerted by the Princess and her friends, for her security in a storm which they must have beheld lowering for some considerable period of time. Lord Churchill had chalked out his own course, and with that decision and prudence which characterized his whole career, had avowed his intentions, and carried them promptly into effect. Prince George, a weaker vessel, had *coquetted* with the winds, and hovered about the shore, before putting out his *barque* of small resolution to sea, trusting to the only gale that ever blew him any importance in the course of his royal existence.

These two, for the time, influential men, the one borrowing all his small lustre from the Princess his wife, the other passionately attached to a woman of rising influence and of strong discernment, could never have desired to conceal their projects, nor even the slightest particulars of their daily movements, from those on whose affections they placed dependence, and whose sentiments were in unison with their own. There can be but little doubt that the plans for the demeanour of the Princess were fully matured before it was necessary to have recourse to action; with the Bishop of London, an avowed enemy to court measures, for her spiritual adviser, Lady Churchill for her friend, and Cavendish, the friend of Russell, for her host.

Whether on this, and on all other occasions of minor politics. Lord Churchill controlled his wife, or his wife controlled him, it is of little purpose to inquire. On this occasion they doubtless were wholly agreed; nor can we view the actions of the Princess Anne from this period until the memorable year 1710, otherwise than with a reference to the opinions and wishes of her presiding genius.

To these observations may be added the rumours, stated by Lediard as facts, that six weeks before she left Whitehall, Anne had ordered a private staircase to be made, under pretext of a more convenient access to Lady Churchill's apartments, but, in fact, to secure a mode of escape whenever her person or her liberty were in danger. The night before Her Royal Highness withdrew, the Lord Chamberlain had orders to arrest the Ladies Churchill and Berkley, but, on the request of the Princess that he would defer executing those orders until after she had spoken to the Queen, he complied with her wishes. The Princess's women, on entering her chamber the morning after her flight, were surprised to find their mistress fled; and the excitement of the people, on the suspicion of outrage to her, was so great, that they threatened to pull down Whitehall, unless the place of her retirement was instantly discovered.[37]

It cannot be disputed but that the Princess acted with a degree of pusillanimity which was a feature in her character, and throughout her subsequent life made her the victim of daring minds, of whose intrigues she was the slave, and at the same time, from her exalted station, the active principle. Anne knew her father too well to suppose, that whilst he retained the power to defend his daughter, he would suffer her to be treated with indignity, or allow violence to be done to her feelings as a wife, or to her opinions as a Protestant. The pretext that it was unsafe for her to remain, on account of the schemes which might be formed against her by the priests, was a needless alarm, and an ungenerous insinuation.

If we are to conclude that Princes may discard natural feeling, and ties of duty, from their consideration, in times of difficulty, we may commend the prudence of Anne in absenting herself from a scene of distress wherein her father was the chief actor; we may excuse her from remaining to receive the deserted and degraded king, justly expiating grave offences by the bitterest mortifications, but stung most by the utter alienation of one daughter, and the heartless discretion of the other. But had Anne continued in London, had she waited to receive the dishonoured King, and, by kindly sympathy and filial affection, which is of no party, endeavoured to soothe the pangs of his return to his gloomy capital—had she thus solaced the most painful hours of a father whom she was to see no more, she would have compromised no party, nor entailed upon herself any responsibility.

She was a passive neutral being; unambitious, and, in those days, whilst her brother and sister lived, comparatively unimportant: any breach of what is called consistency, that fatal word which seems, in a public sense, to be invented to banish sincerity and to smother nature, would, in her, have been attributed to the most amiable source; except, perhaps, by her stern formal brother-in-law, or by her virtuous, wise sister,—a pattern of wives, but an undutiful and heartless daughter, and a cold and ungracious sister.

Anne wanted soul—wanted resolution and character more than heart; and at a critical period, when she might have acted so as to avoid subsequent self-reproach, and might have reaped the satisfaction to her own mind that she had not added to the sharpness of

---

37. *Life of John Duke of Marlborough*, by Lediard.

the "serpent's tooth," she absconded—for the flight had much of that character—under the auspices of Lady Churchill, and guarded by the Bishop of London. It is natural to suppose that the yearnings which in her latter days she felt towards her brother, the Pretender, and her manifest distaste to the Hanoverian succession, proceeded, in a degree, from a too late regret for the part which on this occasion she had been induced to take, and which was quickly followed by her surrender of her right to William the Third.

There is something in the very style of Lady Churchill's exposition of the whole matter, that marks a sense of shame and regret, as she slides rapidly over the particulars of the event.

Fearless herself, one may almost picture to the mind her contempt, when the Princess expressed, in childish terms, her fear of her father. Upon that point, the alleged excuse of her nocturnal flight, Lady Churchill endeavours guardedly to excuse her royal mistress. She dwells with far less minuteness and distinctness on her own motives than on the subsequent explanations of other matters, in which she avows and defends her unequivocal counsels to the Princess, and brings conviction that she acted a sincere and upright part on those occasions.

Her known character for resolutely maintaining her own will, in opposition even to that of Anne, fixed upon her all the ephemeral obloquy with which the Jacobite party assailed the proceeding. It was supposed, and not without reason, that the Princess was even at this time much more under her control, than was the first lady of the bedchamber under that of her mistress, whom she scorned to cajole, but contrived to command.

"Flattery, madam," says her bitterest assailant, "is what you never happened to be accused of, nor of temporising with the humours of your royal patroness. The *peccadillos* you have been supposed answerable for, are of a quite contrary class—of playing the tyrant with your sovereign, of insisting on your own will in opposition to hers, and of carrying your own points with a high hand, almost whether she would or not."[38]

Yet, with the inconsistency which often accompanies invective, this foe of the Duchess adds:

Flattery does not always imply fulsome praises and slavish compliances; none but the grossest appetites can swallow such coarse

---

38. *Other Side of the Question*, p. 11.

food. There is a species, of a much more refined and dangerous nature, which never appears in its own shape, but makes its approaches in so happy a disguise, as to be mistaken for truth, simplicity, and dealing. Your Grace had discernment enough to find that the Princess had an aversion to the first; so you, very adroitly, made use of the last; and, as you confess yourself, found your account in it."[39]

---

39. *Other Side of the Question*, 11.

CHAPTER 4
1688

Surrender of the Crown to William

The Protestant Lords assembled at the Privy Council held by James the Second imagined that the King was altered, and that his powers of mind had forsaken him. They asked each other "where were the looks, and where was the spirit, which had made three nations tremble?"

"They perceived not," says Dalrymple, that the change was not in the King, but in themselves."[1] In their consciousness of the monarch's feebleness, contrasted with former power, consisted the change.

The Princess Anne was not, it is to be presumed, enabled to conquer her fears of encountering her humbled parent, since no mention is found of her return to the metropolis until after all storms were hushed and Mary, "possessing neither the authority of a queen, nor the influence of a wife,"[2] became the presiding power of the concerns of a remodelled court.

The personal character of Mary may be said to have had a considerable influence upon the conduct of Lady Churchill, and upon her position in that purified region, the British court; since, during the whole period of her short reign, the two royal sisters were scarcely ever on affectionate or even friendly terms; and it has been deemed necessary by Lady Churchill to justify herself as the supposed cause of these continual differences, not to say complete though disguised alienation, between those Princesses.

Bishop Burnet has described, in his character of Queen Mary, a perfect model of feminine excellence.

"The queen," he says, "gave an example to the nation, which shined

---

1. Dalrymple, b. 6, p. 232.
2. Macpherson, 1 p. 516.

in all the parts of it." [3] 'Tall and majestic,' of a form exquisitely proportioned, her countenance expressive and agreeable, notwithstanding a constitutional weakness in her eyes, Mary moved with dignity and grace, spoke with equal propriety and spirit, and acted, when occasion required, with masculine resolution. In all that duty and station exacted, she was admirable. She possessed, in its perfection, that quality, "not a science," as Pope expresses it, "but worth all the seven, prudence."

Her intentions for the benefit of her subjects were excellent.[4] Her first and continual care was to promote reform in every department which she superintended. She began by attacking those habits of idleness which had tended to demoralise the court, and exposed its fair ornaments to many temptations. She set the fashion of industry, by employing herself in needlework, working many hours a day herself, with her ladies and her maids of honour similarly engaged around her, whilst one of the party read to the rest. She freed her court from all doubtful or censurable characters, so that there was not a colour of suspicion of any improprieties, such as had been the source of just censure in the preceding reigns. She expressed a deep sense of religion, and formed a standard of principle and duty in her mind, upon the sense of her obligations as a Christian. Industrious and pious, she was consequently cheerful and unconstrained.

Every moment had its proper employment; her time being so apportioned out to business and diversion, to the devout exercises of the closet, and to the polite customs of the court, that the most scrupulous observer could not pronounce her to be too serious or too merry, too retiring or too busy, nor could find out the slightest cause of censure in her well-considered actions, nor in her prudent yet engaging deportment. Her capacity was great; her memory, and the clearness of her comprehension, were particularly remarkable; her attention to everything laid before her was that of a superior and reflective mind. Yet she was humility itself; her distrust of her own judgement was accompanied by an absolute reverence for the King's opinions; and her perfections were crowned, in the sight of the English people, by her firm though unobtrusive adherence to the Protestant faith, of which she was regarded as the chief stay and support, after her merits and her opinions had been fully disclosed.

Such were the qualities assigned to Mary by her zealous panegyrist; but with all these attributes,—admirable in a private sphere, ex-

---

3. Burnet, 4, 193.
4. Noble's edition of *Granger*, vol. 1, p. 13.

cellent in a queen,—like many persons of regular habits, patterns of virtue in a quiet way,—perfect when not put out of their habitual course,—prudent, submissive, and placid, Mary had one grand defect. She wanted heart. Gentle in her nature, whilst free from the passions of pride and anger, she was devoid also of the generosity which sometimes accompanies those defects in character. She rarely gave cause of offence, but she could not forgive. Too good a wife, she sacrificed filial to conjugal duty; forgetting that the Saviour, whose precepts she honoured, throughout all his high vocation, knew no obligation which could obliterate the duty to parents.

But Mary may be held up to the degenerate wives of the present day, as one who would have been at once their model and their reproof, had she been placed under different circumstances. In anything less than the cruel alternative of ceasing to revere and to protect a parent at the command of a husband, or, for the sake of her consort's political views, Mary would have risen pre-eminent in esteem, both immediate and posthumous.

Transplanted early to a foreign soil, she devoted herself with ready submission to the wishes, the pursuits, the very prejudices of a husband whom she could not have loved, had she not possessed feelings different from those of her sex in general. At his command she became sedate and obedient; her naturally good spirits were subdued into the tone which her reserved but not unimpassioned husband deemed becoming in woman, and essential in her who had the honour of sharing his damp climate and cold heart.

This, indeed, became her second nature; yet, at the king's command, the staid, domestic Mary roused herself from her simple habits and matronly reserve, and was converted into a patroness of mirth and folly; for she was enjoined to use every art to entertain, and charm the fascinating Duke of Monmouth, in order to annoy and endanger her father and his throne. William, jealous to a degree, and concealing under his dry exterior a temper of a furious violence,[5] ordered his exemplary wife to attract and to be attractive, and she obeyed. She received visits in private from the Duke; she danced, she skated, because Monmouth loved those amusements.

> "It was diverting," says a contemporary writer, "to behold a princess of Mary's decency and virtue, with her petticoats tucked half-way to her waist, with iron pattens on her feet,

---

5. Burnet.

sometimes on one foot, sometimes on the other."

No less extraordinary was it to hear that Mary was permitted to receive the Duke alone every day after dinner, to teach her country dances in her own apartment.[6] So accommodating was this pattern of conjugal obedience, that she could not only lay aside natural feelings, but, what is perhaps more difficult, dispense with long-cherished habits, and reassume the part of girlhood, after a long period of matronly dignity, which somewhat resembled the precision, without the liberty, of a single life.

In matters of weightier import than learning country dances, or skating on Dutch canals, Mary was equally subservient. The flight of James from London; the arrival of the Prince of Orange at St. James's; the subsequent withdrawal of James entirely from the British dominions; the acknowledgment of the convention summoned by William, that the tranquillity of the country was owing to his administration, and the petition of that body that he would continue to exercise regal power,—were events which would have been regarded by an ambitious woman with the utmost intensity of interest.

The declaration of the Houses of Parliament, five days afterwards, that the crown had become vacant by the desertion or abdication of James, disclosed fully to Mary the realization of those dreams of greatness, which an aspiring or even busy female would have cherished in her heart, in the absence of those natural feelings with which Mary was but little troubled. But the gentle Queen was here again all duty and obedience; her mind was but a reflection of her husband's will and pleasure. Instead of hurrying to occupy the throne to which she might with scarcely an effort have been raised, she remained, at the desire of her consort, patiently in Holland, in order to prevent any intrigues which might be formed in favour of her ruling alone,—a proposal [7] which gnawed into the very heart of the proud, reserved, William.[8]

Upon her being detained still longer in Holland by contrary winds, or perhaps by a secret gale in the form of a conjugal command, the Earl of Danby was despatched for the purpose of detailing to her the debate in Parliament respecting the successor to the vacant throne; and at the same time to intimate that if she desired to reign alone, he doubted not but that he should be able to insure the accomplishment

---

6. Macpherson, vol. 1. p. 308, *apud d'Avaux*.
7. Dalrymple, Burnet, Tindal, Macpherson.
8. Dalrymple, b. 6, p. 269.

of her wishes. The Princess, with a firmness which had something of magnanimity in it, replied, "that she was the wife of William Prince of Orange, and would never be any other thing than what she could share in conjunction with him;" adding, "that she should take it very ill if, under pretext of a concern for her, any faction should set up a divided interest between her and her husband." To confirm this answer, and to prevent misunderstanding, she sent the letter brought to her by Lord Danby, and her answer, to the Prince; and thus prevented any jealousy, on the score of her hereditary right from interfering with her domestic comfort and the confidence of her husband.[9]

Such was Mary, unlike the rest of her imprudent race;—unlike them, perhaps, from the early tuition[10] of her stern husband, a very Utilitarian of the seventeenth century. That she will be fully proved deficient in tenderness—that her feelings were even too much under control—(for we may control our feelings until they cease to exist—extinguished by the constant pressure of a dense and foggy mental atmosphere)—that the good principle within her displayed itself rather in the absence of wrong than in active zeal—that she was amiable without being beloved, and commendable without attaining popularity, was fully shown during her short possession of regal power.

Whilst the debates concerning the monarchy were carried on, the Princess Anne began to manifest some traits of character for which the world had not hitherto given her credit. Unlike her sister, she was not an unconcerned observer of the startling schemes which were bruited, nor of the great changes to which the absence of her father had already given birth. Even her placid temper appears to have been ruffled at the reported desire of William, through the intrigues of his favourite Bentinck, to rule alone; and to exclude her family from the possession of a crown which they were little likely to regain when lost.

But William, checked by the demonstration of English spirit in one of his English adherents, contented himself with a declaration, first, that in case of a regency being proposed, he should decline that office: he would accept of no dignity dependent on the life of another. Secondly, that if it were the design of the people to settle the Princess alone on the throne, and to admit him to a participation of power only through her courtesy, he should decline that proposal also. "Her rights he would not oppose. Her virtue he respected. No one knew

---
9. Tindal, vol. 15, p. 280.
10. Macpherson.

them better than he did. But he thought it proper to let them know that he would hold no power dependent on the will of a woman." And he concluded with an intimation that if either of these schemes were adopted, "he should give them no assistance in the settlement of the nation, but return to his own country, happy in the consciousness of the services which he had, though in vain, endeavoured to do theirs."[11]

This declaration on the part of William had the intended effect. There appeared to men of all parties no alternative between making the Prince of Orange king, or recalling the exiled monarch. The first of these plans was, after much procrastination, adopted.

One obstacle alone was opposed to the decision of the leading partisans of William;—the consent of the Princess Anne to waive her right to the crown was necessary before the accession of William could be accomplished.

The Jacobite party, on the pretext of regard to Anne, but actually for their own factious purposes, supported her in the indecision, not to term it opposition, which the Princess at first evinced, in respect to the proposal to relinquish her right in favour of William.

Anne, after wavering long, after contradicting herself at various times, and keeping all around her and connected with her in suspense, at last consented to postpone her claim in favour of the Prince of Orange; stipulating at the same time for an ample revenue, to support her dignity as next heir to the throne.[12] This step, which was, under all circumstances, the wisest for herself, and the most considerate for the good of the nation, that Anne's counsellors could have advised, was attributed to Lady Churchill,—"one," says Dalrymple, "of the most interested of women, who possessed at that time the dominion of her spirit, and who hoped to serve her own interest and her husband's by betraying those of her mistress."[13]

It will here be necessary, and we think not uninteresting to the reader, to insert Lady Churchill's account of the share which she had in the transaction.

Quickly after this," (speaking of the Princess Anne's flight to Nottingham,) "the King fled into France. The throne was hereupon declared vacant, and presently filled with the Prince and Princess of Orange. The Parliament thought proper to settle the

---

11. Dalrymple, b, 6, p, 270.
12. *Ibid.*
13. *Ibid.*

crown on King William for life, and the Princess of Denmark gave her consent to it. This was another event which furnished simple people with a pretence to censure me. It was intimated that, to make my court to the King and Queen, I had influenced the Princess to forego her undoubted rights. The truth is, I did persuade her to the project of that settlement, and to be easy under it after it was made. But no regard to the King nor the Queen, nor any view of ambition, had the least share in moving me to this conduct, any more than to what inconsiderable part I acted in the business of the Revolution.[14]

Lady Churchill proceeds to say, that, with respect to the Revolution:

> .. it was evident to all the world, that as things were carried on by King James, everybody sooner or later must be ruined who would not become a Roman Catholic. This consideration made me very well pleased at the Prince of Orange's undertaking to rescue us from such slavery. But I do solemnly protest, that if there be truth in any mortal, I was so very simple a creature, that I never once dreamt of his being King. Having never read, nor employed my time in anything but playing at cards, and having no ambition myself, I imagined that the Prince of Orange's sole design was to provide for the safety of his own country, by obliging King James to keep the laws of ours, and that he would go back as soon as he had made us all happy; that there was no sort of difficulty in the execution of this design, and that to do so much good would be a greater pleasure to him than to be king of any country upon earth. I was soon taught to know the world better.
>
> However, as I was perfectly convinced that a Roman Catholic was not to be trusted with the liberties of England, I never once repined at the change of the government; no, not in all the time of that persecution I went through. I might, perhaps, wish it had been compassed by some other man, who had more honour and justice than he who could depose his father-in-law and uncle to maintain liberty and the laws, and then act the tyrant himself in many instances; but I never once wished that the change had not been made.
>
> And as to giving King William the crown, for life, it was the

---

14. *Conduct*, p. 22.

same principle of regard for the public welfare that carried me to advise the Princess to acquiesce in it. It is true, that when the thing was first started, I did not see any necessity for such a measure; and I thought it so unreasonable, that I took a great deal of pains (which I believe the King and Queen never forgot) to promote my mistress's pretensions. But I quickly found that all endeavours of that kind would be ineffectual; that all the principals, except the Jacobites, were for the King, and that the settlement would be carried in Parliament, whether the Princess consented to it or not.

So that in reality there was nothing advisable, but to yield with a good grace. I confess that, had I been in her place, I should have thought it more for my honour to be easy in this matter, than to show an impatience to get possession of a crown that had been wrested from my father. And as it ought to have been a great trouble to the children of King James to be forced to act the part they did against him, even for the security of liberty and religion, (which was truly the case,) so it seems to me, that she who discovered the less ambition would have the more amiable character.

However, as I was fearful about everything the Princess did, while she was thought to be advised by me, I could not satisfy my mind till I had consulted with several persons of undisputed wisdom and integrity, and particularly with Lady Russell of Southampton House, and Dr. Tillotson, afterwards Archbishop of Canterbury. I found them all unanimous in the opinion of the *expediency of the settlement proposed, as things were situated.* In conclusion, therefore, I carried Dr. Tillotson to the Princess, and, upon what he said to her, she took care that no disturbance should be made by the pretended friends, the Jacobites, who had pressed her earnestly to form an opposition.[15]

Having thus explained to Anne the reasons which, in her opinion, rendered it compatible with the honour of the Princess to surrender her right to the crown for the time being, Lady Churchill, aware of the responsibility in which she involved herself, and acknowledging that "she was fearful about everything the Princess did," whilst she was thought to be advised by her, adopted the wise precaution of consulting persons of "undisputed wisdom and integrity," before she permit-

---

15. *Conduct,* p. 22.

ted the Princess to send in her decision upon this momentous point.

The individuals to whom Lady Churchill applied for counsel were such as a woman of discernment, and of right intentions, would desire to consult. The female friend to whom she addressed herself was the illustrious Rachel Lady Russell, the beloved wife, counsellor, friend, the high-minded support and solace, of one of the most noble of men.

The tragedy in which Lord Russell terminated his life, was fresh in the remembrance of the public. Five years before the Revolution, he had been brought before his Peers on his trial, and being told that he might avail himself of the assistance of one of his servants to take notes of the proceedings in short-hand,—"I ask none," was his reply, "but that of the lady who sits by me." And when the assembly beheld the daughter of the virtuous Lord Southampton rising to assist her lord at this extremity, a thrill of anguish moved the spectators.[16]

But very recently, the loyalty, the good faith, the bravery of the Russells, had been recalled to public remembrance, even by the unhappy cause of their heartfelt calamity. When James, in his utmost need, had summoned a council of the Peers to ask their advice, in passing to the council chamber he met the Earl of Bedford, father of Lord Russell, who had offered a hundred thousand pounds for his son's life—a sum which James, then Duke of York, had persuaded his brother to refuse. James, reflecting upon the probity and influence of the Russells, and catching, in his hopeless state, at any straw which could arrest his ruin, said to the Earl, "My lord, you are a good man; you have much interest with the Peers; you can do me service with them today."

"I once had a son," was the heart-broken father's reply, "who could have served your Majesty on this occasion;" and with a deep sigh he passed on.

To the widowed daughter-in-law of this venerable man Lady Churchill addressed herself. Nor would Lady Russell have permitted any step to be entertained, that was derogatory to the honour of her who sought such aid in her judgement; for in this noble woman, faithful in her grief to the memory of him whom she constantly prayed to rejoin, the gentlest qualities were united to the loftiest heroism. Her husband's death was preferable in her eyes to his dishonour. In one long fixed look, in which the tenderness of the fondest affection was controlled on the part of her husband by great and lofty resolves, on

---

16. Dalrymple, b. 1, p. 90.

hers by a fortitude which sprang from the deepest feelings, had the Lady Russell parted from her lord. From the time of his death, Lady Russell, from a sort of common tribute, had taken a high place in society.

She bore her sorrows with the patience of an humble believer in a future state of peace and of reunion with the lost and the beloved; but not all the too late tributes to the motives and excellence of him whom she had lost—neither the reversal of the attainder by parliament, nor the ducal honours conferred upon the family, nor even the universal respect and national sympathy—could recall her to the busy world, bereaved, to her, of all that was valuable. She lived in a dignified and devout seclusion at Bedford House, formerly Southampton House, in Bloomsbury Square, that beloved abode, at the sight of which the eyes of her noble husband had been filled with tears, as he passed to the place of his execution in Lincoln's-inn-fields. Here, consoled by the society of the pious and the learned, cheered by the hopes of an hereafter, and honoured in her dark old age, Lady Russell resided, until death, in 1723, released her from an existence rendered still more mournful by blindness, brought on by continual weeping.[17]

One of the brightest ornaments of the age in which she lived, Lady Russell was as accomplished as she was high-minded. To her counsels the celebrated Dr. Tillotson often recurred. By him, as by all who knew her, she was regarded as the first of women;[18] nor could that woman continue her friend, whose motives were not pure, and whose conduct was not irreproachable.

The other counsellor to whom Lady Churchill put forth her case, was the good, the learned, but calumniated Archbishop Tillotson.

In this selection, also, she showed great prudence. Tillotson was the common friend of both the Princesses, and the spiritual adviser of Mary, who entrusted to him the chief charge of the concerns of the churchy with which William the Third did not consider himself justified to interfere.

Tillotson was of a different temperament from the heroic Lady Russell, and it was perhaps for this very reason that Lady Churchill consulted him. With the soundest judgement and the kindest temper, this revered prelate had a sensitiveness of disposition which tended to render him cautious, perhaps timid, in his measures. "He was," says his dearest friend, "a faithful and zealous friend, but a gentle and soon

---

17. Granger. Edited by Noble. Art. Russell.
18. Dalrymple.

conquered enemy." [19] But he was truly and seriously religious, without affectation, bigotry, or superstition; and it may be supposed that the dauntless thinker, Lady Churchill, whose original mind detested these prevalent defects, delighted in conversing with one of so enlightened a spirit. "His notions of morality were fine and sublime;"[20] and she might well feel that she could not go wrong, with one so scrupulously virtuous to guide her.

The influence of Dr. Tillotson as a preacher, his sermons being then accounted the patterns for all such compositions, might also sway her in requesting his counsels; whilst "the perpetual slanders, and other ill usage," with which, according to his friend, he had been followed, and which gave him "too much trouble, and too great a concern,"[21] might, she may well have thought, have taught him to feel for others, and induced him to double caution in pointing out the right path, to one beginning the weary road of public life, in which she, too, found that vanity and vexation of spirit went along with her on her journey.

It is not to persons such as these that we address ourselves, when we intend to follow a crooked line of policy. We may judge favourably of the purity of our motives, when we determine to question the wise and the good, upon the mode and spirit of our actions; and Lady Churchill, when she hastened to disclose her perplexities, and to unfold her intentions, to two persons of undoubted probity and of known piety, may have felt satisfied that she need not blush to confess them to a higher power.

The result of her deliberations was a determination to influence the Princess to surrender what she could scarcely deem her rights, in favour of William and Mary, during their separate lives; but with precedence to her, and to her children, to any issue which William might have by a second marriage, in case of the death of his Queen. And it might have been inferred that, for this important decision, the gratitude of the King and Queen would have been effectually secured to Lord and Lady Churchill, who had both shared in the good office. But such was not the result.

This obstacle to the settlement of the crown being removed, the Prince and Princess of Orange were declared King and Queen, in accordance with the votes severally of both Houses of Parliament, upon a motion of Lord Danby. The populace, who remembered how

---

19. Burnet, vol. 4, p. 196.
20. *Ibid.*
21. *Ibid.*

the crown had tottered on James's head at the coronation, and who recalled the pleasantry of Henry Sidney, keeper of the robes, who kept it from falling off, remarking, as he replaced it, "This is not the first time that our family has supported the crown,"[22] were now startled by the circumstance, that the day of the proclamation of William and Mary was also that of the accession of the unfortunate James; and the assembled crowds pointed at the statue of the unhappy monarch, with its face turned to the river, and its back to the palace, in bitter and sarcastic allusion.[23]

This event, which took place on the 6th of February, 1689, was, in six days afterwards, succeeded by the arrival of Queen Mary in London. Her singular, and, to a sensitive mind, truly painful situation, raised many conjectures with respect to her probable conduct. But whether, as it is asserted by some, she was warned by William to control her emotions, for his sake, upon her first appearance as a sovereign, the deposer and successor of her father; or whether her extraordinary levity proceeded from the heartlessness of a commonplace character, it is difficult to decide. Political feuds may, indeed, sufficiently, though not satisfactorily, account for hardness of heart, and an oblivion of the dearest ties; and Mary's pliant mind, and warped, but not unaffectionate temper, had been long worked upon, during a series of intrigues, of which her father was the object, and her husband the first agitator.

Whatever was the nature of her feelings, the cold and light deportment which she manifested on her entrance into her palace at Whitehall, the last refuge of her deposed and deserted father, gave considerable offence. Mary, it was thought, might have remembered, with compassion, the unfortunate, and, as far as grave offences were concerned, the innocent Queen, her stepmother, Mary of Modena, who had last inhabited the very apartments into which she was now herself conducted. She might have bestowed one passing serious thought upon that unhappy fugitive, who only two months previously, had left that house privately, with her infant son, the Prince of Wales, then five months old, carried by his nurse; one faithful friend, the Count de Lauzun, the sole companion of her flight.

From this palace she had crossed the Thames, in the darkness of night, unsheltered, in an open boat, the wind, and rain, and swell of the river, conspiring to detain and terrify her, and to add to the gloom of her situation. On this palace, standing for shelter under the walls

---

22. Dalrymple, b. 2, p. 113.
23. *Ibid*. b. 7, p. 272.

of an old church in Lambeth, had the wretched Queen fixed her eyes, streaming with tears, and searching, with fruitless tenderness, for the flitting shadow of her husband across the lighted window; whilst, starting at every sound which came from that direction, the desolate mother sometimes suspended her anxious gaze, to look upon her sleeping infant,[24] unconscious of her miseries, unconscious of the hope deferred, the disappointment, the perplexities which awaited him in his future career, as the penalty to be paid for royal birth.

But if Mary, disliking her stepmother, of whom, indeed, she knew but little, and regarding her as a bigot whose pernicious influence drove James, in the opinion of the Princess Anne, into greater outrages upon justice than he would otherwise have inflicted; if Mary, thus prejudiced, gave not one reflection to her stepmother, nor doubted the reality of her imputed brother's relationship, she might yet have bestowed some few natural tears upon the fate of her father. Many there were who could have told her, had her heart yearned for such or for any intelligence, how James, when his Queen and his son were gone, shuddered at the solitude of his palace; how, in every look from others, he read danger and dark design; how he dreaded alike kindness or distance; and when informed by Lord Halifax (who, to induce him to leave England, deceived him) that William meditated his death, he broke out into the bitter exclamation, "that small was the distance between the prisons of princes and their graves": a saying which he quoted of his father, and which now appeared to his affrighted mind prophetic of his own destiny.

The indecision, the confusion of mind, the helplessness of her father, might rise to Mary's mind, as she entered the hall whence he had been accustomed to issue. The feebleness of majesty without power might occur to her; the hapless King ordering out guards, no longer his, to fight the Prince, and affecting to summon a council which would no longer meet at his command, might have induced some reflections on her own account. But Mary, unmoved, entered the palace, passed through those rooms which scarcely two months before had been opened, the day after James's flight, to receive his expected levee, and walked unconcerned towards her bedchamber, and into the suite of apartments prepared for her. It was, on this occasion, the duty of Lady Churchill to attend Her Majesty, and her account of the Queen's conduct is too lively, has too much an air of truth, to be omitted.

---

24. Dalrymple, b. 6, p. 238.

"I was one of those," says the Duchess, "who had the honour to wait upon her (the Queen) to her own apartment. She ran about, looking into every closet and conveniency, and turning up the quilts upon the bed, as people do when they come into an inn, and with no other sort of concern in her appearance but such as they express; a behaviour which, though at that time I was extremely caressed by her, I thought very strange and unbecoming. For whatever necessity there was for deposing King James, he was still her father, who had been so lately driven from that chamber, and from that bed; and if she felt no tenderness, I thought she should at least have looked grave, or even pensively sad, at so melancholy a reverse of his fortune. But I kept these thoughts in my own breast, not imparting them even to my mistress, to whom I could say anything with all the freedom imaginable."[25]

Two days after the arrival of Mary, both Houses of Parliament went in state to bestow the crown upon her husband and on her. The King, having accepted the gift for himself, and for his consort, was proclaimed with Mary, King and Queen, "in the very hall of that palace," says Dalrymple, "from which the father had been driven; and at the gate of which her grandfather had, by some of those who now placed the crown on her head, and by the fathers of others, been brought to the block."[26] On the following day Lord Churchill was sworn a member of the privy council, and a lord of the bedchamber; and two days before the coronation he was created Earl of Marlborough,—a title which he was supposed to have taken in consequence of a connexion on his mother's side with the family of Ley, Earls of Marlborough, extinct ten years previously. But this famous designation did neither augur unbroken prosperity to the receiver, nor insure to the donor, King William, the devoted fidelity of Marlborough; and the reign upon which we are now entering may be considered to have been, in most respects, a season of anxiety to the spirits, and of depression to the affairs, of Lord Marlborough, and of her who participated in every emotion of his heart.

---

25. *Conduct.*
26. Dalrymple, b. 7, p. 276.

CHAPTER 5

State of the British Court

The English court now presented a strange and gloomy contrast to those seasons of reckless dissipation which had characterised it in the two preceding reigns.

The personal character of the monarch, his weak health and retired habits, had considerable influence in producing this change. William appeared, indeed, almost of a different species to the well-bred and easy-tempered Charles the Second, and to the affable though stately James. Both these monarchs were remarkable for the happy grace with which they bestowed favours;[1] William, as even his warmest panegyrist allows, generally "with a disgusting dryness, which was his character at all times, except in a day of battle, for then he was all fire, though without passion; he was then everywhere, and looked to everything."[2] His "Roman eagle nose," and sparkling eyes, ill corresponding with a weak and emaciated body, gave expression to a countenance otherwise disfigured by smallpox, the effects of which, added to a constitutional asthma, produced in him a deep and constant cough, the surest obstacle to conversation.

Without considering this impediment as having a continual influence over his deportment. King William was one of those cynical personages who adhere to silence as a type of wisdom, and despise the talkative; and who, having seen some mischiefs arise from too great fluency of speech, take refuge from indiscretion in cautious taciturnity. Like most of those who defeat the purpose of society, in thus fencing themselves from animadversion, the King was extremely prone to make severe remarks and hypercritical comments upon others. His very senses, according to Burnet, were provokingly "critical and ex-

1. Macpherson, vol. 1, p. 512.
2. Burnet, 5. 69.

quisite."

Devoid of imagination, which would have stood in the way of his unnatural philosophy, he was an exact observer of men and manners. Nothing escaped his piercing eye, nor was forgotten by a mind endowed with a most extraordinary memory, which never failed him.[3] Like most reserved, phlegmatic men, he imbibed strong and lasting prejudices; and whilst he did not stoop to revenge, he was unable to shake off unfavourable impressions of others, whether founded or unfounded. When to these qualities we add the facts that he could not bear contradiction, his temper being so peevish to a degree, that he could not bring himself to love the English, and that he preferred the retirement of the closet to the brilliancy of the ball-room or banquet, it might be easily foretold, that with good intentions, possessed of sincerity, of religious belief, and of valour, William and his court would become eminently distasteful to the English people.

The Queen endeavoured to the utmost of her power to dissipate the disgust which she could not but perceive to exist in the public mind, since the court was, in great measure, deserted. But as she interfered not in public concerns, and as there was, on that account, little to be gained from her influence, her vivacity, and the redundancy of her conversation, (in which she delighted,) did not attract the gay and the interested, and her efforts were fruitless.

A few days after his accession, William, notwithstanding the advice of his friends, took refuge from that society which he so much despised and disliked, in the retirement of Hampton Court, which he left only to attend the Privy council on stated days; and the people soon found, to their infinite discontent, that it was the design of the sovereign to add to this old and irregular building new tenements, upon an expensive and magnificent scale, for his own and for the Queen's apartments. Thus retired from the gaze of his metropolitan subjects, the King did little to conciliate their affections, as far as the cultivation of those arts extended, which his predecessors had patronised. For his introduction of the Dutch style of gardening into England, the nation has little cause to be grateful. Yet gardening was the only art which seemed to afford him any satisfaction.

In this stately edifice, the proud monument of a subject's wealth, and of a monarch's munificent taste. Lady Marlborough, in her attendance upon the Princess Anne, must have passed a considerable portion of her time.

---

3. Burnet.

It was not long before misunderstandings began to disturb the serenity of that constant intercourse which at first subsisted between the two sisters. On the first arrival of Queen Mary, the Princess, as Lady Marlborough relates, "went to see her, and there was great appearance of kindness between them.

But this," adds the Duchess, "quickly wore off, and a visible coldness ensued; which I believe was partly occasioned by the persuasion the King had, that the Prince and Princess had been of more use to him than they were ever likely to be again, and partly by the different characters and different humours of the two sisters. It was, indeed, impossible they should be very agreeable companions to each other; for Queen Mary grew weary of anybody who would not talk a great deal, and the Princess was so silent that she rarely spoke more than was necessary to answer a question."[4]

It was, however, apparent that the subsequent alienation of the sisters had a deeper foundation than mere difference of taste, or discrepancy of habits, which might naturally be looked for between two sisters separated so early, and passing the season of their youth in scenes widely different, and with characters totally dissimilar. That Mary had received some impressions prejudicial to the friend and counsellor of her sister, previous to her accession, is manifest from the following justification of her favourite, which the Princess had thought necessary, in the preceding year, to write to her sister.

Cockpit, Dec. 29, 1687.

.... Sorry people have taken such pains to give so ill a character of Lady Churchill ...

I believe there is nobody in the world has better notions of religion than she has. It is true, she is not so strict as some are, nor does not keep such a bustle with religion; which I confess I think is never the worse; for one sees so many saints mere devils, that if one be a good Christian, the less show one makes, it is the better, in my opinion. Then, as for moral principles, it is impossible to have better; and, without that, all the lifting up of hands and eyes, and going often to church, will prove but a very lame devotion.

One thing more I must say for her, which is, that she has a true sense of the doctrine of our church, and abhors all the princi-

---

4. *Conduct*, p. 25.

ples of the church of Rome; so that, as to this particular, I assure you she will never change. The same thing I will venture, now I am on this subject, to say for her lord; for though he is a very faithful servant to the King, and that King is very kind to him, and I believe he will always obey the King in all things that are consistent with religion; yet, rather than change that, I dare say he will lose all his places, and all that he has.[5]

This prepossession against the Countess of Marlborough may have originated only in her known and determined spirit; but it was doubtless aggravated by the relationship and correspondence of the Countess with her sister, now Lady Tyrconnel, the warm and busy partisan of the exiled monarch, of whom her husband, Lord Tyrconnel, was an active and influential adherent, the Queen seems to have adroitly thrown her objections to Lady Marlborough into the form of scruples concerning her religious opinions, hoping that Anne's strict notions upon those points might be offended by her favourite's carelessness upon matters of form, then of absolute importance in the tottering state of our national church, and at all times aids and props to devotional exercises, of the greatest assistance to habitual piety. But the insinuations of Mary, in whatever terms they may have been couched, only served to strengthen friendship which a species of adversity still rendered essential to the Princess Anne.

The Countess, however, was retained in her post about the Princess, "a situation seemingly of little consequence," observes Dalrymple, "but which, for that very reason, her pride and spirit of intrigue determined her to convert into a great one."[6]

Like all busy, violent women, especially if their ardent dispositions have a bias to politics, Lady Marlborough seems to have been peculiarly obnoxious to the other sex. There is not an historian who praises her without some reservation; and the majority of those who touch upon the notorious influence which she exercised, mingle admiration for her talents with marked dislike to her personal qualities. Yet, amid the conflicting interests by which even the placid Anne was harassed. Lady Marlborough proved a firm, zealous, and judicious friend, regardless of her own advancement in court favour, and of her husband's military aggrandisement, for which a weaker mind would have trembled, ere it had boldly ventured upon interference in political intrigues.

---

5. Doctor Birch's Notes from the Princess Anne's Letters to her Sister. See Sir John Dalrymple's *Memoirs*.
6. Dalrymple, vol. 2, part 2, b. 1, p. 305.

The first cause of discord between the Queen and the Princess of Denmark was upon a subject of domestic convenience. Upon such themes the spirit of Lady Churchill was peculiarly excitable. In order to understand precisely the nature and merits of a quarrel and a dispute which would have been summarily, and perhaps peaceably settled, had men, instead of women, been immediately concerned in adjusting it, it is necessary to explain the sort of residence which Anne, in common with other branches of the royal family, was obliged at that time to adopt.

It has already been stated that the Princess Anne resided at the Cockpit, Westminster, in apartments which were allowed to her at the time of her marriage, by her uncle, Charles the Second. Concerning these well-situated accommodations, a perpetual irritation, a continual negotiating, intriguing, and consequent ill-will, seems to have been excited. Some description of the localities, and of the advantages which Anne derived from the appropriation of the Cockpit to her use—advantages which sorely vexed her royal sister—may not, therefore, be deemed impertinent.

The ancient Palace of Whitehall, situated beyond Scotland Yard, and on the same side of the street, was obtained by Henry the Eighth, from Wolsey, in 1529, and, until consumed by fire in 1697, was the residence of several of our monarchs, who found their account in thus living in the centre of the metropolitan world, and at the same time in a healthy and airy situation.

In very few years after Henry the Eighth had obtained possession of Whitehall, he procured, in addition to its immediate precincts, the inclosure of the St. James's Park, which he received from the Abbot and Convent of Westminster in exchange for other property, and appropriated to the improvement of the noble structure of Whitehall Palace. One portion of the inclosure he converted into a park, another into a tennis-court, a third into a bowling-alley, and a fourth into a cockpit.

The Cockpit was situated near to what is now called Downing-street; and was the only access from Charing Cross to St. James's Park, and the buildings beyond. Henry, for the accommodation of passengers, erected two gates, one of which opened from the Cockpit into King-street, Westminster, on the north, and the other into Charing Cross. The former of these was known by the name of Westminster Gate, and the other by the name of Cockpit Gate. Both were eminently beautiful; and before the year 1708, that of the Cockpit was still remaining, and added considerable dignity to the entrance into Anne's courtyard, being adorned with four lofty towers, battlements, portcullises, and richly decorated,[7] Westminster Grate had no less a reputation than its neighbour, and is said to have been erected upon a design of Hans Holbein.

Successive innovations in different reigns had, however, long before the Princess of Denmark honoured the Cockpit with her residence, annihilated its uses and original splendour. Apartments had been built over the space, where Henry, with his coarse taste, delighted, in the truly national and disgraceful sport. The Palace of Whitehall, including the Cockpit, was one vast range of apartments and offices, extending to the river. There was even a gallery for statues, accessible to young artists, and rooms to the number of seventy were remaining until lately, [8] The rooms were lent, or given, or let, to different persons who rejoiced in royal favour; and the same tenement, if one so vast and of such a character could be so considered, contained Charles the Second, his court, his queen, the haughty Castlemaine, and the beautiful, dangerous, and devoted Louise de la Querouaille.

The rooms at the Cockpit appear, however, to have been in some respects inconvenient to the Princess of Denmark. Their situation, when all between them and the village of Charyng was an open space, when Westminster Abbey rose uninterrupted to the view, and when St. James's Park, peopled with birds, was daily the scene of all that London could boast of aristocratic splendour, must indeed have been at once gay and commanding. Yet, notwithstanding these advantages, the Princess desired, for certain reasons, to exchange her apartments for others; and she encountered, in that desire, an unkind, and, as it appears, an unnecessary opposition from Mary.

The Duchess of Marlborough thus explains the affair; and as other historians have not thought it worth their notice, we must consider her account of it to be conclusive.

> The Princess, soon after the King's coming to Whitehall, had a mind to leave her lodgings, (the way from which to the Queen's apartment was very inconvenient,) and to go to those that had been the Duchess of Portsmouth's, which the King on her request told her she should have. But the Princess requesting also (for the conveniency of her servants) some other lodgings that

---

7. In 1708 the hinges of the portcullis were remaining.
8. Among others, those near the water were occupied by the late Duchess of Portland.—Smith's *Antiquities of Westminster,* vol. 1, p. 19.

lay nearest to those of the Duchess, this matter met with difficulty, though her Highness, in exchange for all she asked, was to give the whole Cockpit (which was more than an equivalent) to be disposed of for the King's use. For the Duke of Devonshire took it into his head, that could he have the Duchess of Portsmouth's lodgings, where there was a fine room for *balls*, it would give him a very magnificent air.

And it was very plain that while this matter was in debate between the King, the Queen, and Princess, my Lord Devonshire's chief business was to raise so many difficulties in making the Princess easy in those lodgings, as at last to gain his point. After many conversations upon the affair, the Queen told the Princess 'that she could not let her have the lodgings she desired for her servants, till my Lord Devonshire had resolved whether he would have them, or a part of the Cockpit.'

Upon which the Princess answered, 'she would then stay where she was, for she would not have my Lord Devonshire's leavings.' So she took the Duchess of Portsmouth's apartment, granted her at first, and used it for her children, remaining herself at the Cockpit. Much about the same time, the Princess, who had a fondness for the house at Richmond, (where she had lived when a child,) and who, besides, thought the air good for the children, desired that house of the Queen; but that likewise was refused her, though for many years no use had been made of it, but for Madame Possaire, a sister of my Lady Orkney's and Mr. Hill.[9]

Notwithstanding these manifestations of a petty and somewhat tyrannical ill-nature on the part of Mary, the Princess, who was propriety itself, "continued," says the Duchess, "to pay all imaginable respect to the King and Queen." But no humble endeavours on the part of Anne could avail to soothe the irritations of her sister and brother-in law, whilst they perceived that, bred up amongst the people, she was dear to their subjects, and that on important occasions her interests became their cause; and a jealousy, aggravated in its bitterness by the well-known disposition of Anne to befriend her brother, and by her equally certain repentance for her conduct to her father, became a permanent sentiment in the mind of Mary.

It was reasonable in the Princess to expect that having given up her

---

9. *Conduct*, p. 29.

right in the succession, the King and Queen should study to promote her comfort in all essential respects. Her father, at her marriage, had settled upon her a suitable annuity of thirty thousand pounds; and now that a fresh arrangement was to be made, Anne expected that a permanent and independent revenue would be secured to her.

This was in the King's power, the civil list amounting to no less a sum than six hundred thousand pounds a year. But William had no intention of making the Princess independent, if he could possibly avoid such a step; his policy was to keep her in subjection to himself and to her sister, in order, if possible, to insure her fidelity in times when no one around him was exactly to be trusted, and when he was obliged to pardon insincerity, and to be blind even to treachery.[10] The King even expressed some reluctance to continue to Anne the allowance which she had received,—a line of conduct which was viewed with just indignation by his sister-in-law, who had facilitated His Majesty's accession to the throne by her compliance with his wishes, at the time of that revolution which had banished those whom she most loved from the crown.

Stimulated by a sense of this injustice, and prompted by the Countess of Marlborough, Anne resolved to appeal to Parliament, knowing that in that assembly the Tories and the disaffected would warmly support her claims, as the ready means of producing dissension at court, and of rendering William unpopular.[11]

Upon the report of Anne's intentions being conveyed to the Queen, a scene truly singular, as occurring between two royal personages, both celebrated by historians for their moderation and discretion, took place in the heated atmosphere of that scene of faction, Kensington Palace.

The Queen sought an interview with her sister, for the purpose, and to use the Duchess of Marlborough's expression, "one night taking her sister to task about it;" commencing her attack by asking her what was the meaning of those proceedings. To which the Princess, somewhat evasively, replied, "she heard that her friends had a mind to make her some settlement."

The Queen, upon this reply, lost that command of herself for which she had hitherto been remarkable.

"And pray, madam," she thus addressed the Princess, "what friends have you but the King and me?"

---

10. See Dalrymple.
11. *Conduct*, p. 28.

Anne felt the taunt deeply; and resented it with as much warmth as her nature could muster. The intimation of her dependence, conveyed in this speech, appears from the following remarks, penned by her friend and *confidante*, to have stung her severely. How characteristic of that sharp-sighted person is the sarcastic tone of the concluding remark!

I had not the honour to attend the Princess that night, but when she came back, she repeated this to me. And, indeed, I never saw her express so much resentment as she did at this usage; and I think it must be allowed she had great reason, for it was unjust in her sister not to allow her a decent provision, without an entire dependence on the King. And, besides, the Princess had in a short time learnt that she must be very miserable, if she was to have no support but the friendship of the two persons Her Majesty had mentioned.[12]

In justification of the narrow principle adopted by William and his Queen on this occasion, Mr. Hampden, junior, spoke in the House of Commons, representing the impolicy of settling a revenue on a Princess who had so near a claim to the crown, and who might be supported by a number of malcontents. He adduced in favour of his argument the withdrawal of a motion for settling a separate allowance of a hundred thousand pounds a year upon the Queen;[13] but his arguments did not prevail, and the debate was adjourned to the next day. Some of the Princess's friends, encouraged by the general feeling in her favour, even proposed to allow her seventy thousand pounds yearly;—and the King, annoyed at the course which the debate took, and fearful of its issue, prorogued parliament.

Whilst the subject was thus warmly discussed, the Queen, although conversing every day with her sister, observed a cautious silence on the subject of her settlement: and the most strenuous exertions were made, to prevail on the Countess of Marlborough to persuade the Princess to give up the point in dispute. The most intimate friend of the dauntless Sarah was the Viscountess Fitzharding, third sister of Edward Villiers, who was successively created, by William, Baron Villiers and Earl of Jersey.

The family of Lady Fitzharding, though of Jacobite tendencies, exercised over William a prodigious ascendancy, through the influence

---

12. *Conduct*, p. 30.
13. Boyer, p. 6,

of two of its members; the Earl of Jersey, who was himself in high favour with the King; and the Countess of Jersey, though a Catholic, was much esteemed by the Queen: whilst Elizabeth Villiers, sister of the Earl, was the acknowledged mistress of the monarch.[14] Partialities so unaccountable and incongruous are not surprising to the reader who has gone through the private history of courts and kings.

Through this channel Mary now sought to influence Lady Marlborough, the oracle to whom her sister Anne implicitly deferred. Every art was used, either "through flattery or fear,"[15] to dissuade the Princess from the pursuit of a settlement. The Duchess thus describes these ineffectual efforts:—

> My Lady Fitzharding, who was more than anybody in the Queen's favour, and for whom it was well known I had a singular affection, was the person chiefly employed in this undertaking. Sometimes she attacked me on the side of my own interest, telling me, 'that if I would not put an end to measures so disagreeable to the King and Queen, it would certainly be the ruin of my lord, and consequently of all our family.' When she found that this had no effect, she endeavoured to alarm my fears for the Princess by saying, 'that those measures would in all probability ruin her; for nobody, but such as flattered me, believed the Princess would carry her point, and in case she did not, the King would not think himself obliged to do anything for her. That it was perfect madness in me to persist, and I had better ten thousand times to let the thing fall, and to make all easy to the King and Queen.'

Little could Lady Fitzharding understand the character of her gifted friend, when she attempted to dissuade her from any undertaking in which she had resolutely engaged. On the contrary, the Duchess, persisting the more strenuously in her determination the more it was opposed, with a true feminine spirit writes:

> All this, and a great deal more that was said, was so far from inclining me to do what was desired of me, that it only made me more anxious about the success of the Princess's affair, and more earnest, if possible, in the prosecuting of it.

For, as she further declares, she would rather have died than have sacrificed the interests of the Princess, or have had it thought that

---

14. Coxe, vol. 1, p. 60.
15. *Conduct*, p. 30.

she had herself been bribed or intimidated into compliance with the wishes of the court.

Lady Marlborough, therefore, employed all the powers which she possessed, to forward the settlement She justly reflected, as the Princess's friend, that anything was better than dependence upon William's generosity, of which she had no opinion. For Lord Godolphin told her that the King, speaking of the civil list, "wondered very much how the Princess could spend thirty thousand pounds a year, although it was less," adds the shrewd Duchess, "than some of His Majesty's favourites had."[16]

Meantime King William and his Queen were perfectly aware, as it appears, with whom the resistance to their plans originated, and they took measures, accordingly, to appease and to satisfy her who already held "that good sort of woman,"[17] their royal sister, in a kind of subjection to her will and opinion. Accordingly, a few days before the question was put to the vote, a message was despatched to Lady Marlborough, offering, on the part of the King, to give the Princess fifty thousand pounds a year, if she would not appeal to parliament.

The person employed on this delicate embassy was Charles Talbot, Duke of Shrewsbury, whom the King had taken into his favour, although once a Catholic, and the godson of Charles the Second. This nobleman, according to William, "the only man of whom both Whigs and Tories spoke well," was an enemy to those party distinctions by which even great and good men were betrayed into the violence of faction. Easy, graceful in his deportment, and accomplished, he was peculiarly adapted, from his charms of manner, and even of countenance, notwithstanding the loss of an eye,[18] to act the part of mediator between the irritating and the irritated, especially when of the gentler sex.

Empowered by William to use his own discretion in the mode of persuasion to be adopted, the Duke obtained an interview with Lady Marlborough. He unfolded the object of his mission, which he sought to strengthen.

The result of these negotiations was favourable to Anne. She gained her point, and an income of fifty thousand pounds was settled on her by parliament. Some of the members persisted in proposing an allow-

---

16. Conduct, p. 32.
17. See *Private Correspondence.*
18. He was called in Ireland, when he was appointed by Anne lord lieutenant, Polyphemus, or Ireland's Eye.—Noble's *Granger*, vol. 1 p. 51.

ance of seventy thousand pounds, but the Princess was advised by her friends to accept of the smaller sum, and not to combat the point any longer against the influence of the crown.

Notwithstanding this arrangement, the Countess thought it incumbent upon her not to allow the Princess to accept of the settlement without further advice. She sent, therefore, to ask the opinion of the Earl of Rochester, who was then "just creeping into court favour,"[19] by means of the interposition of Bishop Burnet, who recommended him to the Queen's regard and forgiveness. For Rochester was one of those who had wished for a regency instead of a king, and who endeavoured to instil into his own party those notions of arbitrary government which he had imbibed in the reign of Charles the Second, under whom he had held several high ministerial appointments.

Lord Rochester, like all party men in his time, had his admirers and his censurers. Although considered a man of abilities, and although his private character was highly respectable, there were some points in his conduct of which an adversary might take advantage, to question this nobleman's integrity.[19]

Having refused to turn Catholic, in King James's time, the earl had received an annuity of four thousand a year, on his life and on that of his son, settled upon him as a compensation of the Lord Treasurer's staff, which had been taken from him on that occasion. Lady Marlborough's observation upon the opinion which this nobleman now delivered to her is therefore peculiarly pungent.

> "Nevertheless," she says, "I was so fearful lest the Princess should suffer for want of good advice, that after I had heard of the Commons voting 50,000*l*. a year, I sent to speak with my Lord Rochester, and asked his opinion whether the Princess ought to be satisfied, or whether it was reasonable she should try to get more. (I did not then know how much his heart was bent on making his court to the Queen.) His answer to me was, that he thought not only that the Princess ought to be satisfied with 50,000*l*., but that she ought to have taken it in any way the King pleased; which made me reflect that he would not have liked that advice in the case of his own 4000*l*. a year from the Post-Office, settled on him and his son."[20]

---

18. *Conduct.*
19. Tindal, vol. 16, p. 502.
20. *Conduct*, p. 35.

"But I was not," she adds, "so uncivil as to speak my thought, nor so foolish as to struggle any longer. For most of those who had been prevailed with to promote the settlement were Tories, among whom my Lord Rochester was a very great man. Their zeal on the present occasion was doubtless to thwart King William, for I never observed that on any other they discovered much regard for the Princess of Denmark."[21]

The success of the affair was justly attributable, as she affirms, not to any faction making the passive Princess the plea for a vexatious opposition to the court, but, as she forcibly expresses it, "to the steadiness and diligence of my Lord Marlborough and me; and to this it was imputed, both by those to whom the result was so exceedingly disagreeable, and by her to whose happiness it was then so necessary."[22]

Anne was at this time deeply sensible of all that she owed to the firmness and zeal of these devoted servants. "She expressed her gratitude in a manner generous to a very high degree;" and from this time, until many years afterwards, the interests and the happiness of the Churchill family were the objects of her solicitude, and of a munificence certainly conferred with delicacy, and often rejected on their part with a spirit of independence and disinterestedness.

---

21. *Ibid*, 37.
22. *Ibid*.

Chapter 6
1789

Attachment of Marlborough to his wife

Whilst encountering many enemies, both male and female, whose hostility the Countess of Marlborough might set down to the score of envy, she possessed one friend who, through life, influenced all her actions, and who has been supposed to have gained her affections.

It would be a libel upon human nature to imagine, that the cherished wife of John Duke of Marlborough could be fascinated by the lesser constellation of talents and of virtues, displayed in the character of the minister Godolphin. The impure and consequently illiberal judges of conduct, who pride themselves on what is called knowledge of the world, may decree that a cordial and confidential friendship, in the simple acceptation of the word, cannot exist between the two sexes, where similarity of age is joined to congeniality of temper and taste. But, happily for society, some men are honourable, some women high-minded; reliance may gratify one party, and approbation and esteem secure the kindly feelings of the other. A friendship firm, generous, and delicate, may exist between persons of different sexes; and where it has this pure source, it will ever be found beneficial, permanent, and delightful.

Resembling, in one respect, his distinguished friends, Godolphin had early in life been attached to the service of the Stuart family. The first situation that he held was that of page to Charles the Second; the last appointment that he retained under the Stuarts was the painful and precarious office of lord chamberlain to the blameless and unhappy Mary of Modena, for whose beauty, misfortunes, and interests, he ever expressed admiration, compassion, and regard.[1]

Queen Anne, it is said,[2] had been touched by the merits of one whom it required merit to appreciate, and had loved Godolphin when young, but was prevented by state necessity from marrying a subject.[3] After the revolution, in the progress of which Lord Godolphin acted the part of an honest statesman, yet forgot not the duty of a grateful subject, he was approved and retained in the Treasury by William, who appointed him also one of the Lords Justices of the kingdom in his absence. Godolphin, indifferent to the blandishments of rank, absolutely declined the honour of the garter; and raised, unwillingly, to the Peerage, was as disinterested in respect to the gains, as in regard to the honours of successful ambition.

In this particular he displayed a character totally unlike that of the gifted woman for whom he has been said, by Tory writers, to have cherished a passion which influenced his political bias.[4] His disposition, in other respects, little resembled hers. He was of a reflective, inquisitive turn of mind; slow but unerring in his conclusions; possessed of exquisite judgement in all the affairs of life; yet of a temper so peculiarly amiable, possessed of sentiments so unusually lofty, that he might have lived in the most innocent retirement, from the purity of his motives and the elevation of his general character.

Superior to the low practices by which weaker spirits toiled for ascendency, Godolphin never condescended to a courtier's arts. His promise was inviolate; he detested not only falsehood, but, what in his situation was most difficult, he never permitted himself to have recourse to the more prevailing, and as it is believed safer, form of that vice, dissimulation. Like Marlborough, Godolphin, when asked to confer favours, softened his refusals with a kindness and frankness which propitiated even the disappointed.

The notions of economy, which this great minister adopted, not grounded on a passion for wealth which sullied the brightness of the great Churchill's virtues, were applied with the same rigid care to the public means, as to the expenditure of his own private fortune. Grave even to sternness, he won universal esteem from his inflexible justice, and in society was the object of affection, no less than of respect. Disfigured in countenance by the smallpox, and severe in expression,

---

1. Noble's edition of *Granger*, vol. 2, p. 18
2. Macpherson.
3. Noble, art. Godolphin.
4. Dean Swift's *Four Last Years of Queen Anne*, p. 12.

there was yet something bright and penetrating in his eye, something engaging in his smile, which procured him the favour of the female sex,—to whom, with all his profound experience of men and manners, with all his infallibility of judgement, and his gravity of deportment. Lord Godolphin was, during the whole of his life, passionately devoted.[5]

The name of Godolphin (signifying a white eagle) was of ancient origin. His immediate progenitors, country gentlemen of the county of Cornwall, were distinguished for their loyalty to the Stuarts during the civil war.[6] According to Dean Swift, who mentions the circumstance in that casual, careless way which answers the intentions of malice without wearing its aspect, Godolphin was intended for some trade, until his friends procured him the office of a page at the court of Charles the Second.[7]

From this humble station he rose rapidly into political consequence; for he sat in the first Parliament after the Restoration, as member for Helston in Cornwall, and was shortly afterwards employed in various high offices, until appointed to the commissionership of the Treasury, at the same time that he was called to the House of Peers. During the reign of James the Second, Godolphin enjoyed the favour of Queen Mary, to whom he was chamberlain, and of James, who reappointed him one of the Lords of the Treasury. Educated in high church tenets, Godolphin, like his friend Lord Marlborough, became a Whig when the Protestant succession was in danger.

Yet, whilst he managed, with consummate prudence, to act as one of the commissioners appointed by James to treat with William at his landing, and was so skilful and so fortunate as to retain his situation of Treasury Lord upon the accession of William,—Godolphin, courageous, and, like most courageous men, tender-hearted, was among the few of the deposed monarch's courtiers who gave him the solace of their attendance and sympathy. He accompanied the abdicated King to the seaside when he quitted England, and maintained a correspondence with him until his death.

It is not always possible to calumniate noble and popular characters, but it is generally easy to ridicule the greatest and the best. Lord Godolphin's weakness, according to one whose inimitable strokes of satire sink into the memory, were love of play and vanity.

---

5. Boyer, p. 17.
6. *Ibid.*
7. Swift, p. 12.

"Physiognomists would hardly discover," says Dean Swift,[8] "by consulting the aspect of this lord, that his predominant passions were love and play—that he could sometimes scratch out a song in praise of his mistress with a pencil and a card—or that he hath tears at his command, like a woman, to be used either in an intrigue of gallantry or politics."

Conformably to this devotion to dames and damsels was his lordship's romantic admiration of the beautiful exiled Queen, Mary of Modena, whom he used to address in letters, in which love was ambiguously mingled with respect; "whilst little presents of such things as ladies like"[9] accompanied these epistles,—such tokens of regard to one so unfortunate and so interesting being always first shown to King William, though with the knowledge of James's Queen. But in these minor traits, mentioned as inconsistencies and follies, there is a touch of generous sentiment, at the disclosure of which Lord Godolphin, amidst all his vast concerns and political pursuits, need not have blushed.

It was to this valued friend, both her own and her husband's best counsellor, that the Countess of Marlborough applied for advice, about a year after the settlement on the Princess had been made, in a matter of some delicacy. The Princess, from gratitude for her friend's exertions, wrote to offer her a pension of a thousand pounds. The manner in which this proof of a generous friendship was offered, speaks honourably for Anne's goodness of heart and propriety of feeling.[10]

I have had something to say to you a great while, and I did not know how to go about it. I have designed, ever since my revenue was settled, to desire you would accept of a thousand pounds a year. I beg you will only look upon it as an earnest of my goodwill, but never mention anything of it to me; for I shall be ashamed to have any notice taken of such a thing from one that deserves more than I shall be ever able to return."

Some delay having taken place in the payment of this annuity, the Princess wrote a letter, couched in terms of the most sincere affection, to her "dear Mrs. Freeman," begging her not to think meanly of her faithful Morley for the negligence of her treasurer.

Upon this the Countess began to take seriously into consideration the propriety of accepting Her Highness's kindness. The circum-

---

8. *Four Last Years*, p. 12.
9. Swift.
10. *Conduct*, p. 37.

stances of her family were not, as she alleged, great; yet she was far from catching at "so free and large an offer," until she had sent the first letter from the Princess to Lord Godolphin, and consulted him upon the matter.

Lord Godolphin's opinion was favourable to the wishes of the Princess. He replied, that there was no reason in the world for Lady Marlborough to refuse the pension, knowing, as he did, that it was entirely through her activity, and the indefatigable industry of Lord Marlborough, that the Princess had obtained her settlement;[11] and the proffered income was gratefully accepted.

The good understanding which had subsisted between the two royal sisters had never been based upon sincere affection, and the slightest accident served to discompose, and even to annihilate, their apparent friendship. Anne, who had repented, with tears, of. her conduct to her father,[12] and was not consoled for filial disobedience by her husband's expected aggrandisement, was doubtless scandalised by the manifest determination of her sister to encourage every demonetarisation of public opinion which her father had discountenanced. An occasion soon offered. The only dramatic exhibition which the retiring Queen witnessed was the play of the *Spanish Friar*, which had been forbidden by the late King.

But Mary was duly punished for this want of good taste, to say the least of it, or deficiency in filial feeling. The repartees in the drama happened to be such as the spectators, hearing them with preoccupied minds, could readily appropriate to the Queen. Mary was abashed, and forced to hold up her fan, and, to hide her confusion, turned round to ask for her palatine, her hood, or any article of dress she could recollect; whilst the audience, not yet softened towards her by those respectable qualities which afterwards gained their esteem, directed their looks towards her, whenever their fancy led them to make any application of what was said, to the undutiful and unpopular daughter of James; and the Queen, upon another diversion of this kind being proposed, excused herself upon the plea of some other engagement, whilst the affair furnished the town with discourse for a month.[13]

It was evidently the policy or pleasure of Mary to retain the different members of her family, as much as circumstances permitted, in

---

11. Conduct, p. 38.
12. Macpherson.
13. Letter written soon after the Revolution, by Daniel Finch, Esq. of Nottingham. Dalrymples *Mem.* vol. 2, p. 79.

subjection. In particular she insulted her sister by a marked indifference to Prince George, her brother-in-law, who, though remembered by posterity as the "*Est-il possible*" of King James, was a man of respectable conduct, of valour, humanity, and justice.[14] William, however, held his brother-in law in utter contempt; and the manner in which he repaid the Prince's desertion of his father-in-law, would have been peculiarly galling to a gentleman of a warmer temper than, fortunately, the Prince appears to have been.

When William was obliged to go to Ireland, and to enter upon that memorable campaign which finally decided the peace of the United Kingdom, Prince George involved himself in a great expense to attend His Majesty, with a zeal returned only by ungracious and unbecoming conduct,—William not even suffering the Prince to go in the same coach with him; an affront never before offered to any person of the same rank.[15]

Prince George, a pattern of patience, one of those characters who have not, and who cannot have, a personal enemy, submitted not only to this indignity, but to every possible species of irreverence, during the whole campaign. He distinguished himself at the battle of the Boyne, and was yet treated by the King, says the Duchess in her *Conduct*, "with no more respect than if he had been a page of the backstairs."[16]

These slights and disappointments came to a crisis, when the ill-used Prince, determined not again to be exposed to such contumely, requested permission of the King to serve him at sea as a volunteer, without any command. The King, who was going to Flanders, embraced him by way of *adieu*, but said nothing; and silence being generally taken for consent, the Prince made preparations, and sent his baggage, arms, &c., on board. But the Queen, according to the Duchess, had "her instructions neither to suffer the Prince to go to sea, nor to forbid him to go, if she could so contrive matters as to make his staying at home appear his own choice."

Mary, in conformity with her invariable practice, followed to the very letter the wishes of her royal husband, and endeavoured to make the Countess of Marlborough her agent upon this occasion. But Her Majesty had yet to learn the fiery temper of her with whom she attempted to deal.

---

14. Boyer, p. 357.
15. *Conduct*, p. 88.
16. *Ibid.*

"She sent a great lord to me," says the Duchess, "to desire I would persuade the Princess to keep the Prince from going to sea, and this I was to compass without letting the Princess know that it was the Queen's desire."

The Countess's reply was, that she had all the duty imaginable for the Queen, but that no consideration could make her so treacherous to her mistress as she should consider herself, if she attempted to influence her in that matter, without telling her the reason; and she intimated that she "would say what Her Majesty pleased to the Princess, if she were allowed to make use of the Queen's name."

The affair ended in Prince George's submission to a peremptory message, forbidding him to go to sea, and conveyed through the Earl of Nottingham. He justly felt himself rendered ridiculous to the public, by being obliged to recall his preparations, to obey like a schoolboy, and to remain at home.

Whilst these minor events were disturbing the peace of the royal household, the first campaign in Ireland called Marlborough away from the home and the wife whom he loved so well. Every letter to the Countess which he penned during his absence, breathes a devotion which time and distance seem only to have heightened. In the hurry of military movements, in the excitement of unparalleled triumphs, his heart was ever with her. "I am heart and soul yours," was his constant expression. "I can have no happiness till I am quiet with you." "I cannot live away from you."[17] Again, he beautifully concludes one letter: "Put your trust in God as I do, and be assured that I think I can't be unhappy as long as you are kind."

So true and elevated was the attachment of that affectionate heart. "Pray believe me," he says, writing in 1705, immediately after the battle of Ramilies, "when I assure you that I love you more than I can express."[18] These and other innumerable fond asseverations, even when his wife had passed the bloom of youth, and, it appears, no longer possessed (if she ever did) equanimity of temper, speak an attachment not based upon evanescent advantages. With a candour inseparable from a great mind, he generously took upon himself the blame of those contentions by which the busy and harassing middle period of married life, that period in which love often dies a natural death, is, in all stations, apt to be embittered.

---

17. *Correspondence*, vol. 1, p. 44.
18. *Ibid.* p. 27.

On one occasion, after thanking her, as for a boon, for "very many kind expressions" to him in a letter, he says:

. . . .in short, my dear soul, if I could begin life over again, I would endeavour every hour of it to oblige you. But as we can't recall what is past, forget my imperfections, and as God has been pleased to bless me, I do not doubt but he will reward me with some years to end my days with you; and if that be with quietness and kindness, I shall be much happier than I have ever yet been.

This longing for home, and for the undisturbed enjoyment of all that home gives, appears in every effusion of that warm heart, the natural feelings of which neither the dissipations of a court, nor the possession of power, nor the incense of nations, could alienate from the fondest objects which life presents to a mind not vitiated by selfishness. Marlborough, amidst all his troubles, was happiest in his nursery. There the guilelessness, the freshness of the infant mind appeared to him in beautiful contrast with the measured phrase, and the mask of prudence, adopted insensibly in the world; the petty cares and wants of children, so easily solaced—their unconsciousness of all that is painful, all that is anxious—operate as a charm on the sickened heart and harassed mind, and bring to the wearied passenger through life some sense of happiness, some trust and hope that all is not disappointment and deception in this probationary state. Those parents who turn with disgust and indifference from children, as merely sources of care, may picture to themselves the great Marlborough the playfellow of his little girls.

"You cannot imagine," he writes from Tunbridge to Lady Marlborough, "how I am pleased with the children; for they, having nobody but their maid, are so fond of me, that when I am at home they will always be with me, kissing and hugging me. Their heats are quite gone, so that against you come home they will be in beauty.

"If there be room I will come on Monday, so that you need not write on Sunday.

"Miss is pulling me by the arm, that she may write to her dear mamma; so that I shall say no more, only beg that you will love me always as well as I love you, and then we cannot but be happy."

To this charming and natural letter the fond father added, in his own handwriting, the following little postscript from his daughter:—

I kiss your hands, my dear mamma.—Harriet.[19]

Happy and amiable Marlborough! and blessed the parents, to whom still the affectionate though unconscious dependence of their children brings a thousand minute and indescribable enjoyments!

With the affections of such a man, Lady Marlborough might have been the happiest, as well as one of the most distinguished of women, had she risen superior to the temptation of intrigue, and discarded the workings of tea-table politics with the scorn which they deserved. But her unquiet spirit allowed her no real happiness. External circumstances, which were peculiarly in her favour, contributed to ruin her peace, by fostering her domineering and busy temper. Indulged by her husband in living at her birthplace, he gratified her inclination still further, by purchasing the respective shares of her sisters, Frances and Barbara, joint co-heiresses with herself, and built a mansion on the spot, called Holywell House.

At this place Lord and Lady Marlborough resided, the house being described as one of great magnificence, and they left it only to enter upon the yet more majestic pile of Blenheim House, when repeated success had raised them to the climax of their greatness. The birth of six[20] children successively—of two sons and four daughters—added to their domestic felicity, whilst yet those children were spared to them, and continued amenable to the domestic control. Some troubles, incident to human nature generally, were allotted to the distinguished parents, but mitigated by advantages so abundant, that the early portion of their married life must be considered as peculiarly blessed.

During the first two years after the accession of William, Lord Marlborough only enjoyed his home and country at brief intervals, that were tantalising even to one who felt himself destined to high offices, and framed for glorious enterprises. On his return from the Netherlands, the King, though secretly nettled at his interference in the affair of the settlement, was obliged to acknowledge that it was to Marlborough that the success of his troops at the siege of Walcourt, a small town in the Low Countries, was to be chiefly attributed.[21]

In the close of the year 1690, Marlborough was entrusted with the command of troops sent to Ireland, in which country he had refused

---

19. Coxe, vol. 1, 4 to. p. 18.
20. Lediard.
21. Coxe.

to act whilst James the Second, his former benefactor, remained in that island. But when James retired to France, Marlborough prepared to use his utmost exertions, in conjunction with others, to reduce the remainder of that kingdom to obedience. The success of his endeavours enabled him to return to England on the 28th of October, and to experience a favourable reception from King William; but he was obliged almost immediately to resume his command in Ireland, where he remained during the winter.

The following year found him still active in military affairs, serving under William himself in Flanders, with a distinction and success that wrung praises from his enemies. Even William was forced to acknowledge that "he knew no man so fit for a general who had seen so few campaigns;"[22] and to the praises of the Prince de Vaudemont, who prophesied of Marlborough that he would attain a higher point of Military glory than any subject William possessed, the phlegmatic monarch relaxed so far from his usual taciturnity as to reply with a smile, "he believed that Marlborough would do his part to make his words good." But all these services were obliterated shortly afterwards from the royal mind; and a cloud of adversity, though not of disgrace—for nothing can disgrace the virtuous—lowered over the fortunes of Marlborough.

---

22. Lediard, p. 103.

Chapter 7
1689
Disgrace of Lord Marlborough

In order to understand the vicissitudes of favour which Lord and Lady Marlborough experienced, some insight into the state of parties, and some acquaintance with the characters of public men, are essential; although a lengthened discussion upon the subject, in a work of this nature, would be wearisome and inconvenient.

Scarcely had William the Third ascended the throne, than he found that "his crown was encircled with thorns."[1] In the hurry and stir of events, carried away by the strong current of sympathy, the Tories had promoted his elevation; but when dangers were past, they remembered, too late to retrieve, what they considered to be their error—that in so doing they had departed from all their established maxims; they recollected, not only that they had dethroned James, but that they had preferred his daughters and the Prince of Orange in the succession, to the infant Prince of Wales; and, to excuse their inconsistency, they were forced to pretend a mere submission to events which they had actively promoted. This faction, reluctantly styled by Burnet, in the portion of his history[2] relating to this period, "Tories," were therefore avowedly hostile to the court, and yet not to be considered as its sole, nor indeed as its most dangerous enemies.

The clergy, the majority of whom had inveighed from the pulpit against the right of infringing upon the order of succession, were, from motives of the same description, inimical also to the Calvinistic King, whose known attachment to Dissenters inspired a jealousy of him, and towards his numerous adherents of the same tenets with

---
1. Dalrymple.
2. Dalrymple, part 2, b. 1. p. 300.

himself, which was quickly manifested by the Bishops. Among the seven prelates who had been persecuted by the late King, only one, the Bishop of St. Asaph, did homage to the new monarch, and took the oaths. And when Mary sent to ask Sancroft's blessing, the cutting reply of the Archbishop was, "that she must seek her father's first, otherwise his would not be heard in heaven."[3]

Thus repelled, William looked in vain for a servile compliance from the Whigs; they had the plea of consistency to shackle the support which they might be expected to give the royal minion of their power; and, having always opposed the crown, they were unwilling to relinquish that jealousy of its prerogative for which their party had hitherto been distinguished.

After the happy termination of the war in Ireland, factious spirits, like gnats after rain coming forth in the sunbeam, began to show themselves, and to congregate for action. Whilst some complained of the great standing army kept up after the contest with James and his adherents was finally and triumphantly concluded—whilst some murmured at one grievance, some at another—Englishmen of all parties were disgusted with the preference given to the Dutch, on whom alone the confidence of the sovereign was bestowed. Nor did William take any means to ingratiate himself in the affections of his adopted country.

He shut himself up all day, attended chiefly by Bentinck, whom he had created Earl of Portland, and who shared his favour with Henry Sidney, the only Englishman whom the King really liked. By degrees, a new feature in the character of the chosen successor of James, alienated from him that party who had placed him on the throne, and who began to think that there was something contagious around that unenviable position. Naturally cautious, and ignorant of our constitution, William took offence at the warmth of those who professed liberal opinions, mingled with notions of republicanism, from which he recoiled with as much dread as his prerogative-loving predecessors. The name of liberty became intolerable to him; and it was soon found that his love of monarchy, and his sense of its high privileges, were far greater than could possibly have been expected, in a prince whose pretensions rested upon the suffrage of the great body of the nation.[4]

These opinions were supposed to be cherished in William by the Earl of Nottingham, who was chosen Secretary of State with the Earl

---
3. Dalrymple, part 2, b. 1, p. 300.
4. Tindal, Dalrymple, Burnet.

of Shrewsbury. Lord Nottingham had opposed the settlement of the crown with vehemence, and in *copious orations;* declaring, however, when the party opposed to him had prevailed, that "though he could not make a king, yet, upon his principles, he could obey one better than those who were so much set on making one."[5] It was this minister's successful endeavour to infuse distrust and dislike of the Whigs into the mind of his sovereign—to gain every species of information which could assist his efforts, from the lowest sources and by the lowest means—every angry speech in political meetings being reported to His Majesty's ears, and making a deep impression on the mind of William.[6] Yet Nottingham has been said, even whilst holding his office of secretary, to have always kept "a reserve of allegiance to his exiled master;"[7] whilst the necessities of a numerous family induced him to take an employment in the existing government.

The great ambition of this nobleman was to be at the head of the church party. Regular in his religious duties, strict in morals, and of a formal, unbending character of virtue, the zeal of Nottingham, affected or real, aided by a solemn deportment, and by a countenance the inflexible gravity of which accorded with his disposition,—it was not until years afterwards that his actual insincerity was discovered, and that it was found that the principles which he professed had been all along at variance with those which he actually entertained.[8]

Amongst sundry Tories and Jacobites who, by the influence of Nottingham, were preferred, Lawrence Hyde, Earl of Rochester, contrary to all expectation, was made a privy counsellor. His near relationship to the Queen, his niece, had not hitherto secured royal favour. He was accounted a man of abilities, although immeasurably inferior in that respect to his celebrated father; he wrote well, but was an ungraceful speaker. Devoted to the exiled monarch, Rochester, whilst he perceived the errors of his royal brother-in-law, opposed the act of settlement, and voted for a regency—a step which Queen Mary found it difficult to forgive; nor was it until after Bishop Burnet had wrought upon her mind, that she consented to receive her uncle, or to forget his opposition to her reign.

By degrees, however, he rose in her regard, and attained a degree of influence which was exerted against Lady Marlborough in particular,

---

5. Burnet, vol. 4, p. 2.
6. *Ibid.* p. 5.
7. Swift's *Four Last Years of Queen Anne,* p. 16.
8. Swift,

and of which she felt the effects. Lord Rochester, with many excellent and respectable qualities, united a spirit somewhat too zealous to be productive of benefit in the state affairs at that time; he was considered as the leader of the high church party; and, refusing the oaths of allegiance to William and Mary, remained a non-juror until his death.[9]

The more placid, but more steady opposition of Bentinck, Earl of Portland, to all that Lady Marlborough proposed and desired, was supposed by her to be even more effective than the turbulent temper of Lord Rochester. Brave, faithful, disinterested, charitable, a favourite without presumption, a consummate statesman without forgetting the higher duties, Bentinck would have been a valuable and a devoted friend, had Lady Marlborough been so fortunate as to possess his esteem; nor is there any reason to suppose that he was at any time her implacable enemy, although his interests, and even his affections, were centred in the monarch whom Lady Marlborough has treated, in her *Conduct*, with so little respect.

Descended from an ancient family in the province of Guelderland, Bentinck was first page to William Prince of Orange, and afterwards gentleman of the bedchamber. When William was made *stadtholder*, Bentinck continued near him, and was with him when the Prince was attacked with the smallpox, a disease which had been peculiarly fatal to the *stadtholder's* family. On this occasion, and during the progress of a disorder then shunned with as much alarm and horror as the plague and cholera have since been, and the first symptoms of which were regarded almost as the signal of death, Bentinck never deserted the sick room of the Prince. He administered medicines to his master, and was the only person who lifted him in and out of bed.[10]

The first day of the Prince's convalescence was the commencement of Bentinck's illness. He begged of William to allow him to return home, as he could no longer combat against the symptoms of disease. Happily, William had not to grieve that the life of his devoted servant had been sacrificed by his tender care. From that time Bentinck was peculiarly favoured by the reserved but not ungrateful Prince; yet so little dependence is there to be placed on human affections, so constantly are we to be admonished that nothing is stable, nothing wholly satisfactory, in this life of chances and changes, that the generous Bentinck afterwards found himself supplanted in his sovereign's regard by Keppel Earl of Albemarle; and, whilst he still retained

---

9. Boyer, App.; Tindal, Burnet.
10. Sir William Temple's *Memoirs*. See Boyer, App. p. 49.

the confidence of William, perceiving that his personal influence with the King was gone, in 1698 he retired from court, leaving those offices which he had so long held in the household to be performed by deputy.

During the first six or eight years of the reign of William and Mary, Lord Portland, however, enjoyed all that favour and those distinctions which his prudence, and the courage which he had displayed both in military and civil affairs, so well justified. The avowed favourite of the King, and deriving considerable grants from the crown, he spent the sums for which he was indebted to the Treasury and to British lands, in promoting the welfare of the English peasantry. Besides daily extensive charity among his poor neighbours, Lord Portland built and endowed a charity school on his estate in Buckinghamshire; and passed his days in the domestic, and dignified, and useful retirement of an English nobleman of the old school; visiting Holland every summer, but living mostly in England. It was before going as ambassador to negotiate the peace of Ryswick, that he endeared himself to the English nation by being actively instrumental in saving the noble edifice of Whitehall, in which a fire had broken out, which was chiefly checked by the zeal and liberal aid of this noble foreigner graft upon our English nobility.[11]

The Earl of Portland became eventually one of the richest subjects in England. But, as there is a dark spot on all human brightness, he rendered himself unpopular to many, notwithstanding his extensive charities—notwithstanding his profusion "in gardening, birds, and household furniture,"—qualities truly English,—by a frugality which, in the continental nations, is carefully instilled into youth by education and practice, but which is uncongenial to the habits of the English nation. The resentment of Queen Anne and of the Duchess of Marlborough was shown in a manner not displeasing to the public, when, on her accession, the Queen deprived Portland of "the post of Keeper of Windsor Great Park."[12]

Whilst we accord to Bentinck every merit due to one so estimable, it must be allowed that his relationship to the Villiers family contributed greatly to the support of that rank which he held in the King's esteem, whilst it was at the same time the cause of the hostilities afterwards declared between his lordship and the vehement lady whom he had the fortune mortally to offend. By his first marriage with Mrs.

---

11. Boyer, Appendix, p. 57.
12. Noble, vol. 1, p. 61.

Villiers, fourth sister of the Earl of Jersey, Lord Portland strengthened his interests doubly. Lady Jersey was the *confidante* of Mary; Lord Jersey was in high favour with William; whilst Elizabeth Villiers, afterwards Lady Orkney, was the mistress of the gloomy and grave, but, as it seems, not altogether faithful husband of the subservient and devoted Mary Stuart.

There was, however, an intermediate person, a third sister of Lord Jersey, the Viscountess Fitzharding, one of the favoured few who were prized by the Countess of Marlborough, but, as it seems, a spy upon her friend, and a betrayer of her secrets. This lady held a confidential situation in the household of the Princess of Denmark, and was also one for whom Lady Marlborough entertained what she truly calls "a very singular affection"—a possession of which she shamefully availed herself, by repeating all that she heard, and perhaps more than what she heard, in the Princess's family.

The pernicious effect of such repetitions, even between relatives affectionately attached, may readily be conceived; but in the dissensions of two sisters, whose earliest instructions, when they referred to conduct to each other, had in all probability been those of distrust—whose interests clashed, whose relative position was every way awkward, whose husbands were on indifferent terms, and who resembled each other only in one respect, that of displaying filial ingratitude to a misled and culpable monarch, but an affectionate father—it was certain that a spark would kindle a flame between spirits so ready for combustion.

At length the smothered discords between Mary and her sister broke out, and once blazing, they were never entirely extinguished. The imprudence, vulgarity of taste, or rather deficiency in feeling, of the Princess and of her favourite, in their ordinary conversation and correspondence, cannot be justified. It is often from errors apparently trivial, though originating from coarseness of mind and violence of temper, that the most serious inconveniences, sometimes the greatest misfortunes, originate. The Princess and her favourite considered it high diversion to vent their dislike to the King, in applying to him opprobrious terms, the most decorous of which was "Caliban," whilst others will not bear repetition.[13]

These offensive expressions, though, after the death of Queen Anne, carefully expunged by the Duchess even from her original let-

---

13. See Coxe, note, vol. 1, p. 61.

ters, as well as in her *Conduct*, were, however, acknowledged by Lady Marlborough, in the indorsements of letters from Lady Orkney to her ladyship; and they were carefully collected and repeated by Lady Fitzharding, whom the malcontents supposed to be in their confidence. The hour of disgrace was, however, at hand—disgrace inflicted in the tenderest point, and calculated to humble, if anything could humble, the lofty spirit of Lady Marlborough. That, however, which would have crushed a gentler spirit, scarcely pressed upon hers; as appears by her subsequent effrontery, which even her own skilful defence could not extenuate.

But even if the comparative grossness of the times, and the aggravations received from the court, cannot justify the Princess and her "dear Mrs. Freeman," neither can the petulance, meanness, and love of power which Queen Mary displayed, be excused.

There is always something in feminine altercations that is ludicrous as well as painful. Few women know how and where to stay the course of anger; when it once begins to flow, every charm, every grace so fondly prized by the sex, is obliterated, when retort follows retort, and retaliation grows vigorous; and dignity, to assert which the lair sex is oftentimes so valiant, takes its departure immediately we become vociferous in its defence.

One evening, in the interregnum between the quarrel concerning the settlement and their final feuds, the Queen, who had lived outwardly on tolerable terms with her sister for some time, "began," as the Princess Anne expressed it, "to pick quarrels," upon the sore subject of the annuity, and to intimate that supposing some twenty or thirty thousand pounds were to be taken off the fifty thousand allowed, the Princess, she presumed, could live upon it "as she had done before;" upon which an indecorous altercation ensued.[14] On the following day, Lord Marlborough, after performing his usual duties as lord of the bedchamber, received, through Lord Nottingham, the humiliating intimation that he was dismissed from all his employments, both civil and military, and forbidden the court. This blow is said to have been totally unexpected by the Earl, from whom the King had parted on that very morning in the usual manner.[15]

Lord Marlborough received the intelligence communicated by Lord Nottingham with the composure of a superior mind.

"He retired," says one of his biographers, "with the calmness

---

14. Coxe, p. 59.
15. Lediard, p. 107.

of the old Roman dictator, wishing to be succeeded by a better servant, and by one more concerned for his Highness's honour."[16]

Of course, innumerable causes for this unlocked for occurrence were started by the public, always curious on such occasions. By some it was said that a letter had been intercepted, which gave rise to suspicions unfavourable to the Earl. By others the disgrace of Marlborough was ascribed to the resentment of Lord Portland, whom Marlborough was in the habit of designating "*un homme de bois;*"[17] by many, the interference of Marlborough and the Countess in the matter of the settlement was referred to as the cause of his loss of favour and office, without taking into account that it was then two years since that affair, and that Marlborough had been in the mean time so employed and distinguished by the King as to have obtained from the Marquis of Carmarthen the invidious appellation of the "General of favour." But, whilst it has been allowed that these various causes, severally and conjointly, might have, in some degree, effected the result so painful to the Earl and so aggravating to the Countess, the recent boldness of Marlborough, in representing to His Majesty the detrimental effects of his undue partiality to the Dutch, was the immediate source of the King's marked displeasure.

"It was said," relates Lediard, "that all the resentment was, for the liberty he had taken to tell the King, that though himself had no reason to complain, yet many of his good subjects were sorry to see his royal munificence confined to one or two foreign lords."

French historians make no scruple to name the Earl of Portland and Rochford, both Dutchmen, to be the lords here hinted at; and add that the King turned his back upon the Earl without making any answer, and soon afterwards sent him a dismissal from his employments, and forbade him the court Those who considered the jealousy or envy of foreign officers a reason for his lordship's disgrace, assert it to be a confirmation of their opinion that the Earl was not employed again, nor recalled to council, until this motive ceased, and an end was put to the war by the peace of Ryswick.[18]

The Countess of Marlborough, however, makes no allusion to this

---

16. *Ibid.* p. 105.
17. Coxe, p. 69.
18. Lediard, vol. 1, p. 105.

ungrateful and petulant behaviour of the King.[19]

"This event may be accounted for," she says, speaking of the dismissal of his lordship, "by saying that Lord Portland had ever a great prejudice to my Lord Marlborough, and that my Lady Orkney, (then Mrs. Villiers,) though I had never done her any injury, except not making my court to her, was my implacable enemy. But I think it is not to be doubted that the principal cause of the King's message was the court's dislike that anybody should have so much interest with the Princess as I had, who would not obey implicitly every command of the King and Queen. The disgrace of my Lord Marlborough, therefore, was designed as a step towards removing me from about her."[20]

Lord Rochester, the Countess proceeds to say, was also her foe, having warmly opposed her coming into the Princess's family in the first instance, and wishing at that time greatly for her removal; believing that if he could compass it, he should infallibly have the government of both the sisters, his nieces, although he had never done anything to merit the confidence of the Princess.

There was, however, still another reason assigned for the event which caused so much speculation. The beautiful Frances Jennings, the "glass and model" of her fair countrywomen in the days of Charles the Second, had twice changed her condition since she had officiated, in the bloom of youth, at the court of the Duchess of York. The first affections of Frances were bestowed on the noted Jermyn, for whose unworthy sake she rejected the brave Talbot, marrying, in a temper of mind betwixt pique and ambition, Sir George Hamilton, a *maréchal-de-camp* in the French service, and grandson of the Earl of Aberdeen.

In 1667, Lady Hamilton becoming a widow, and the attachment of Talbot being unchanged by time, she became his wife; a marriage unfortunate, as far as ambitious views were concerned, as the high rank which Talbot afterwards obtained as Duke of Tyrconnel was not acknowledged at the court of William.

Between the Duchess of Tyrconnel and her sister Lady Marlborough, there never subsisted any very cordial intercourse,[21] nor was the connexion likely to prove anything but a source of suspicion towards the Earl and Countess. The Duchess of Tyrconnel, on the part of Wil-

---

19. *Conduct*, p. 42.
20. *Conduct*, p. 43.
21. *Notes to Grammont*, vol. 2,. p. 324.

liam, exercising the ingenuity with which nature had endowed her, in tormenting those admirers who were too importunate, or, when she ceased to attract those who were too cold, turned her lively talents to political intrigue, in which she played a deep game: but her cabals were often detrimental to the cause which she espoused, and terminated finally in her becoming one of those needy Jacobites about the court of St. Germains, whom the beset and unfortunate exiled monarch—as unfortunate in his friends as in his enemies—was obliged to satisfy with some portion of his own pension.[22]

The Duke of Tyrconnel, united as he was to this busy spirit, had qualities which would have adorned a better cause than that for which, with zeal and address, he long combated in the sister country.

"He was," says Clarendon, "a very handsome man, wore good clothes, and was, without doubt, of a clear, ready courage, which was virtue enough to recommend a man to the Duke's good opinion; which, with more expedition than could be expected, he got, to that degree, that he was made of his bedchamber."

To this qualified praise must be added the undoubted stigma attached to the conduct of Tyrconnel, having in his youth been one of those "men of honour," so termed by Grammont, who acted as counsel to James the Second, when Duke of York, in order to facilitate his nullifying the marriage contract between His Highness and Miss Hyde. If such were the arts by which he recommended himself to James, and obtained, added to various other means, a fortune, as we are told, of forty thousand a year, they are not much to his credit.

The first object of Tyrconnel's admiration was Miss Hamilton, to whom he offered his hand and fortune; and further proffered as many sacrifices as she could desire of the letters, hair, and pictures of a former flame, the Countess of Shrewsbury; and although these articles had no intrinsic value, they testify strongly—such, at least, is the opinion of that competent judge, Count Grammont, of a lover's "sincerity and merit."

Refused by Miss Hamilton, whose affections were engaged to the gay, the captivating, the admired, the profligate Grammont, Lord Tyrconnel had next wooed, and nearly won, the capricious Frances Jennings. In both these instances he had the good sense and good taste (only to be mentioned as remarkable in such days as those) to select women of reputation—without modern ideas, we can scarcely say

---

22. Granger and Grammont, from Coles's State Papers.

of virtue—for the objects of his adoration. But whilst he laid at Miss Jennings' feet the honours, in prospect, of a peerage, and the present respectability of an ancient name, though represented by an impoverished family—though his wealth tempted her, and the elegance of his person and manners, in a court where the art of good-breeding was the only art studied, were acknowledged, he had been again, as it has been seen, unsuccessful.

In this mortification the vanity of the rejected suitor was solaced by the languishing attachment of the automaton, Miss Boynton, one of those young ladies who enjoyed the reputation of performing fainting-fits upon the slightest occasion, and who had formerly won his regard by swooning away upon his account at their first interview. To this languid lady, a contrast to the lively Frances Jennings, Lord Tyrconnel had been eventually united. Affected in manners, weak in mind, and uninteresting in person, she proved perhaps a better helpmate to this determined Jacobite than his equally resolute and more intriguing second wife, to whom, after the death of her first husband, he was united.

Such is the account of that historical romance by Grammont, to which we owe the very questionable advantage of an intimate acquaintance with the court of the second Charles.

To those personal gifts which appeared so dangerous in the eyes of Miss Boynton,[23] the Duke of Tyrconnel added the still more important acquisition, derived from the habit of frequenting the best company, of knowing how to recommend himself to others by that knowledge, which seems in a man of the world a sort of instinct, of the dispositions, the weaknesses, and wishes of those with whom he converses. With prodigious vanity, much cunning, and little principle, Tyrconnel displayed some noble qualities. By James the Second he had been appointed to the command of the army in Ireland; by James raised to the Peerage—first to an earldom, then a dukedom; by James he was appointed Viceroy of Ireland. Upon the invasion of Ireland by the Prince of Orange he bravely defended it, nor could the offers which were held out to induce him to submit, make any impression upon his integrity.[24]

Tyrconnel sank into insignificance after the battle of the Boyne in 1651, but the English court still jealously watched his movements;

---

23. She was the daughter of Sir Matthew Boynton, and sister-in-law to the famous Earl of Roscommon.
24. *Notes to Grammont*, vol. 2, p. 328.

and his close connexion with the Earl and Countess of Marlborough was not forgotten by those who envied the high qualities of the one, and disliked the proud spirit of the other, and aggravated, doubtless, the secret dislike which Queen Mary indulged towards the Countess of Marlborough. Since the origin of most mischief is attributed to women, an imputed act of indiscretion, on the part of that lady, was alleged, at any rate, to have been made an excuse for the sudden disgrace of her husband.[25] The Earl, it was reported, had mentioned to his wife, in confidence, a scheme which had been confided to him, to surprise Dunkirk—a project which had been concerted by William, and had proved abortive. Lady Marlborough, as it was also rumoured, had spoken of this plan to the lady of Sir Theophilus Oglethorp;[26] and it had been carried, in some manner, of course, to Lady Tyrconnel, and from her to the French court.

The author of *The Other Side of the Question*, in confirmation of this report, has stated, but on no assigned authority, that four persons only in England were privy to the design on Dunkirk; namely, "the King, Lord Marlborough, and two more; that one"[27] of these four communicated the secret to his wife, who, as it was said, sold it to Lady for what she could get: that in consequence, the said design miscarried, and those concerned in it abroad were hanged: that upon this, the King sent for his three confidants, and having with some trouble found out the leak, expressed himself, on the occasion, in his dry way, as follows—"My lord, you have put a greater confidence in your wife than I did in mine."

This conjecture, or tradition, however,—for though a prevalent report at the time, it is nothings more,—is refuted by the fact that the design against Dunkirk was not projected until the month of August, 1692, whereas the Earl had been dismissed from his employments in the previous January;[28] and although every possible obloquy that could be cast upon the Countess of Marlborough was likely to be propagated in the court, where she was known to be out of favour, yet it is certain that no misconduct of hers, nor indiscretion on the part of her husband, on the score of the projected siege of Dunkirk, could have occasioned the harsh usage which his lordship had experienced.

Lord Marlborough, although disgraced, was not without advocates,

---
25. Lediard, p. 111.
26. *Ibid.*
27. *Other Side of the Question*, p. 70.
28. Coxe, vol. 1, p. 63.

as the King soon perceived. Admiral Russell, one of a family noted for magnanimous courage in the cause of justice, "put himself on ill terms with the King," as Lediard relates, by pressing to know the grounds of the Earl's disgrace; and almost reproached William with his oblivion of the Earl's services, who had, as he said, "set the crown on the King's head."[29]

This generous interference, and the regret for the occasion of it which the Princess of Denmark evinced, only irritated the King and Queen more and more against their oppressed sister-in-law and her favourite. On the twenty-ninth of January, the Princess received an anonymous letter, informing her that a dangerous cabal was formed among the Portland and Villiers family against the Earl and Countess of Marlborough, and apprising her that their misfortunes would not end with the Earl's dismissal, but that he would be imprisoned as soon as the prorogation of Parliament had taken place. The unknown friend who wrote this letter, added, that the interview which Marlborough had held with his friends Godolphin and Russell, on the day of his disgrace, had excited the jealousy of the court; whilst the tears which the Princess had herself been seen to shed since that event, had added to the irritation of her sister and brother.[30]

Perhaps the Princess Anne might, in the midst of her tears, remember with a pang the indulgent conduct of the father whom she had deserted, and who, according to a writer contemporary with her favourite, had twice paid debts which the mercenary spirit of that favourite, according to the same account, which must be taken with some reservation, had led the Princess to incur.[31]

Whatever were Anne's feelings, those expressed by Lady Marlborough were quite in accordance with her high spirit, which, with a hardihood which certainly has the effect of disguising our faults far more than the varnish of dissimulation, she avows in her own peculiar way.[32]

> But to come to the sequel of the King's message: I solemnly protest that the loss of my Lord Marlborough's employments would never have broke my rest one single night upon account of interest; but I confess, *the being turned out* is something very disagreeable to my temper; and I believe it was three weeks be-

---

29. Lediard, p. 111.
30. Coxe, vol. 1, p. 61.
31. *Other Side of the Question*, p. 48.
32. *Conduct*, p. 42.

fore my best friends could persuade me that it was fit for me to go to a court which (as I thought) had used my Lord Marlborough very ill. However, at last they prevailed, and I remember the chief argument was urged by my Lord Godolphin, who said that it could not be thought that I made any mean court to the King and Queen, since to attend the Princess was only to pay my duty where it was owing.

The consequence of this advice, upon which Lady Marlborough so much relied, was, that "she waited on her mistress to Kensington." Particulars of the interview may readily be conceived. The offended dignity of Mary, the suppressed vexation of the tearful Anne, the flush of anger on the brow of the haughty lady in waiting, that subdued but not intimidated favourite, nature struggling with etiquette, as she bent before the Queen whom she hated, and followed the Princess whom she governed and despised;—all these circumstances combined must have formed a fine scene for the pen or the pencil.

Unfortunately, no details of the meeting are permitted us, but the effect which it had upon the temper even of the mild and prudent Mary, may be inferred from a letter which the Queen wrote to her sister on the ensuing day.

After premising that she had something to say which she thought would not be very pleasing to the Princess, the Queen reminded her sister that nobody was ever "suffered to live at court in my Lord Marlborough's circumstances." It was therefore incumbent on Her Majesty, as she thought, though much against her will, to tell her sister how very unfit it was that Lady Marlborough should stay with the Princess either; "since that," added the Queen, "gives the husband so just a pretence of being where he ought not."

"Taking everything into consideration," the Queen, therefore, plainly intimated to her sister, that, since she had allowed Lady Marlborough to accompany her to Kensington on the forgoing night, Her Majesty was reduced to the necessity of plainly telling her, that her lady of the bedchamber "must not stay," and "that she had all the reason imaginable" to look upon Anne's bringing her as "the strangest thing that ever was done; nor," added the Queen, "could all my kindness for you, (which is ever ready to turn all you do the best way at any other time,) have hindered me from showing you that at the moment; but I considered your condition, and that made me master myself so far as not to take notice of it then."

"But now," adds the Queen, "I must tell you, it was very unkind in a sister, would have been very uncivil in an equal, and I need not say I have more to claim, which, though my kindness would make me never extort, yet when I see the use you would make of it, I must tell you I know what is due to me, and expect to have it from you. 'Tis upon that account, I tell you plainly. Lady Marlborough must not continue with you in the circumstances her lord is,"

This assumption of the Queen towards her offending sister, Mary softened by kinder terms. "I have all the real kindness imaginable for you," she added, "and as I ever have, so will always do, my part to live with you as sister's ought;" and neither the King nor she were willing, as she said, to have recourse to harsher means.

But, notwithstanding the resolution expressed in the foregoing paragraph,—"the sight of Lady Marlborough," the Princess proceeds to say, "having changed her style, does naturally change her thoughts."[33]

"She could pass over most things," and "live with her sister as became her, but she complained of the want of common civility exhibited by that sister, in not comprehending her wishes, and avoiding the contact with which she had placed her with Lady Marlborough.

This reproof was felt severely by Anne, and gave dire offence to her who had courted the rebuke, and it afforded Mary the desired opportunity of putting a direct affront upon her. Nor could numbers of affectionate expressions, nor what the Duchess of Marlborough calls, in the conclusion of the epistle, "useless repetitions," intended "to remind her sister of the distance between them," heal the wounds thus made, nor reconcile Anne to a sister who had incurred the displeasure of one whom she loved better than all the world besides.

From this time the firebrand of discord, thrown between the two royal sisters, was never extinguished except by death. The mortification inflicted upon Lady Marlborough was bitterly commented upon by her, years after she had outlived the effects of other changes in those whom she served, and those whom she endeavoured to serve. This first humiliation was, perhaps, her bitterest pang of the sort; and she, to "whose temper the being turned out was not very agreeable,"[34] must have writhed under the banishment from that court, in whose atmosphere she had been accustomed from her early youth to consider herself as a privileged individual.

Queen Mary, having struck the first blow, was resolved not to relax

---

33. See Appendix, No. 4, for the rest of this letter, and for others upon the same subject.

34. *Conduct.*.

in her displeasure. The Duchess, in recalling this period of her life, endeavours to show the inconsistency of the Queen, in expelling from her sister's service one whom she had formerly designated as a "kind, dear friend, from whom she hoped that her sister would never part."[35] But Mary then knew the Countess only by letter, and by report, as the beloved wife of an influential man disposed to liberal measures, and devoted to Protestantism,—as a Whig in principle herself, and having influence enough to make her husband turn round to her opinions; as a woman to be feared, encouraged, courted.

Even after her arrival in England, Mary behaved towards her subsequent foe with a consideration which would, says the Duchess of Marlborough, have engaged "some people to fix the foundation of their future fortunes in her favour;" nor could anyone, she asserts, have had a greater chance to rise in it than herself, "if she could have broken the inviolable laws of friendship;" but this transient sunshine was now over-clouded, and events succeeded each other, which added to the darkness of the storm.

The Princess Anne returned an answer to the Queen's letter the day after she had received it, having first consulted her uncle, Lord Rochester, requesting him, with the greatest earnestness, to assist her in this affair, and to convey her letter to the Queen; an office which his lordship declined, promising, however, that he would speak to the Queen upon the subject. The epistle, in consequence of his lordship's refusal to act as a mediator, was therefore sent to Mary by one of the Princess's own servants. The reply, probably penned only by Anne, and composed either by her who was termed her "Dictatress,"[36] or by Godolphin, is couched in calm but resolute terms.

No apology is tendered for the act which had offended the Queen; no possible reason for the dismissal of Lady Marlborough is allowed: she is justified throughout; whilst a reference to Lord Marlborough's conduct, which might have called down an answer, is prudently avoided.

It is to the unkindness of her sister to herself personally, that the Princess principally objects. The whole letter bespeaks a stronger mind to have been employed in its careful construction than the Princess of Denmark possessed; doubtless, he who gave the advice to go to court, and she who followed her there, were its authors.[37] Lord Rochester,

---

35. *Conduct*, p. 48. See Appendix 5 for Queen Mary's two letters to Lady Churchill.
36. *Other Side of the Question*, p. 75.
37. *Conduct*, p. 55, See Appendix.

who had only recently crept into royal favour, was wise enough not to convey the offensive document. No other answer was returned to it than a message by the Lord Chamberlain to the Countess of Marlborough, to forbid her remaining any longer at the Cockpit

The residence designated by this undignified name has been already described, and its appropriation to the Princess Anne, at the time of her marriage, specified. It appears to have been only sufficient for the Prince and Princess of Denmark and their household, their children being established in the Duchess of Portsmouth's former apartments in the palace, whither it had formerly been the wish of Anne to remove.[38]

The Cockpit being, however, within the precincts of Whitehall, the command issued by Queen Mary for the removal of the Countess of Marlborough was certainly an undue exertion of authority, since it was disputed by several people whether the King had power to remove any individual from the Cockpit.

At the time of the Princess Anne's marriage, Charles the Second had bought this house from the Duke of Leeds, and settled it on his niece, and on her heirs. It was, therefore, clearly her own property, and the attendants whom she chose to retain under its roof were separately and especially her servants.

But Anne, though she might, says the Duchess, have insisted on her right "of being mistress in her own house," was resolved to avoid all risk of irritating the King and Queen; and she determined, consequently, upon retiring from the Cockpit, instead of continuing to brave the displeasure of these royal personages by retaining her favourite in that abode. She wrote, therefore, respectfully, but not submissively, to her sister, declaring that since all that she had said, and all that Lord Rochester had urged, could not prevent the Queen from exacting a mortifying sacrifice from her, she was resolved to retire, and to deprive herself of the opportunity of assuring her of that duty and respect which she had always been, and which she should always be, desirous of showing Her Majesty.[39]

The Princess took prompt measures for her departure. She sent to

---

38. Whitehall, partly rebuilt by James I., who found it in a ruinous state, comprehended within its walls, although unfinished, different suites of rooms, in which the various members of the royal family, their several retinues, the great officers of state, and in the times of Charles the Second and James, the female favourites of those monarchs who could sanction their pretensions.—*Pennants London*, v. 1. p. 191.

39. *Conduct*, p. 58. See Appendix 6.

desire an interview with the Duchess of Somerset,[40] from whom she requested the temporary loan of Sion-house; and the Duchess, with many professions of service, after retiring to consult with the Duke her husband, waited on Her Highness, to acquaint her, in a very respectful manner, that Sion-house was at her service.

As soon as this arrangement was known, the King, according to the Duchess of Marlborough, sent for the Duke of Somerset,[41] and did all he could to persuade his grace to retract his promise to the Princess; "but in vain; so," as the Duchess contemptuously remarks, "there was an end of that matter."[42]

Previous to Anne's removal from the Cockpit, however, she deemed it incumbent on her to wait upon the Queen at Kensington, and to make "all the professions that could be imagined;" but Mary met all these advances with a cold disdain; or, in the words of the Duchess, "was as insensible as a statue;" and when she did answer her sister, it was in the same imperative and offended style as that in which her letter had been dictated.

This alienation of the royal sisters was, however, fully explained by events which reflect no honour either upon Lord or Lady Marlborough. Even the panegyrists of the great Churchill have not attempted to extenuate, whilst they were unable to deny, his political intrigues at this epoch.

No individual in the British dominions was more fully aware of the fact, that King James still lived in the hearts of the English, than he who held the unenviable post of his successor. The progress of the French arms abroad contributed greatly to the unpopularity of William, which at the universities, and amongst churchmen of all ranks, the divine and indefeasible nature of hereditary right was still strenuously, and by the Archbishop of Canterbury, with eight bishops in his

---

40. Elizabeth Percy, Duchess of Somerset, daughter and sole heiress of Joceline Percy, Earl of Northumberland. This lady had been affianced to Henry Cavendish, Earl of Ogle, only son of Henry Duke of Newcastle, but his early death, in 1680, prevented the completion of the nuptials. The Duchess afterwards supplanted the Duchess of Marlborough in the confidence of Queen Anne.—*Granger*, vol. 3, p. 437.
41. Charles Seymour, commonly called the proud Duke of Somerset.
42. It may here be observed, that probably this firmness and propriety of conduct on the part of the Duke and Duchess of Somerset laid the foundation of that partiality which Anne evinced towards them, to the prejudice, as it proved, of her earlier friends. The Duchess, or, as the Duchess of Marlborough was wont to call her, "the great lady," was an avowed opponent of the Tory party, and became in after life a most influential, as well as a most active friend to Whig principles.

train, publicly maintained.

The retired habits of the King, his cold exterior, his uniform preference of his Dutch followers in all appointments about the court, the vast expense and indifferent management of the war in Ireland, the presence of foreign troops, and the neglect of the navy, all grievous and tender points with the English nation, produced a secret but universal discontent The Marquis of Halifax was heard to declare, that if James could be prevailed on to make advances to the Protestants, it would be impossible to keep him four months longer out of the kingdom.[43]

Under these circumstances, there were, even in the British cabinet, not a few who regretted, and even repented, the part which had been so recently enacted in the late settlement of the crown. The dissolution of the Parliament, or Convention as it was called, irritated these discontents; a secret correspondence was held, even from the very centre of the court, with the monarch at St. Germains; the Duke of Bolton, the Marquis of Winchester, the Earls of Devonshire and Montagu, the Marquis of Carmarthen, one of the principal abettors of the Revolution, were all more or less implicated in the conspiracy.

At this critical period, the fidelity, the honour, and the prudence of Marlborough, sank beneath the powerful temptation of avenging upon William the slights which he had suffered, and of raising his own fortunes by restoring the Stuart dynasty. Historians have been at a loss to comprehend the motives of one who had so recently sacrificed all private considerations to what he justly deemed imperative necessity.[44] Ambition, and, in the mind of Marlborough its too frequent attendant, the love of gain, sufficiently account for his defection from William, who, prejudiced, as the Duchess asserts,[45] by Bentinck, availed himself of the services of Marlborough in war, but was little disposed to recompense his toils by appointment to lucrative civil offices.

Whatever might be the motives of Marlborough's culpable correspondence with the exiled King, the fact itself was not long concealed from William, who was cruelly compelled to employ many to whose dissimulation he was not a stranger; whilst James was equally unable to rely on the assurances of those whose perfidy to another did not augur the most perfect fidelity to his own cause.[46] All classes in society

---

43. Notes to *Berwick's Memoirs*, vol. 1 p. 424.
44. *Conduct.*
45. Tindal, vol. 16, p. 517.
46. Dalrymple's *Memoirs.*

were now, however, more or less infected with Jacobitism. Those who were dissatisfied with the treatment of the British court were secretly addressed by the agents of James, whilst the lower classes were stimulated by means of the press, which formerly had published many libels against the Duke of York, but which were now loud in his favour.[47] It was not long before this conspiracy, the first of the many ineffectual attempts which were made to restore James, began to assume the distinct and fearful form of a threatened invasion.

In the latter end of the year 1690, James despatched into England Colonel Bulkley, whose daughter was afterwards married to the Duke of Berwick,[48] and Colonel Sackville, with instructions to probe the sentiments of the people, and to attach to him the disaffected. Bulkley first addressed himself to Lord Godolphin[49] by allurements and promises. At their interview he inquired, in a tone of despondency, but kindly, respecting the court of St. Germains; but, on being asked by Bulkley what he would sacrifice in order to serve the cause of the deposed monarch, Godolphin started from his chair, and exclaimed that he would leave the office in which he had lately been replaced, that of first lord of the Treasury,[50] in order that he might be free to promote the restoration of James.

Lord Halifax was the next of William's ministers who received Bulkley with open arms; and his ready profession of loyalty to James encouraged the more wary measures of Godolphin and Marlborough. Bulkley, however, meeting these two noblemen in the park, solicited them to return with him home to dine at his lodgings: the invitation was accepted, and Colonel Sackville was summoned to join the conference, and to receive the declaration of Marlborough's penitence. The Earl could neither eat, nor drink, nor sleep, as he assured Colonel Sackville, from the pangs of conscience; and he protested that he would risk the ruin of all his fortunes to redeem his apostasy.

But, in fact, Marlborough, although employed by William in situations of high trust, had never entirely broken off all correspondence with James's adherents. When he, in conjunction with other great men, had invited William Prince of Orange to England, he had,

---

47. Notes to *Berwick's Memoirs*, p. 426.
48. Marshal Berwick, the son of James II., and the nephew of Marlborough, was twice married. His first wife was a daughter of the Earl of Clanricarde, and in 1699 he married a lady attached to the court of the exiled Queen of England, and niece of Lord Bulkley.—*Memoirs of the Duke of Berwick*, vol. 1,. p. 17.
49. *Autobiography of James II.*, edited by Macpherson, p. 235.
50. *Ibid.*

perhaps, in common with many others, no expectation that William would become king. His connexion with the Duke of Berwick, his nephew, and with Earl Tyrconnel, had enabled him to maintain a secret but continued correspondence with those active agents of the exiled King.

Marlborough had long since made his peace with James. He had been the first to give intelligence to the Jacobite party of William's intention to visit Ireland, and was the chief person to despatch timely notice to any of that faction who were threatened with warrants of the privy council, of which he was a member. Yet the services which he had performed in the taking of Cork and Kingsale somewhat abated those hopes of his defection from William, which James had never entirely abandoned.

The conference with Bulkley was not the first step of Marlborough's treason;—for such, in fact, after the settlement of the crown by the voice of Parliament, oaths of allegiance taken, and offices of military trust exercised, it must be deemed.

In January, 1689, the year preceding the visit of Bulkley, Marlborough had addressed James by letter. He had petitioned for the forgiveness of the exiled King, and for that of the Queen. He had promised that the influence of Lady Marlborough to bring back the Princess Anne to her duty should be exerted. Upon this assurance pardon had been granted;[51] and in consequence of this reconciliation further measures were resorted to by Marlborough.

The Duke of Shrewsbury was next brought into the plot; yet both the Duke and Godolphin were urged by Marlborough, the one to continue in office, the other to endeavour to regain it, that they might more effectually serve their liege lord and sovereign. Lord Carmarthen also was willing to be reconciled, though cautiously neither giving nor refusing promises; whilst Marlborough went so far as to proffer his exertions to induce a revolt of the army in England, and to urge an invasion of twenty thousand men from France with James at their head, acknowledging that all schemes for his restoration must be visionary, unless they were seconded by the King of France.[52]

At length an arrangement for striking this decisive blow was completed. The two admirals, Russell and Carter, were drawn into the scheme, and Louis the Fourteenth was assured that the army would

---

51. Dalrymple, b. 7, part 2, p. 493.
52. Dalrymple, p. 2, b. 7, p. 493.

be conducted by Marlborough, the fleet by Russell,[53] and informed that the management of the church was to be left to the judgement and responsibility of the Princess Anne. That Princess, instigated by her friends, had already sought a reconciliation with her father; her motives, it is to be feared, being of a very mixed nature, resentment towards William and Mary actuating her far more than a late return of filial duty.

The admirable energy and sound judgement of Queen Mary, it is well known, saved the country from the threatened invasion, and defeated the designs of the conspirators. In the absence of William, whilst her mind was saddened with anxiety for the King's safety, not knowing whom to trust, she summoned the Parliament by proclamation; she issued warrants against the disaffected, amongst whom were many persons of high rank; and, collecting the militia of Westminster, and the trained bands of London, in Hyde Park, she appeared amongst them at two days' review, and commended their readiness and loyalty. By a master-stroke of policy she prevented the defection of the navy, and is acknowledged to have contributed greatly to strengthen the tottering adherence of her naval commanders.

Being apprised, in the absence of the King, that several of the English officers were disaffected, she desired Lord Nottingham to write to Admiral Russell, informing him that she would change none of the officers, and that she imputed the reports which had been raised against them to the contrivance of his enemies and of theirs. The officers returned an assurance, that they were ready to die in her cause and that of their country; and her generous and wise confidence was justified in the event.

The battle of La Hogue, in which Russell retrieved the credit of the navy, and proved his valour and his restored sense of loyalty, saved our country.[54]

The same high policy adopted by Mary, magnanimous, it must be acknowledged, as well as prudent, was pursued by William. Upon his return from Holland, after the battle of La Hogue, he reproached Godolphin with the correspondence he had carried on. The minister

---

53. Russell avoided an engagement with the French fleet: he never failed entreating King James to prevent the meeting of the two fleets, assuring him that as an officer and an Englishman, he could not avoid firing on the first French ship that came in his way, even if he should see the King on the quarter-deck.—Notes to *Berwick's Memoirs*.

54. Tindal, 16, p. 531.

denied the fact; but William, placing a letter in his hand, which had been stolen from the cabinet of the exiled Prince, desired him "to reflect on the treachery of those whom he was trusting, and the mercy that was shown him." The generous mind of Godolphin was touched, and he remained ever after a faithful servant to William.[55] The Duke of Shrewsbury was won over by a similar line of conduct. With the Earl of Marlborough a more severe policy was adopted.

1692. On the 5th of May, a fortnight before the engagement of La Hogue, Marlborough was suddenly arrested, along with two other noblemen, and Dr. Spratt, Bishop of Rochester, on a charge of high treason. The Duchess thus scornfully mentions the occurrence:—

> Soon after the Princess's going to Sion, a dreadful plot broke out, which was said to be hid somewhere, I don't know where, in a flowerpot, and my Lord Marlborough was sent to the Tower.[56]
>
> To commit a peer of the realm to prison, it was necessary there should be an affidavit of the treason. My Lord Romney, therefore, Secretary of State, had sent to one Young, who was then in gaol for perjury and forgery, and paid his fine, in order to make him what they call a legal evidence; for, as the court lawyers said, Young, not having lost his ears, was an irreproachable witness. I shall not dwell on the story of this fellow's villainy, the Bishop of Rochester having given a full account of it in print.[57]

The miscreant named Young, whose negative virtue Lady Marlborough thus describes, was at that time imprisoned in Newgate for the non-payment of a fine. This man, being an adept at counterfeiting hands, drew up an association in favour of James the Second, annexing to it the signatures of Marlborough, the Bishop of Rochester, and others. He also forged several letters from Marlborough; and, after secreting the pretended document of association in the palace of the Bishop of Rochester, at Bromley in Kent, he gave information of its being lodged there. Measures were instantly taken to secure the supposed delinquents.

In this season of adversity, new to Marlborough, some tried and faithful friends proved their respect for his honour, by rejecting the infamous accusation with contempt. Lady Marlborough thus describes

---

55. Dalrymple.
56. *Conduct*, p. 60.
57. *Conduct*, p. 63.

the conduct of friends and of relatives. Her testimony adds one to the many bitter convictions which the narrative of life presents, that the ties of blood are sometimes found inferior in strength to the close bonds of friendship, in those on whom we have no other claim.[58]

And though these considerations had no weight with the King, they had so much with my Lord Devonshire, my Lord Bradford, and the late Duke of Montagu, that they thought it infamous to send my Lord Marlborough to prison on such evidence; and therefore, when the warrant for his commitment came to be signed at the council table, they refused to put their hands to it, though at that time they had no particular friendship for him. My Lord Bradford's behaviour was very remarkable, for he made my Lord Marlborough a visit in the Tower; while some of our friends, who had lived in our family like near relations for many years, were so fearful of doing themselves hurt at court, that in the whole time of his confinement they never made him or me a visit, nor sent to inquire how we did, for fear it should be known.

The affectionate heart of the Princess of Denmark produced a prompt letter of condolence upon the arrest of the Earl; an event, which it appears, from one passage, was to be succeeded by a less abrupt, though equally strict, mode of imprisonment of Anne and her husband. But William was probably fearful of the consequences of such a step as that to which Anne alludes; and the degradation of the Princess into a private station, with the loss of all public honours usually paid to one of her rank, seems to have been the only penalty imposed upon his sister-in-law.

"I am just told by pretty good hands,"[59] the Princess writes, "that as soon as the wind turns westerly, there will be a guard set upon the Prince and me. If you hear there is any such thing designed, and that 'tis easy to you, pray let me see you before the wind changes; for afterwards one does not know whether they will let one have opportunities of speaking to one another. But let them do what they please, nothing shall ever vex me, so long as I can have the satisfaction of seeing dear Mrs. Freeman; and I swear I would live on bread and water, between four walls, with her, without repining: for as long as you continue kind,

---

58. *Conduct*, p. 62.
59. Coxe, vol. 1, p. 34.

nothing can ever be a real mortification to your faithful Mrs. Morley, who wishes she may never enjoy a moment's happiness in this world, or in the next, if ever she proves false to you."

These expressions of affection are reiterated in various forms, in several other letters which the Countess of Marlborough at this time received from her royal mistress.[60] These epistles speak well for the generosity of feeling and good-breeding of Anne. The utmost delicacy towards the inferior, the warmest sentiments for the friend, prevail; and those obstacles, which gave the character of heroism to their mutual regard, were doubtless highly favourable to the Countess's influence. A little love of opposition reigns in all female bosoms; to oppose their wishes, is to strengthen those wishes until they become ardent passions. This, indeed, seems to have been exemplified in the warm intercourse of Mrs. Morley and Mrs. Freeman, and in the midst of state intrigues, dangers, invasions, and treasons, to have thrown a character of romance over their difficulties and their separations, which must have proved consolatory at least to the disinterested party in a friendly alliance which has met with undeserved ridicule.

The anxieties' of the Countess probably produced an indisposition to which her friend, in one of these letters, refers. After telling her friend, "for God's sake, to have a care of her dear self, and give way as little to melancholy thoughts as she can," she suggests a trial of ass's milk, and regrets the necessity of her dear Mrs. Freeman's being "let blood." [61]

The proud, imperious Countess writhed under the disgrace of her lord; and the world might also assign another reason for her distress, and for the passionate expression of her dislike towards his enemies, and towards those of the Lord Treasurer, which even in her latter days dictated the pages of her personal narrative. Amongst the political enemies of Lady Marlborough, the most celebrated, and the least scrupulous, was the celebrated Dean of St. Patrick. Swift, who patronised the authoress of the *Atalantis*, the infamous Mrs. Manley, and who procured that most abandoned woman remuneration from the Tories, for the imprisonment which she sustained for some of her lampoons,[62] has adopted one of her falsehoods gravely, and as a matter of acknowledged fact, into his *Remarks upon the four last years of Queen Anne's reign.*

---

60. See Appendix, 7.
61. *Conduct.*
62. Note in Coxe, vol. 1, p. 9.

In his character of Lord Godolphin, he says:

His alliance with the Marlborough family, and his passion for the Duchess, were the cords which dragged him into a party which he naturally disliked, whose leaders he personally hated, as they did him.

This assertion, in which the reputations of two persons are sacrificed by a side-blow, alludes to a report prevalent during the prosperous years of Lady Marlborough's life, and called into being by that very prosperity. It originated with Swift's tool, Mrs. Manley, or, as she chose to call herself, Rivella, who was subsequently employed by the Tory party in their periodical, *The Examiner,* after Swift had relinquished his part in it: but he has not blushed to acknowledge that he supplied this disgrace to her sex with much of the venom poured out upon the Whigs, in that noted publication.[63]

By the agency of Mrs. Manley, a rumour was spread abroad reflecting on the nature of that friendly connexion between the Marlborough family and Godolphin, which a closer tie afterwards cemented. An intrigue of the grossest character was described, by the pen of that wretched woman, as having taken place between the Lord Treasurer and the Countess of Marlborough; whilst even her de voted husband was alleged to have been acquainted with it, and to have connived at it for purposes of his own interest, and from party motives.[64]

These calumnies, which, says the anonymous author of the *Duchess's Life,* "however improbable it seems, we remember the time when many people believed more firmly than they did their creed,"[65] originated in the intimacy, both personally and in correspondence, not only between the Earl of Marlborough and the Lord Treasurer, but between Godolphin and the able and influential woman whose intellectual sway asserted an enduring power over both these good and distinguished men. In all the difficulties and anxieties of the Earl and Countess, Godolphin participated.

Their opinions, their feelings, were in unison with those of the Lord Treasurer. Like him, nurtured in high church and Tory principles, they had abandoned with reluctance those doctrines when the spirit of the age no longer went with them. Like him, their early prepossessions, their maturer affections, leaned to the Jacobite cause. The

---

63. Coxe.
64. *Life of Sarah Duchess of Marlborough,* p. 41.
65. *Ibid,* p. 39.

Countess, indeed, being younger when the mischievous tendencies of those bygone notions of prerogative and divine right were disclosed to her, had more thoroughly imbibed sentiments of the Whig party than Lord Marlborough and Godolphin; but in essential points this celebrated triumvirate accorded.

It was easy for the opposite faction to raise conjectures, and to disseminate calumnies, upon the basis of a friendship so closely cemented, that neither the Earl nor the Countess ever acted without first consulting him whom they regarded as their best friend. It is easy to demolish, by the blast of malignity, every fair fabric which the best affections of our nature raise up; it is easy to put the worst construction upon intimacies, the sources of which the innocent mind would gladly lay bare to the whole world. Endowed with beauty, with wit, fearless in her temper, unbending in her opinions. Lady Marlborough was not, nevertheless, one of those individuals whom the infections of slander could eventually taint. She was of too independent a nature to be readily susceptible of the tender passions. Her domestic character, as a mother, acknowledged to be exemplary even by those who commended her not,[66] afforded the best refutation to the corrupt passions of which she was accused.

The neglect of daily duties is generally the first signal of a woman's ruin—the first indication that her mind is unsettled, her inclinations gone astray, her peace and composure destroyed. The virtuous, blameless character of the Princess, who gave the Countess of Marlborough her favour and countenance, was, in a minor degree, a refutation of the malignant charge, raised doubtless in the hope of rending asunder the unanimity of three powerful persons, by awakening the gnawing pangs of suspicion, and the dread of an endangered reputation, to disturb their repose.

The uniform confidence of the most devoted, if not the best beloved of husbands; the pride, the virtuous pride, which he felt in her great qualities; the undying love which he bore her through the toils of campaigns and the turmoil of politics, triumphantly assert the innocence of that woman, of whose misdeeds there would have been abundant willing witnesses, eager to offer their testimony to the absent and injured husband. But the Earl left her, as it appears, without a misgiving with respect to her moral conduct; and trusted her to the honour, as he often commended her to the advice, of that friend whom he loved to his dying hour, and whom he bitterly regretted

---

66. Burnet.

after his death.[67]

It is impossible to unveil the secrets of the human heart; but to those who believe in the existence of virtue, honour, friendship, all the probabilities are in favour of Lady Marlborough's innocence of this hideous charge. From this period of her life, however, when Godolphin became her acknowledged ally, must be dated the influence which that firm and notable friendship began to exercise over her opinions and conduct, as well as the ascendency of her own political influence.

Godolphin, who, according to the Duchess herself, "conducted the Queen, with the care and tenderness of a father or a guardian, through a state of helpless ignorance, and who faithfully served her in all her difficulties," [68] now shared the counsels, as he had participated in the scheme of Marlborough to restore James. According to his female friend, he was admirably calculated for an adviser; being, as she describes him, "a man of few words, but of a remarkable thoughtfulness and sedateness of temper; of great application to business, and of such despatch in it, as to give pleasure to those who attended him in any affair." [69] Thus provided with an able and efficient counsellor, less bigoted, perhaps, to her virtues than her still enamoured husband, and, by the equability of his temper, well adapted to calm what Dr. Burnet terms her "impetuous speech,"[70] Lady Marlborough succeeded in steering through the rest of this reign in far more tranquillity than could possibly have been anticipated from its commencement.

---

67. Coxe, vol. 6, p. 216.
68. Opinions of the Duchess of Marlborough. See *Private Correspondence, Colburn,* 1837, vol. 2, p. 125.
69. *Ibid.*
70. Burnet.

CHAPTER 8
1694
Release of Marlborough from Prison

The pretended association and audacious forgery of Young were discovered immediately upon his being confronted with the Bishop of Rochester. The Earl of Marlborough was consequently released, but not until the 15th of June, that being the last day of Term. He was then admitted to bail, the Marquis of Halifax and the Duke of Shrewsbury being his sureties; an act of kindness for which they were, however, erased shortly afterwards from the list of privy counsellors.[1]

Sometime afterwards, when Young was on the point of suffering the penalty of death for another offence, he confessed, with pretended contrition, that he had obtained the Earl of Marlborough's seal and signature by addressing him under the character of a country gentleman, inquiring the character of a domestic. This avowal completely exonerated Marlborough, who had been himself startled at the similarity of the signature, subscribed to the association, to his own handwriting.

Conscious, perhaps, of deserving disgrace, Lord Marlborough remained during the latter years of William's reign chiefly at Sandridge, sometimes exchanging his residence for apartments at Berkeley House, which Lady Marlborough, in virtue of her office about Queen Anne, inhabited on the removal of the Princess thither from Sion House. The Countess of Marlborough meantime devoted herself to the care of the Princess, who was confined, at Sion House, of a lifeless infant, whilst yet altercations between her and her sister were rife. Anne,

---
1. Coxe, vol.1, p. 69

however, sent due intelligence of her confinement to Queen Mary, first by Sir Benjamin Bathurst, and then by Lady Charlotte Beverwart, who waited until the Queen should have held a conference with the Earl of Rochester, before she could see Her Majesty. The delivery of her message produced a visit to Sion House, of which the Duchess gives the following account.[2]

> She (the Queen) came attended by the Ladies Derby and Scarborough. I am sure it will be necessary to have a good voucher to persuade your Lordship[3] of the truth of what I am going to relate. The Princess herself told me, that the Queen never asked her how she did, nor so much as took her by the hand. The salutation was this: 'I have made the first step, by coming to you, and now I expect you will make the next, by removing my Lady Marlborough.' The Princess answered, that she had never in all her life disobeyed her, except in that one particular, which she hoped would some time or other appear as unreasonable to Her Majesty as it did to her. Upon which the Queen rose up and went away, repeating to the Prince, as he led her to the coach, the same thing that she had said to the Princess.

Lady Derby, one of the Queen's ladies in waiting, took up the cue from her royal mistress, and never even went up to the bedside to inquire how the Princess was. The Queen, indeed, upon her return, was heard to say, "she was sorry for having spoken to the Princess," whose agitation she had observed was so great, that "she trembled, and looked as white as the sheets."[4] Nevertheless, soon after this visit, all company was forbidden to wait upon the Princess, and her guards were taken from her.

The King was not in England when these indignities were offered to the Princess, and Mary and her constant adviser, Lord Rochester, were alone responsible for the harshness with which an only sister was treated. But Anne, as the presumptive heir apparent, was dear to a people who dreaded the horrors of civil war, and of a disputed succession. In coming from Sion House to London, without guards, her coach was attacked by highwaymen, a circumstance which produced many severe animadversions on the danger to which the heir of the throne was exposed, without an escort, at a period when such adventures

---

2. *Conduct*, p. 74.
3. Lord Cholmondeley, to whom the Duchess addressed her *Vindication*.
4. *Conduct*, p, 74.

were not unknown even in Piccadilly.[5]

Lady Marlborough, distressed at being the manifest cause of the indignities offered to her gracious mistress, entreated Anne to allow her to leave her, and used every argument her thoughts could suggest to persuade the Princess to that effect. These well-meant endeavours were unavailing; for "when I said anything that looked that way," the Duchess relates, "she fell into the greatest passion of tenderness and weeping that is possible to imagine;[6] and though my situation at that time was so disagreeable to my temper, that could I have known how long it was to last, I could have chosen to have gone to the Indies sooner than to endure it, yet, had I been to suffer a thousand deaths, I think I ought to have submitted rather than have gone from her against her will."

The result of the Princess's vexations was a fever, after her confinement, on recovering from which she sent to Dr. Stillingfleet, Bishop of Worcester, hoping through his mediation to convey to Mary her sense of the honour which the Queen, in her last heartless visit, had conferred upon her. Dr. Stillingfleet, whom the Princess found, in her conversation with him, to have become very partial to the Queen, undertook to be the bearer of a letter, in which Anne requested permission to pay her duty to her sister.

The Queen's reply evinced a determined, and, if not an unkind, almost persecuting spirit. She began by telling her sister that since she had herself never used compliments, "so now they will not serve." She declared that "words would not make them live together as they ought;" there was but one thing she had required, "and no other mark would satisfy her."[7] But she must have been ignorant of the tenacity of her sister's disposition, and only partially aware of the influence which the Duchess exercised over the easily moulded Anne, if she could have expected such a sacrifice.

Meantime Lord and Lady Marlborough had the misfortune to lose their infant son, Lord Brackley,—an event to which Anne alludes in the following terms.

> I am very sensibly touched with the misfortune that my dear Mrs. Freeman has had of losing her son, knowing very well what it is to lose a child; but she knowing my heart so well, and how great a share I bear in all her concerns, I will not

---

5. See Horace Walpole's Letters to Sir Horace Mann.
6. *Conduct*, p. 73.
7. *Conduct*, p. 79.

say any more on this subject, for fear of renewing her passion too much. Being now at liberty to go where I please, by the Queen's refusing to see me, I am mightily inclined to go tomorrow, after dinner, to the Cockpit, and from thence privately in a chair to see you sometime next week. I believe it will be time for me to go to London, to make an end of that business of Berkeley-house.

This letter of condolence contained a copy of the cold and arbitrary reply of the Queen to the Princess; the original, Anne specifies, being kept by her, in case it should be necessary to show it for her own justification. At the same time she observes, that having extorted an admission from Dr. Stillingfleet that she had made "all the advances that were reasonable," she thought that the more "it was noised about that she would have waited on the Queen, but that she refused to see her, the better; and therefore that she should not scruple saying so to anybody, when it came in the way."[8]

Not, however, satisfied with the perpetual assurances of the Princess, that "only death should part her from her dear Mrs. Freeman"—that if her dear friend should ever leave her, "it would break her faithful Mrs. Morley's heart"—and other repeated declarations of the same nature, the Countess sought to ascertain the sentiments of the Prince George, upon the subject of her quitting the Princess's service. The reply of the warm-hearted, and certainly at this period of her life, the generous Anne, was equally distinct upon this point as upon the other bearings of the question.

"In obedience to dear Mrs. Freeman, I have told the Prince all she desired me, and he is so far from being of another opinion, that, if there had been any occasion, he would have strengthened me in my resolutions, and we both beg you would never mention so cruel a thing anymore."

"Can you think either of us so wretched," she continues, "as for the sake of twenty thousand pounds, and to be tormented from morning to night with flattering knaves and fools, we should forsake those we have such objections to, and that we are so certain are the occasion of all their misfortunes?"

"No, my dear Mrs. Freeman," she thus addressed her in another part of her letter, "never believe your faithful Morley will ever submit. She can wait with patience for a sunshiny day, and if she

---

8. *Conduct*, p. 80.

does not see it, yet she hopes England will flourish again. Once more give me leave to beg you would be so kind never to speak of parting more, for, let what will happen, that is the only thing that can make me miserable."[9]

It is curious, but to the experienced observer of all that passes among the social relations of life, whether of friendship, love, or kindred, not surprising, to find these letters so full of tenderness, and of disinterested attachment, and so acceptable at one time to Lady Marlborough, thus characterized, when she dipped her pen in gall to write the character of her former patroness.

"Her letters," says the plain-spoken Duchess in her private memoranda, "were very indifferent, both in sense and spelling, unless they were generally enlivened with a few passionate expressions, sometimes pretty enough, but repeated over and over again, without the mixture of anything either of diversion or instruction." [10]

Thus firmly fixed in the affections of the Princess, none of the numerous efforts which were made by different members of the household, many of whom had been promoted to their situations by the Countess, availed to induce Anne to allow her favourite to be removed—Lord Rochester, her uncle, in vain working to effect that end. The result was a direct and unhappily prolonged hostility between the Queen and the Princess, and it was made a point of duty with regard to the one sister, that no courtier should visit the other.

Lady Grace Pierrepoint was one of the few ladies, with the exception of some female members of Jacobite families, who determined to make her election between the two courts in favour of Anne; other ladies of high rank made their visits very rare, paying their respects only on certain occasions. A more decided mark of royal spleen was testified, through the agency of Lord Rochester, when the Princess visited Bath. This nobleman, who loved pageants and addresses, "wrote to the Mayor of Bath, a tallow-chandler, forbidding him, or any of his brethren of the corporation, to show any respect to the Princess Anne, without leave from the court."

"But it must be owned," says the Duchess in her contemptuous way, "that this lord had a singular taste for trifling ceremonies. I remember, when he was treasurer, he made his white staff be carried by his chair-side, by a servant bare-headed; in

---

9. *Conduct*, p. 18.
10. *Opinions of the Duchess. Private Correspondence*, vol. 2, p. 120. Colburn.

this, among other things, so very unlike his successor, my Lord Godolphin, who cut his white staff shorter than ordinary, that he might hide it, by taking it into the chair with him."[11]

"My Lord Rochester," however, must, the Duchess imagines, "have been disappointed, if he expected that the Princess regarded this petty exertion of power with anything but contempt," Anne was, in fact, infinitely more vexed to observe a frown on the brow of her favourite, than to be precluded from the honours usually paid her.

"Dear Mrs. Freeman must give me leave to ask her," writes the submissive Queen, on one occasion, "if anything has happened to make her uneasy. I thought she looked tonight as if she had the spleen. And I can't help being in pain whenever I see her so." [12]

With respect to the mayor's omission of the wonted respect of going to church with her, Anne thought it was a thing to be laughed at; nor was she probably disturbed in her general placidity by "another foolish thing," as the Duchess calls it, a trifling, but characteristic proof of Mary's unsisterly vengeance. When the Princess resided at Berkeley House, it was her habit to attend St. James's church; and the preacher, in compliance with custom, ordered a copy of his text to be laid upon her cushion. But Mary, carrying her resentments into that sacred edifice without whose porch worldly passions should be left, ordered that this observance also should be abandoned: the minister, however, refusing to comply, unless an order were given in writing, which the Queen and her advisers "did not care to do," "that noble design," as the Duchess terms the Queen's prohibition, "was dropt."[13]

Berkeley-house, to which the Princess about this time removed, was the scene of all those cabals, those fears and resentments, those heart-burnings and bickerings, by which a minor court, in open hostility with the more powerful, but less popular head of the family, is tolerably sure to be infested. Berkeley-house, standing on the site of Devonshire-house, and giving the name to Berkeley-square, was at this time the last house in Piccadilly, a distinction which Devonshire-house also possessed until long often the year 1700.[14]

The Princess lived here with her favourite and other friends in a

---
11. *Conduct*, p. 98, 99.
12. *Ibid*.
13. *Conduct*, pp. 98, 99.
14. Pennant, p. 171.

very quiet manner, never seeing the Queen, who still, through Lady Fitzharding and other mediators, insisted upon the dismissal of Lady Marlborough as the condition of reconciliation between herself and Anne; whilst Anne, with her native obstinacy, adhered to her friend in preference to her kindred.

The unkindness of the Queen, however, could only injure the Princess in one way, that of stopping her revenues; but Lord Godolphin was Treasurer, a man too useful to the court to be offended, and who, as the King knew, would quit his office in preference to refuse paying an annuity which had been voted by act of Parliament, Between these discordant sisters, one stay, one common subject of interest and source of affection, there still how ever was, to mitigate the anger of Mary, and to preserve the semblance of a bond of union between the family. The hopes of the nation, the pride of his family and his preceptors, and the promising representative of weak parents, the infant Duke of Gloucester was now the sole object of mutual interest, for to their common parent the royal sisters could not look conjointly for comfort.

Anne had, indeed, already reconciled herself to that culpable monarch, though injured parent, whom she had deserted in the hour of trial; and, upon the threatened invasion of James, had written to assure him that she should fly to him the instant she heard of his landing, saying, "She could ask for his forgiveness, being his daughter, but how could she ask him to present her duty to the Queen?"[15] But Mary, at variance to her dying day with her father, could not join with her sister in those expressions of duty and sentiments of affection, which might have proved a bond between her and Anne, but which were all turned to bitterness in the mind of one who loved her husband, to use her own habitual expression, "more than she loved her life."[16]

William Duke of Gloucester, a child, at this time, of three years old, was now, therefore, the only bond between these disunited sisters. This Prince, subsequently the favoured charge of the great Marlborough, and of the celebrated Bishop Burnet, was the only surviving offspring of the Prince and Princess of Denmark, of six children, most of whom had died as soon as they were born, and only one of whom, a daughter, had attained the age of a twelvemonth. Both William and Mary appear to have regarded this promising but premature scion of their house as their own peculiar possession; and William, especially after the death

---
15. Dalrymple, b, 7 p. 508.
16. See *Mary's Letters to William III*. Dalrymple. Appendixi p. 129..

of his Queen, manifested the tenderest solicitude for the health and welfare of the young. Prince; a circumstance which seemed to imply that the Duke had been dear to his deceased and lamented wife.[17]

The Duchess of Marlborough, indeed, intimates that whenever Her Majesty made the young Prince any present of "rattles" or other playthings, "she took especial care to have her attention inserted in the *Gazette*. Whenever the Duke was ill, she sent a bedchamber woman to Camden-house, to inquire how he did. But this compliment was made in so offensive a manner to the Princess, that I have often wondered how any mortal could hear it with patience. For whoever was sent, used to come without any ceremony into the room where the Princess was, and passing by her, as she stood or sat, without taking more notice of her than if she had been a rocker, go directly up to the Duke, and make their speech to him, or to the nurse, as he lay in her lap."[18]

The Princess, however, happy in her favourite circle, seems to have received these indignities with her wonted apathy, whilst she testified her affection for Lord and Lady Marlborough by the offer of a pension of a thousand pounds a year, creating a new place in her household as an excuse for that granted annuity to one whom she considered as a victim in her cause. But Marlborough, though his income was materially reduced by the loss of his lucrative employments, respectfully declined the generosity of his kind patroness.[19]

These bickerings between the Queen and the Princess were soon, however, painfully and effectually terminated. The smallpox at that time raged fearfully in London. Thousands died of the disease, and apprehensions were entertained for the safety of the Queen, who had never had the cruel distemper. Mary had a short time previously been much concerned at the sudden decease of Archbishop Tillotson, who was struck with palsy whilst performing service in Whitehall Chapel. She had spoken of this revered prelate with tears, and her mind had been considerably disturbed at the loss of so valuable a friend.

Whilst still grieving for this event, she fell ill; but her natural spirits sustained her. The disease seemed to subside; and to Bishop Burnet, who was with her for an hour on the day of the attack, she complained of nothing. On the following morning she went out; but returned oppressed with the cruel malady to her closet. There she shut herself

---

17. Conduct, p. 103.
18. *Ibid.*, edition 1742, p. 109.
19. *Conduct*, p. 285.

up, burnt many of her papers, and put the rest in order. Nevertheless, thinking it might be only a transient indisposition, she used some slight remedies: these were ineffectual to relieve her, and in two days the smallpox appeared in its most malignant form. The Princess Anne was at this time indisposed, and remaining, by her physician's advice, upon one floor, lying constantly on a couch. Yet, upon hearing of the Queen's illness, she sent a lady of the bedchamber with a message of kindness and respect, begging that Her Majesty would allow her the happiness of waiting on her, and declaring that she would run any risk in her present situation to have that satisfaction.

To this message, which was delivered to the Queen herself, a reply was returned, in the King's name, that the Queen would send an answer on the following day. Accordingly a letter arrived, announcing that, since the Queen was ordered to be kept as quiet as possible, the writer. Lady Derby,[20] was Lady Derby was Lady Elizabeth Butler, daughter of Thomas Earl of Ossory; married to George ninth Earl of Derby, who died in 1702, and was succeeded by James tenth Earl, who had been groom of the bedchamber to William the Third.—Burke's Peerage, ordered by the King to request that the Princess would defer her visit.

The construction which Lady Marlborough put upon this "civil answer was, that poor Queen Mary's disease was mortal, more than even if the physicians had told her that it was;" yet she added also the uncharitable interpretation, "that the deferring the Princess's coming was only to leave room for continuing the quarrel, in case the Queen should chance to recover, or for reconciliation with the King (if that should be thought convenient) in case of the Queen's death."[21]

Be that as it may, the two sisters never met again. The King, overwhelmed by a knowledge of the Queen's danger, seems to have been occupied with far different thoughts than those imputed to him by the Duchess; and probably consulted only the Queen's well-doing, when he prohibited a harassing interview between her and the Princess, which might have hastened the approaching event. On the third day of Mary's illness, the stem, reserved monarch was completely bowed down by the intelligence that the medical advice called to supersede the erroneous treatment of Dr. Ratcliffe, was resorted to too late. He called

Dr. Burnet into his closet, and with a burst of anguish exclaimed,

---
20. Burnet, 4. p. 149.
21. *Conduct*, p. 106.

that there was "No hope of the Queen; that, from being the happiest, he was now going to be the most miserable creature upon earth." The Queen bore the awful consciousness of approaching death with far more composure than he, for whom she had sacrificed every other tie, could assume. When apprised by Archbishop Tenison that all hope of her recovery was at an end, she quickly comprehended the reverend prelate's intention, for which he sought to prepare her by degrees. She evinced no agitation. She said, she thanked God that she had always resolved that nothing should be left to the last hour; she had then nothing to do, but to look up to God, and submit to his will. Indeed, as one who loved this virtuous Princess observes, "her piety went farther than submission, for she seemed to desire death rather than life."[22]

Whilst this solemn scene was passing at Kensington, the Princess sent every day to inquire after the state of the Queen, but received no encouragement to urge her desire of an interview. On one occasion, the Lady Fitzharding, who had the charge of the Duke of Gloucester, broke into the room where the dying Mary lay, and declaring the Princess's message to her, endeavoured to impress Her Majesty with a sense of her sister's distress. The Queen, according to the Duchess of Marlborough, returned no answer but "a cold thanks."[23] Nor did she ever, in the course of her illness, send any message whatsoever to the sister from whom she was estranged. In extenuation of this seeming inconsistency in one so devout, it must be stated, that she had so far adopted the stoical notions of her husband, as to preclude him and herself from the trial of a last farewell. After causing to be delivered to him a small casket, in which she had formerly written her sentiments, she devoted her time to prayer.

The Archbishop of Canterbury administering, and all the bishops standing round, Mary received the Holy Communion—that solemn service, in which, even in the fullness of health, we cannot participate without an awful consciousness of the immediate presence of our Maker. Faint but calm, the dying Queen followed the whole office; and, when that was concluded, she composed herself to meet her God. She slumbered sometimes, but she was not refreshed; for, "*like others who labour and are heavy laden*," nothing refreshed her but prayer. At last her strong reason began to be obscured, her speech to falter; she tried in vain to say something to the King; she endeavoured to join in the holy offices of the archbishops. Cordials were given her; but all

---

22. Burnet.
23. *Conduct*, p. 107.

was ineffectual; and she sank about one o'clock in the morning of the twenty-eighth of December, her disorder having first displayed fatal symptoms on Christmas Day.[25]

In this beautiful picture of an exemplary deathbed, but two objects are wanting: a father reconciled, a sister restored to affection. But the father, who regretted more that his daughter died unforgiven by him, and undutiful, than her death itself, was at a distance; his pardon and his blessing could not have been obtained. The sister prayed for admission, and was refused. Such is the effect of party violence, which ruled even in the breast of the pious, affectionate, and strong-minded Mary! If it be said, *"how hardly shall a rich man enter the kingdom of heaven,"* it may also be a matter of consideration how difficult it must prove for the soul, torn by the strong contending passions which darken a political career, to enter into that blessed rest, where selfishness and ambition can find no mansion!

The Princess Anne, unchecked by indifference to her amiable advances, by the advice of Lord Sunderland and others, wrote to the King, shortly after the Queen's death, a letter expressive of her "sincere and hearty sorrow for his affliction," and declaring herself "as sensibly touched by his misfortune," as if she had not been so unhappy as to fall under her sister's displeasure. Her letter found the King too dejected, and too much humbled by his calamity, to think of refusing her petition. During the Queen's illness, his anguish had broken out into violent lamentations; after her death his spirits sank so low, that many persons feared that he was following her.

In this depression of spirits and strength, he betook himself to those aids of religion which, with a due seriousness, and a respect for sacred subjects, he had never, during his busy intercourse with the great world, resorted to with heartfelt earnestness, as the only solace, the only cure for bereavements which leave us heartbroken, dependent, and wretched beings.

Whilst William was in this state of mind, the great and good Lord Somers, who had long lamented the feuds which disturbed the royal family, visited him at Kensington, for the purpose of interceding with a view to reconciling these differences. He found the King sitting at the end of his closet in an agony of grief, little to be expected from one who rarely betrayed the passions by which his spirits were now overwhelmed. The King, lost in his own bitter reflections, paid no at-

---

25. Burnet, p. 199.

tention to the entrance of Lord Somers, until that nobleman, remarkable for his courtesy and prudence,[26] broke the silence by expressing a hope that now all disunion between His Majesty and the Princess Anne might cease. "My lord, do what you will; I can think of no business," was the agonised reply of the King; and to all the observations which Somers made, he returned no other answer.[27]

The Duchess of Marlborough, however, imputes the reconciliation to Lord Sunderland, who had, on all occasions, as she says, shown himself to be a man of sense and breeding, and had used his utmost endeavours, before the Queen's death, to make up the breach between the two sisters, though, she thinks, he never could have succeeded during the lifetime of Mary. Although the reconciliation was opposed by the Earl of Portland, yet the quarrel was at last adjusted; and Anne visited the King, who received her with cordiality, and promised her that St. James's palace should in future be her residence.[28]

"And now," says the Duchess, "it being publicly known that the quarrel was made up, nothing was to be seen but crowds of people of all sorts flocking to Berkeley-house, to pay their respects to the *Prince* and *Princess*: a sudden alteration which, I remember, occasioned the half-witted Lord Caermarthen to say one night to the Princess, as he stood close by her in the circle, "*I hope your highness will remember that I came to wait upon you when none of this company did*; which caused a great deal of mirth."

But although matters were thus publicly made up, the King, at least in the opinion of the Duchess, never cared to testify the slightest public respect for Anne, nor to conciliate her regard. From the beginning of his reign, when he committed the heinous offence on which much stress was laid, that of disappointing the Princess of a plate of peas on which she had set her mind,[29] to the last hour, he was still mightily indifferent to the placid, but, it must be acknowledged, somewhat uninteresting Anne. But all his affronts were borne with imperturbable patience by the Princess.

When she waited upon His Majesty at Kensington, no more respect was shown her than to any other lady, "till the thing caused some discourse in town, after which Lord Jersey waited upon her once or

---

26. Swift. *Last Years of Queen Anne's Reign*, p. 6.
27. Coxe, vol. 1, p. 74.
28. *Conduct*, p. 110.
29. *Conduct*, p. 115.

twice downstairs, but not oftener. And if any one came to meet her," continues the Duchess, "it was a page of the back-stairs, or some person whose face was not known. And the Princess, upon these occasions, waited an hour and a half, just upon the same foot as the rest of the company, and not the least excuse was made for it."[30]

All this submission was very galling to the proud, high-spirited favourite, who would have braved William in presence of his whole court, had she been the Princess, rather than have paid one tribute of respect to the careless and contemptuous monarch. Lady Marlborough looked on indignant, and was of opinion that the Princess conciliated a great deal too much. She could not endure that her royal mistress should move a single step that she would not have taken in her place; nor was there a single advance on Anne's part of which she approved, except her last letter to the Queen, and her offer of visiting her dying sister.[31] This candid acknowledgment she makes with an almost indecent boldness, not to be wondered at in one who, in her later days, defended herself, in a court of justice, a suit against her grandson.[32]

It must, indeed, be allowed, that the list of petty grievances with which the Duchess swells the indignities offered to the Princess Anne, appears, at this distance of time, puerile and vexatious. Her complaints are detailed with a solemnity which seems ridiculous, now that all the stirring passions which gave importance to those incidents are at rest. Her narrative, sarcastic as it is, was unfortunately polished by the hired assistance of Hook, the historian, and, after repeated revisions, which must have shorn many pungent and characteristic passages, was given to the disappointed public, respectably moderate. Still these "annals of a wardrobe," as Horace Walpole designates them, this "history of the back stairs," possess—as even he who speaks of "old Marlborough" with bitter contempt is fain to allow—some "curious anecdotes, some sallies of wit, which fourscore years of arrogance could not fail to produce in so fantastic an understanding." [33]

With the account of the death of Queen Mary, much of the Duchess's caustic satire subsides. Still she has a few touches reserved for William. Even the sorrow which the monarch experienced, and his desolate situation in a foreign country, where he reigned unloved, did not soften the unceasing aversion and contempt with which the

---
30. *Ibid.* P. 111.
31. *Conduct.*
32. Walpole's *Reminiscences*, p. 315.
33. Walpole's *Noble Authors*, p. 190.

Duchess regarded the royal widower.

His first grave offence, after Mary's decease, was his silence in regard to a letter written by the dutiful and subservient Anne, congratulating His Majesty upon the honour done to his name and adopted country, by the taking of Namur, Probably the King would have received congratulations with a better grace, from any one than from her, who might regard herself as having a sort of partnership interest in the glory of England. Good wishes from Anne were somewhat like the next heir to an estate setting forth a strain of rejoicing, on the growth of timber, or on the improvement of lands, to him who was actually in possession. The King took no notice of the humble epistle, or, in the Duchess's words, "showed his brutal disregard for the writer," by never returning "any answer to it, nor so much as a civil message."[34]

The next offence, and it certainly was one which spoke ill of William's good breeding, was his compelling Prince George to wear coloured clothes on the royal birthday, almost immediately after the death of his brother, the King of Denmark. The Prince, knowing that deep mourning was sometimes allowed in certain instances, requested, through Lord Albemarle, permission to keep on his mourning when he paid his respects to His Majesty.[35] William's ungracious reply was, that he should not see his brother-in-law unless he came in colours; and the subservient Prince was forced to comply.

"I believe," says the Duchess, after relating this instance of William's contemptuous conduct "I could fill as many sheets as I have already written, with relating the brutalities that were done to the Prince and Princess in this reign. The King was, indeed, so ill-natured, and so little polished by education, that neither in great things nor in small had he the manners of a gentleman." [36]

The Duchess makes no allowance for His Majesty's habits and character. Precise as he seems to have been in the article of Prince George's attire, William hated formalities, and especially those public addresses which must be so peculiarly tedious to a sovereign. Respecting this very siege of Namur, touching which he gave so much offence to the Duchess, he committed an act of ill-breeding towards no less an individual than the mayor of a borough. This worshipful

---

34. See Appendix, 8.
35. *Conduct*, p. 114.
36. *Conduct*, p. 115.

person having come to court to present an address, combining the two dissimilar topics of condolence for the death of the Queen, and congratulation for the success at Namur, introduced himself by saying that "he came with joy in one hand and grief in the other."

"Pray put them both into one hand, good Mr. Mayor," was the King's laconic remark, heedless of the impression which he made upon formal courtiers and ladies in waiting, who, like the Duchess of Marlborough, could sooner pardon a defect in morals, than a solecism in manners."[37] It was probable, from His Majesty's known aversion to compliments, public and private, that he intended no offence to the Princess Anne, when he committed the "brutality" of not answering her letter.

Notwithstanding the spirit manifested in these animadversions by the Countess of Marlborough, the Earl sought every opportunity of maintaining the good understanding between the Princess and the court.[38] This he justly thought of importance, possibly for the reason avowed by Dalrymple, that an apparent reconciliation between the royal family had all the good effects of a real one, "because it obliged inferior figures to suspend their passions by the example of their superiors."[39] But Marlborough, although taking an active part in the House of Lords, was not at present allowed to enter the royal presence, though having a "fair and very great reversion" of favour.[40]

The only adverse event during the remaining portion of William's reign, which particularly affected Lord and Lady Marlborough, was the conspiracy of Sir John Fenwick, one of the most active Jacobites of the day. With this party, though not personally with Fenwick, Marlborough, it cannot be denied, had been deeply and culpably implicated.

No considerations can excuse the dishonourable intercourse which Marlborough, in conjunction with Godolphin and others, had carried on with the exiled monarch. It resulted from a temporising and mean policy, which sought to secure an indemnity from James in case of his restoration, or of the accession of the Prince of Wales. If the reasons which engaged Marlborough to aid the accession of William were valid, and sprang from a pure source, those reasons were still in force to promote the peaceable rule of the reigning monarch, and to support

---

37. Dalrymple, b. 4. p. 78.
38. Coxe, vol. 1, p. 74.
39. Dalrymple, b. 3, p. 56.
40. Coxe. From the Shrewsbury Papers.

him on his throne.

The rash encouragement which Godolphin and Marlborough had given to James's emissaries, now involved them in a serious dilemma. Fenwick, convicted, upon the evidence of an intercepted letter to his wife, of being concerned in the plot formed at this time to assassinate William, sought to avert the justly merited sentence from which he afterwards suffered, by a disclosure of the names of those whom he declared to have been concerned in the conspiracy. He was instructed in the details of his pretended confessions, by Lord Monmouth, afterwards the noted and eccentric Earl of Peterborough. He accused the Duke of Shrewsbury, the Earl of Marlborough, Godolphin, and Russell, of treasonable practices; and of having, in particular, accepted pardons from the late King.

These noblemen were, however, fully cleared of the charges made against them by Fenwick; and Marlborough, standing up in his place in the House of Lords, solemnly denied ever having had any conversation whatsoever with Sir John Fenwick during the reign of the present King. Lord Godolphin vindicated himself in the same manner. Fenwick was executed, and Monmouth stripped of all his offices, and sent to the Tower; but was saved from further punishment by the mediation of Bishop Burnet.[41]

Cleared, therefore, from this atrocious accusation, Marlborough, who, with his wife, had suffered much uneasiness whilst the proceedings against Fenwick were pending, experienced, in the end, the security which a subject derives from the dominion of a rightly thinking and high-minded prince, and the superior strength and wisdom of such a government to the uncertain rule of passion and despotism. It was William's policy to make large allowance for the transient defection of his subjects; to endeavour to bring them back to duty by mildness and forgiveness; and to show no petty spleen, nor undue displeasure at the lingering fondness which they might cherish for their absent and justly-deposed monarch.

Sometime, however, elapsed before Marlborough received any outward proof of his sovereign's restored confidence. William, indeed, openly regretted that he could not employ a nobleman who was great both in military affairs and as a cabinet minister, and "one who never made a difficulty." [42] But, at length, either the King's scruples were

---

41. Coxe, p. 82.
42. Coxe, p. 86. From the *Duchess's Narrative*. Green Book.

overcome: or, as he allowed, in any enterprise, choosing to act upon the principle of converting an enemy into a friend, he appointed Marlborough to a situation of the highest trust.

CHAPTER 9
1697, 1698

Appointment of Marlborough

The peace of Ryswick, in 1697, was accompanied by two acts, intended, on the part of William the Third, to relieve and indemnify his predecessor for some of his disappointments and afflictions. On the one hand, the King bound himself to pay fifty thousand pounds a year to Mary of Modena, the wife of James; a sum which would have been her jointure had she continued Queen of England. By another act William consented that the son of James the Second, afterwards known as the Pretender, should be educated in England in the Protestant faith, and should inherit the crown after his own death.[1] Such were his just intentions; but, in consequence of the distinct refusal of James on both these points, the Pretender lost his crown, and his mother her jointure; and the hopes of the country, and the kindly feelings of the King, were henceforth centred in William, the young Duke of Gloucester, the only surviving child of the Prince and Princess of Denmark.

The Duke was now entering his tenth year; and, it was thought advisable to withdraw him from the care of female instructresses, and to place him under the guidance of the learned and the valiant. He was a child of singular promise, and of a precocious capacity, foreboding weakness of body and premature decay. The King long hesitated before he could resolve to comply with the wishes of the Princess Anne, who earnestly desired that Marlborough might be appointed her son's governor. The situation was first offered to the Duke of Shrewsbury, but was declined by that nobleman, whose infirm health rendered him, at that time, desirous of retiring from public life.

---
1. Dalrymple, book 5, p. 88.

There was a considerable struggle in the mind of William before he could decide to place, in so responsible an office as that of governor, the man upon whom all the most enlightened of his advisers had fixed, as the proper tutor for the Prince. At length, the persuasions of the Earl of Sunderland, and of Lord Albemarle, who had succeeded Lord Portland in the royal favour, induced the monarch to bestow the honour upon Marlborough. It was conferred with these remarkable words: "Teach the Duke of Gloucester, my lord, to be like yourself, and my nephew cannot want accomplishments."[2] On the evening of this appointment, June 19th, 1698, Lord Marlborough was sworn one of the privy council.

This sudden restoration to good fortune and to the King's confidence acted doubtless beneficially upon the disposition of Lord Marlborough, who, like all superior natures, received benefits with the kindly spirit with which they were proffered. But no conciliation could mollify the implacable spirit of Lady Marlborough, nor reconcile her to the monarch who had once consented to the indignity offered to her, of forbidding her the court. Instead, therefore, of softening her tone when she discusses the events of this period, or of acknowledging the distinction conferred on Lord Marlborough, she refers to the arrangements respecting the household of the young Duke, as plainly proving that the Princess judged rightly, when she refused, on a former occasion, to leave her settlement to the generosity of the King.

William, as the Duchess affirms, obtained from Parliament a grant of fifty thousand pounds a year for the settlement of the young Duke, but allowed the young Prince five thousand pounds only of that sum, refusing even to advance one quarter for plate and furniture, which the Princess Anne was therefore obliged to supply out of her own funds.[3] The Princess received, also, a promise from His Majesty that she should have the appointment of all the household, excepting to the offices of the deputy-governor and gentlemen of the bedchamber. The message which brought Anne this assurance was, what the Duchess calls, "so humane," and had so different an air from anything the Princess had been used to, that it gave her "extreme pleasure;" and she instantly set about to fill up the appointments, making various promises to her own, and undoubtedly to her favourite's, friends. What then were the consternation of the Princess, and the fury of

---

2. Lediard, p. 118.
3. *Conduct*, p. 117.

the Countess of Marlborough, when, after a long delay in confirming these appointments, they were apprised that the King, who was going abroad, would send a list of those persons whom he had selected for the Duke's household.

The cogitations of two ladies, on such an occasion, may be imagined. The disappointment of various friends, the affronts sustained by others—the loss of patronage—the sure gain of contempt and ridicule—all the awkwardness of the affair must have ruffled even the placid Anne, who was probably, however, not half sufficiently incensed to satisfy the far more irritable and indignant Countess.

Anne, too, was in that condition which rendered any annoyance to her a matter seriously to be dreaded. She had settled who were to be grooms of the bedchamber, and who were to be pages of honour, and was not by any means disposed to unsettle these appointments.

All this was duly represented to the King by Lord Marlborough, who respectfully hoped that His Majesty "would not do anything to prejudice the Queen in her present state;" but this intercession produced no other effect than a violent fit of passion in the King, who declared that the Princess "should not be Queen before her time," and that he would make a list of what servants the Duke should have.

At length, however, Keppel Earl of Albemarle, who had more influence than any other courtier with the King, undertook to settle the affair. He took the list of the household made out by the Princess, and, whilst they were in Holland, showed it to the King. The list was, as it happened, approved by William, with very few alterations. But that was not, the Duchess declares, owing to the King's goodness, but "to the happy choice which the Princess had made of the servants." Nay, she further insinuates that the reason of William's desiring to alter the list was, that he might place in the household some of the servants of the last Queen, and by that means save their pensions.[4]

At length, however, the arrangements were completed. It must be acknowledged they were made somewhat too soon for the benefit of the royal child. The young Prince, delicate in frame, would have been happier perhaps, and, in the event of his living, stronger in mind as well as in body, had nature, and not etiquette, been made the rule of his youthful pursuits, and if state and ceremonials, too fatiguing for his infancy, had been postponed until his childish powers could better sustain their injurious effects upon his health. But the little vic-

---

4. *Conduct*, p. 119.

tim, who had struggled into boyhood, the only one of his family, and who was doomed to be the national hope, and the sole object of the monarch's care, was to be rendered valiant, theological, wise—a hero, a wonder—in short, that miserable being, a prodigy.

Marlborough was to teach him military tactics and the theory of war. The boy delighted in all that boys of simpler habits, and in a happier sphere, usually delight in. He learned with facility all the terms of fortification and of navigation; knew all the different parts of a strong ship, and of a man of war; and took pleasure in marshalling as soldiers a company of boys who had voluntarily enlisted themselves to form his troop.[5] All this the great Marlborough himself taught him. In the departments of classical literature and theology, the Duke had another preceptor, scarcely less celebrated.

Dr. Gilbert Burnet, whom William now appointed governor to the Duke of Gloucester in conjunction with Marlborough, was at this time Bishop of Salisbury, a see which he wished to resign on being appointed preceptor to the young Prince; being conscientiously averse from holding any preferment, the duties of which he could not in person superintend. Dr. Burnet was the intimate friend of the Countess of Marlborough; and probably he had had some share in forming her political opinions, and in weaning her from the Tory party, in whose principles the Countess had been reared.

It was scarcely possible for the Countess to possess a more valuable friend, nor the Duke of Gloucester a more enlightened preceptor, than this able, uncompromising advocate of civil and religious freedom—this pious divine, this disinterested, scrupulous, and zealous man. Burnet was of Scotch descent, and his character exhibited some of the noblest features which distinguish the inhabitants of the north of the Tweed, in all varieties of situation and circumstance. Like many great men, he owed much of his eminence, and most of his religious impressions, to his mother. She was a Presbyterian, a sister of the famous Sir Alexander Johnston, Lord Warristoun, who headed the Presbyterians during the civil wars, and whom no alliance nor kindred could bend to show any lenity to those who refused the solemn league and covenant.

Dr. Burnet's father, differing from these opinions, from the conviction that the Presbyterians did not intend to reform abuses in the Episcopal church, but to destroy that church itself, resolutely rejected

---

5. Boyer, p. 7.

the league and covenant; and was, on that account, at three several times, obliged to fly from his native county of Aberdeen; and, during one occasion, to remain five years in exile. Such were some of the consequences of fanatic *zeal*, in those disturbed and uncomfortable times.

By his father, himself a barrister, Burnet was educated, until he attained ten years of age, when, being a master of the Latin tongue, he was removed to Aberdeen College, and at fourteen began to study for the bar; such was the precocity of his intellect; in some respects, the effect of the custom of the day.

Fortunately for the Church of England, Burnet, after a year's application to the law, changed his course of studies, and applied himself to divinity, for which his father had originally destined him. When eighteen years of age, he was put upon his trial as a probationary preacher, the first step in Scotland towards an admission into orders, both in the Episcopal and in the Presbyterian church. From this epoch in his career, he devoted his life to the service of the church. He improved his notions upon many matters, in those times still unsettled, relative to the rites and ceremonies of the church, by conversing with the learned at the English universities. By foreign travelling, he enlarged his ideas concerning the differences into which learned and pious men fall, upon points of discipline and matters of doctrine.

Whilst residing in Holland, he became acquainted with the leading men of the various persuasions tolerated in that country; the Arminians, Papists, Unitarians, Brownists, and Lutherans, all passed under review in his reflecting mind; and, from the observation of the pious dispositions and high motives, of which he met with instances among all professing Christians, he drew this satisfactory and benevolent conclusion, that nothing but general charity could be acceptable to the great Ruler of men; he learned to abhor severity, and to see the beauty and wisdom of universal toleration.

Thus prepared for the eminent station which he afterwards filled, and for the great part which he had to act, Burnet, during a protracted intercourse with the kings and nobles of the land, held fast his integrity. When chaplain to Charles the Second, he remonstrated with him on his licentious course of life, fearless of the consequences to himself. He laboured with as little success to convert James from the doctrines of papacy. At a time when silence would have best aided his preferment in the church, he published his History of the Reformation, for which he received the thanks of both Houses of Parliament.

Nor did he lose any opportunity of publicly admonishing, and of privately reclaiming, the abandoned members of the aristocracy; and of calling sinners of all ranks and conditions to repentance. His preaching was earnest, unstudied, emphatic, effective. He improved upon the Scottish mode of giving premeditated discourses from memory, and by allotting many hours of the day to meditation on any given subject, and then accustoming himself to speak upon those aloud, he attained a remarkable facility in that mode of religious instruction, which is, of all others, when well acquired, the most effective.[6]

It was whilst this excellent and energetic man was chaplain to Charles the Second, an unwilling witness of the corruptions of the court, that he was requested to visit a female of abandoned character, who had been treading the paths of destruction with the celebrated Wilmot Earl of Rochester. Burnet, at this time without any parochial duty, never refused his aid to those who sought it. He went to the sinner, and left her penitent; but the good which he did ceased not here, but shed its beams forth in a "naughty world." The Earl of Rochester, hearing of the manner in which the divine had reclaimed the unfortunate partner of his guilt, sent for Burnet; and during a whole winter, once in every week, went over with him all those topics by which infidelity attacks the Christian religion.

The judgement of the sceptic, Rochester, was convinced; his conviction of the importance of moral duty established; his proud spirit laid prostrate; his opinions and his deportment entirely changed. He died a sincere penitent; whilst Burnet, in bequeathing to posterity the memorial of the sceptical difficulties, of the true contrition, of this misled and sinful man, has left to the infatuated and to the erring a legacy of inestimable price. In the words of Dr. Johnson, speaking of the bishop's account of these conferences, entitled *Some Passages in the Life of John Earl of Rochester,* "the critic ought to read it for its elegance, the philosopher for its argument, the saint for its piety." [7]

Burnet, both by his own account and that of his biographer, appears to have been very unwilling to undertake the charge now of-

---

6. It is told of Burnet, that on the consecration of some bishops. Bishop Williams was appointed to preach the sermon at Bow Church. The clerk had twice given out the psalm, and still the bishop, detained by some accident, did not appear. Burnet was desired by the Archbishop of Canterbury to supply his place. He did so, and preached one of the best sermons he had ever been known to deliver.
7. Johnson's *Lives of the Poets,* Art. Rochester. See also *Life of Bishop Burnet,* by Thomas Burnet, Esq. Burnet, *Hist. of his own Times,* vol. 4, p. 307.

fered to him by the King, and pressed upon him by the Princess. "I used," he says, "all possible endeavours to decline the office."

Having once, however, consented, he devoted himself with his usual ardour to the important task of educating the Prince. His admirable observations on education, in the conclusion of his History, show how excellently qualified the bishop was for the task. He went beyond his age, and was devoid of the narrow views and prejudices of his time. The great design of instruction was, as he justly thought, to inculcate great and noble sentiments, to give general information, to avoid pedantry, and to represent virtue and religion in the true light, as the only important, the only stable acquisitions in this sublunary state. He looked with regret on the errors committed by parents of the highest rank, who, lavish in other respects, were narrow in their notions of expenditure on education; he regarded education as "the foundation of all that could be proposed for bettering the next age." He considered that "it should be one of the chief cares of all government."[8]

With such a preceptor, it may readily be supposed how exact, and how earnest, would be those lessons guided by such high principles. "I took," says the bishop, "to my own province, the reading and explaining the scriptures to him, the instructing him in the principles of religion and the rules of virtue, and the giving him a view of history, geography, politics, and government;" instructions which the peculiar though simple eloquence of the bishop might have rendered invaluable in any other case.

But such advantages as these were adapted to one of riper years, and of a more hardy constitution than the feeble Prince. His progress was indeed amazing. Under the guidance of the bishop he attained a religious knowledge which was, says Burnet, "beyond imagination." His inquiries, his reflections, his pursuits, were those of a precocious and highly endowed mind. The custom of the times authorised this hot-bed culture to the infant mind. Our nobles and gentry were generally members of the universities at a period of life when now they would be schoolboys. But the approved mode of rearing a vigorous plant cannot be pursued with a tender and delicate shoot.

Henry Prince of Wales, the wonder of the court of James the First; and the Duke of Gloucester, the last remaining object of the Princess Anne's maternal affection, are instances of excellence too prematurely developed to be permanent. The event of two years showed, indeed, that the care and zeal bestowed upon the powers of the Duke's mind

---

8. *Ibid*. Vol. 4, p. 207.

might with advantage have been postponed, however admirable the intentions, and valuable the instructions, of his distinguished preceptors.

Whilst Marlborough, with his eminent colleague, was training up the young Prince to prove, as they hoped, an honour to his country, the great general's own family were growing up around him, displaying more than the ordinary graces and promise of youth. At this time, five children, one son and four daughters, formed the domestic circle of Lord and Lady Marlborough. Yet they were not destined to derive unalloyed felicity from these fondly prized objects of paternal affection. Their eldest son, afterwards Marquis of Blandford, a youth of considerable attainments, and of great moral excellence, was eventually consigned by his disconsolate parents to an early grave. The beauty and talents of their daughters were counterbalanced by defects which occasioned many heart-burnings, and much "home-bred" infelicity, in the latter period of Lady Marlborough's life.

Henrietta, the eldest daughter of these distinguished parents, inherited much of her mother's spirit, with more than Lady Marlborough's personal charms, and with a great portion of that mother's less enviable temper. When old age and bitter humiliation had added to the Duchess of Marlborough's native moroseness, which they ought rather to have subdued, their eldest daughter and she were long at variance, and never reconciled.

Yet, in a happier season, better expectations and brighter hopes were formed in the prospect of an union between Lady Henrietta, and the son of Lord and Lady Marlborough's most intimate and valued friend. At this time, in her eighteenth year, the Lady Henrietta had already attracted many admirers. The intimacy of her parents with Lord Godolphin directed, however, her inclination to one object, Francis, Lord Rialton, the eldest son of the Earl. The attachment between these two young persons began at a very early age, and was viewed with approbation by the parents on both sides, although the advantages to be derived from the projected marriage were chiefly, in worldly respects, on the side of Lord Rialton; Godolphin having, two years previously, resigned his situation as first lord of the Treasury, at the time of Sir John Fenwick's accusations, and, whilst he conducted the public finances, he had rather impaired than improved his own property.

But similarity of political opinions, a close intimacy, mutual confidence and respect, rendered the prospect of a near alliance with Godolphin not only agreeable, but advantageous; and Marlborough, in his subsequent campaigns, and after Godolphin was reinstated in his office, experienced the benefit of possessing a friend at the head of that important department, in which Lord Godolphin, as first lord of the Treasury, aided all the great general's designs, by a prompt attention to a supply of those means without which the most skilful projects could not have succeeded.

When Lady Henrietta had completed her eighteenth year, the marriage with Lord Rialton took place. The fortune of Lord Marlborough did not, at this time, authorise him to bestow a large portion on his daughter; yet he prudently and honourably declined the ample settlement which the Princess Anne, with kindness of intention, and delicacy of manner, offered to make in favour of the lovely bride. The sum which her royal highness proposed was ten thousand pounds; one half of which was accepted by her favourites, who added five thousand pounds to the liberal gift. And with an establishment ill suited to their rank, but probably sufficient for happiness, the young couple were obliged to be content.

Lady Anne Churchill, next in age to Lady Rialton, and according to Horace Walpole, "the most beautiful of all Lady Churchill's four charming daughters,"[9] excelled her sister Henrietta in sweetness of disposition, as well as in external advantages. Her amiable manners, and the possession of mental qualities beyond her age, particularly endeared this beautiful and affectionate daughter to her parents. She was the object of admiration, as well as of affection.

Lady Anne received, before her marriage, the flattering tribute of complimentary verses from Lord Godolphin, who delighted to relieve the duties of the great master of finance by the fascinating attempts of the poetaster.[10] Lord Halifax, of whose poetry, we must agree with Dr. Johnson, that "a short time has withered the beauties,"[11] celebrated also the charms of Lady Anne, in verses somewhat better, though not above mediocrity. Yet it was not the fate of this admired young lady, at first, to inspire that ardent attachment in the husband selected for her by her parents, which her beauty and her goodness of disposition merited.

Amongst the most intimate of Lord Marlborough's friends, Robert Spencer, Earl of Sunderland, secretary of state and president of the council to James the Second, had proved himself, at the time of Marl-

---

9. *Reminiscences*, p. 341.
10. Coxe, vol. 1, p. 92. See Note.
11. *Life of Halifax*.

borough's disgrace at court, the most zealous of his advocates. Sunderland, who had encountered a variety of accusations for countenancing popery to please King James, and for betraying that monarch afterwards to William, was now in high favour with the reigning sovereign, over whom he exercised a remarkable ascendency. Although beloved neither by Whig nor Tory, his ministry was more efficient than any which succeeded it in the time of William.

Of disputed integrity, but of acknowledged talents, Lord Sunderland was, however, constrained to bend beneath the violence of party. He withdrew about this time from public life, notwithstanding the earnest entreaties of the King that he would remain near him; and, fearing that in the attacks made upon him by the Tories he would not be supported by the Whigs, Sunderland fled from the censures for which he felt there was too real a foundation, in his conduct during the preceding reign.[12]

Between the Countess of Sunderland and Lady Marlborough there existed a friendship of an enthusiastic, almost a romantic character. This affectionate intimacy was accounted for by mutual obligations and common misfortunes, shared by the two great statesmen, the husbands of these two ladies.

After the revolution, Marlborough had exerted his influence to assist Sunderland in exile and distress. When Marlborough fell into disgrace, Lord Sunderland had pleaded his cause, and adhered to him with a grateful constancy; advocating with the King the expediency of placing Marlborough in the office of preceptor to the young Duke of Gloucester. The warm attachment between the two Countesses sometimes aroused even the jealousy of the Princess Anne, who considered Lady Sunderland as her rival in the affection of the spoiled and flattered Lady Marlborough,[13] and envied the terms of equality which rendered the friendship of the two Countesses a source of mutual happiness. Not devoid of romance in her early years, though in her latter days she degenerated into coarseness of mind and vulgarity of manners, Anne felt, it seems, the insuperable barrier which her exalted rank had placed between her and the delights of a true, disinterested friendship. Charles Lord Spencer, the only son of the Earl and Countess of Sunderland, reported to have been famed alike for "his skill in negotiations and his rapid equestrian movements,"[14] was the object to

---

12. Burnet, vol. 4, p. 302.
13. Coxe, p. 94.
14. *Granger*, vol. 2, p. 373.

whom the ambition of his parents now pointed, as a probable bond of union between their family and the powerful houses of Marlborough and Godolphin. The lovely Lady Anne was god-daughter to the Countess of Sunderland. Her beauty, her accomplishments, and the favour which she already enjoyed with the Princess Anne, were all cogent reasons for promoting the match, in the eyes of the veteran courtier and statesman, Sunderland, The first proposals in the affair seem to have originated on his side. In one of the letters written on the subject he says:[15]

> "If I see him so settled, I shall desire nothing more in this world but to die in peace, if it please God. I must add this, that if he can be thus happy, he will be governed in everything, public and private, by Lord Marlborough, I have particularly talked to him of that, and he is sensible how advantageous it will be to him to do so. I need not, I am sure, desire that this may be a secret to everyone but Lady Marlborough."

Notwithstanding their friendship for the family of the Earl, the suggestion of a closer bond was not at first received by Lord and Lady Marlborough with encouragement. Perhaps they might regard the betrothing of their favourite daughter to Lord Spencer somewhat in the light of a sacrifice. That young nobleman had displayed a character of mind both uncommon and repulsive: grave, cold, and staid in his deportment, an ardent, impetuous, and somewhat haughty spirit was concealed beneath that icy exterior.[16] His political principles were those of republicanism; his notions of filial duty were tinctured by the actions of his schoolboy studies.

Already had he anathematised his father in the House of Commons, with all the powers of a ready eloquence, and declared against the crafty Earl for protecting traitors, and for permitting his mother to harbour her own daughter, the wife of the attainted Lord Clancarty. For this act of Roman heroism, Lord Spencer had been extolled by the violent party, and his loyalty to the King eulogised; since, to serve His Majesty, he would not scruple to expose his father. But cautious observers had questioned this unnatural display, which was supposed to be concerted between the young lord and his father; and Lord Spencer had lost some friends from the supposition.[17]

---

15. Coxe, vol. 1, p. 95.
16. *Ibid.*
17. Cunningham's *History of Great Britain,* book 4,. p. 171.

The detestation which Lord Spencer expressed for his father's opinions, and especially for those which he had adopted on his conversion to the Church of Rome, was, however, sincere. On the death of Lord Sunderland, he took care to manifest his unseemly disrespect, by casting out of the library which his father had collected, all the works of the holy fathers, or, as he called them, "dregs of antiquity," which he considered well replaced by the works of Machiavel.[18] This self-opiniativeness characterised his whole career.

Though professing himself a devoted adherent of Lord Somers, Lord Spencer had neither the moderation nor the true patriotism of that great and good man.[19] He carried all his notions to extremes; mistook violence and recklessness for zeal, and bluntness for sincerity; and his private deportment was ill calculated to obliterate the unfavourable impression which his public career had imparted. To this dark picture we must add, however, before we consider the portrait of Lord Sunderland to be complete, some, though few, enlivening touches. Eager for distinction, or at least for notoriety, this nobleman was, nevertheless, exempt from the mercenary motives by which many public men were debased. His high spirit led him, though not rich for his station, to reject a pension offered him by Queen Anne, when, during her reign, he was left out of the administration.

The same indifference to his pecuniary interests caused him to reject, with indignation, the attempts made by his mother-in-law to reinstate him in his employments, in the reign of George the First.[20] And when it is stated that he discarded the "holy fathers "from his library, after his father's death, it must be added that he replaced them by numerous works of great value, forming a library of considerable extent, and selected with admirable judgement.

To this ungenial partner the young and lovely Anne was eventually consigned. At first, indeed, her parents made many objections to the marriage. The coldness and indifference of Lord Spencer to their daughter was the chief obstacle. He was now a widower, having recently lost, in the Lady Arabella Cavendish, a wife whom he idolised, and for whom he still mourned with all the depth of feeling, and tenacity of a man of strong passions, and reserved nature. His political violence was another impediment, in the opinion of the rightly-judging mind of the great Marlborough, who saw in the times nothing to justify, but everything to deprecate, temerity and factious heats.

---

18. *Granger*, vol. 2, p. 46.
19. Coxe, p. 96. 20. Cunningham's *History of Great Britain*, book 5, p. 301.

But the Countess of Marlborough, more disposed to Whig opinions, viewed that objection to Lord Spencer with far less anxiety than his coldness to her darling child, and the increased gloom of the young nobleman's deportment and countenance.

From those she augured little of happiness to a daughter for whom she evinced true maternal apprehensions, and who lived not to harass and aggravate her, when the once fascinating Countess, degenerated into "Old Marlborough," had become captious and vindictive. High-minded, though faulty, Lady Marlborough dreaded that her daughter should be sacrificed to a man who loved her not, and who might be induced to marry whilst his affections were buried in the grave of another. The eagerness of Lord and Lady Sunderland for the promotion of the match—their remonstrances, the earnest solicitations, which they addressed to their son— all added to her apprehensions, and occasioned her to draw back somewhat from the first steps in her projected alliance.

By degrees, however, the grief of the gloomy young widower yielded to the loveliness and youthful graces of the Lady Anne. He began not only to tolerate, but to cherish, the idea of a second marriage. The growing attachment became ardent, as his other passions; and his mother, eagerly communicating the change in his feelings to her friend, urged Lady Marlborough to hasten an union now anxiously desired by her once reluctant son.

Lady Marlborough found some scruples, some objections on the part of her husband, still to overcome. But her influence was paramount.

In spite of many forebodings, induced by the headstrong nature of Lord Spencer, he gave his consent; but his prognostications, that political differences between him and his future son-in-law would ere long arise, were unhappily justified.

The marriage, however, after a series of negotiations which lasted eighteen months, was solemnised at St. Albans in January 1699-1700, the Princess Anne bestowing a dowry of five thousand pounds upon the bride, and her father adding as much more."[21]

The young couple appear to have lived happily together, though not without some alloys from the habits and circumstances of Charles Lord Sunderland. Lady Sunderland became the centre of a political and fashionable circle, and, as the "Little Whig," (so called from the smallness of her stature,) took the lead in that party in the great world.

---
21. Coxe.

Years afterwards, the solicitude which Swift evinced to conciliate her ladyship's favour, when, during the struggle for power between the contending parties, the influence of the "Little Whig "might avail his selfish pursuits, proves the estimation in which Lady Sunderland's fascinations were held.[22]

The Lady Elizabeth, Countess of Bridgwater, third daughter of the Earl and Countess of Marlborough, is said to have eclipsed her three sisters in beauty of countenance, eminently gifted as they were in personal advantages, whilst she was inferior to none in excellence of disposition. Her face is described to have been remarkable for symmetry: and its sweet and intelligent expression lent that indescribable charm to beauty which, in Lady Elizabeth, captivated some singular and highly-gifted admirers. Pope ventured to admire, and admiring, first depicted her face, and then her mind.

Hence Beauty, waking, all her forms supplies,
An angel's sweetness, or Bridgwater's eyes.[23]

Yet the poet threw all the drawings which he is said to have made of this amiable lady into the fire. "She was," says the monumental inscription to her memory in Little Gaddesden church, Hertfordshire, "a lady of exquisite fineness, both of mind and body; agreeably tall; of a delicate shape and beautiful mein; of a most obliging, winning carriage; sweetness, modesty, affability, were met together; whatsoever is virtuous, decent, and praiseworthy, she made the rule of all her actions; her discourse was cheerful, lively, and ingenuous; pleasing, without ever saying too much or too little; so that her virtue appeared with the greatest advantage and lustre; her address was as became her quality, great, without pride; admired and unenvied by her equals; and none condescended with greater grace and satisfaction to her inferiors."[24]

For this accomplished being a suitable settlement in life was provided; and, at a very early age, she was united to Scrope, Earl, and afterwards Duke, of Bridgwater.

If we may judge from the inscription on her monument, this union appears to have been as replete with happiness as the fondest parents could have wished. "Happy," says the epitaph, "her lord in such a wife; happy her children in such a mother; happy her servants that duly attended upon her. Being arrived at the highest pitch of worldly felicity,

---

22. See Swift's *Letters*.
23. *Granger*, vol. 2 p. 372.
24. Clutterbuck's *Hist. Hertfordshire*, p. 19.

in full enjoyment of tenderest love and esteem of her entirely beloved husband, universally admired and spoken of for every good quality."[25]

Such were the terms employed in describing this beloved child of the Marlborough family, whose early fate, like that of her sister, Lady Sunderland, afterwards embittered their father's old age, and hastened his death by the effects of grief.

His youngest daughter, Lady Mary, Pope's *Angel Duchess Montagu*, married, in 1705, John Montagu, Duke of Montagu, Grand Master of the Order of the Bath, and the trusted servant of successive sovereigns.[26] The Duchess of Montagu became, eventually, one of the bedchamber ladies to the Princess of Wales, afterwards Queen Caroline, towards whom her mother, the Duchess of Marlborough, imbibed a strong aversion. *The Angel Duchess Montagu*, beautiful as her sisters, appears not to have verified that name in her subsequent conduct to her mother, with whom she was long at bitter variance. At this epoch of the Duchess of Marlborough's life. Lady Mary was, however, yet a child, and her mother's temper had not shone forth, as afterwards it became apparent, in her conduct.

Thus, in the exalted stations which her children attained, the ambition of Lady Marlborough, as a mother, may be supposed to have been fully gratified. But whilst she accomplished for them, aided by their personal advantages, connexions all advantageous, though not equally splendid, she omitted to sow the good seed of filial subjection, which is ever best secured by cultivating the affections. In her family she may be said to have been peculiarly unhappy. Not many years elapsed after Lord Marlborough was raised to a dukedom, before his son, the Marquis of Blandford, the sole male representative of his father's honours, was summoned to an early grave. The title eventually descended in the female line, and Lady Godolphin became Duchess of Marlborough. With this daughter Lady Marlborough was many years embroiled in endless contentions, and the latter period of the illustrious Marlborough's life was employed in the vain attempt to mediate between two fierce and grasping combatants. Money, as usual, was the cause of the combustion, and a total alienation the result.

Lady Sunderland died young, but her sons became at once the delight and the torment of their grandmother in the decline of her long-lived importance, and, as it almost appeared, of her judgement and sense of decorum.

---

25. See Appendix 8. The Epitaph of Lady Bridgwater.
26. Collins's *Baronage*, vol. 2, p. 319.

Lady Bridgwater also died too early for *her* contentions with her mother to be signalised; but she left a daughter, the Duchess of Bedford, afterwards married to Lord Jersey, between whom and the Duchess of Marlborough a running warfare was long maintained.

With her youngest daughter, the Duchess of Montagu, the irritable Duchess was on terms equally unhappy. The Duke of Marlborough was heard to observe, speaking to his wife of this daughter, "I wonder you cannot agree, you are so alike!"—a speech which augurs ill for the Duchess of Montagu's temper. The lively and amiable Duchess of Manchester, granddaughter of the aged and morose Sarah, and described by one who knew her as "all spirit, justice, honour," possessed that influence over her grandmother which gay and open characters often seem to acquire, by the unpremeditated frankness which charms whilst it half offends. "Duchess of Manchester," said her old grandmother to her one day, "you are a good creature, but you *have* a mother."—"And she *has* a mother," was the arch and fearless reply.[27]

Such were the anecdotes in circulation at a later period. In her own youth Lady Marlborough rendered the beauty and accomplishments of her daughters serviceable in her own elevation to power. She afterwards obtained for so many of them posts about the Queen, that Anne was said to have her court composed of one family.[28] Yet the Duchess lived to prove, in the joyless isolation of her old age, how completely all our wishes may be realised without producing happiness.

---

27. Horace Walpole, *Rem.* p. 315.
28. Cunningham.

Chapter 10

1700

Illness and Deathbed of William

The death of the Duke of Gloucester cast a gloom over the last year of King William's life, whilst it caused not only maternal grief, but scruples of serious import, in the mind of the young Prince's mother, the conscientious but weak-minded Anne.

The Earl and Countess of Marlborough were at Althorp when they were apprised of the dangerous illness which had attacked the young Prince.[1] The Duke was of delicate frame, and for some years had been languishing. It was not to be supposed that a child could live in health or enjoyment whose premature intellect was, before the age of eleven, stocked with "Greek and Roman histories," the gothic constitution, and the beneficiary and feudal law,'" added to various other acquirements, equally obnoxious to the natural tastes of children, and therefore to be gradually and slowly introduced into their progressive capacities. Neither could the visits of five cabinet ministers, once a quarter, to inquire, by the King's orders, into his progress, have been otherwise than stimulating and fatiguing to the unhappy child.[2]

On the 24th of July, 1700, he attained his eleventh year. On the ensuing day he was taken ill; "but that," says his Episcopal tutor, "was imputed to the fatigues of a birthday, so that he was too much neglected." On the following day he grew much worse, and at the end of the fourth day he was carried off, his complaint proving to be a malignant fever. His mother, the Princess, attended him throughout his illness "with great tenderness," according to Burnet, "but with a grave composedness that amazed all who saw it: she bore his death with a

---
1. Coxe, p. 88.
2. Burnet, vol. 4. p. 358

resignation and piety that were indeed very singular."³

The Earl of Marlborough hastened to Windsor upon the first intelligence of the fatal disease, but arrived only in time to receive the last sigh of his young and interesting charge. Thus died the last of seventeen children that the Princess Anne had borne, dead and living, and thus William expressed his feelings on the event, in reply to the letter sent him upon this occasion by the Earl of Marlborough.

"I do not think it necessary to employ many words in expressing my surprise and grief at the death of the Duke of Gloucester. It is so great a loss to me, as well as to England, that it pierces my heart with affection."⁴

By this melancholy event the strength of the Jacobite party was considerably augmented. The Princess, indeed, still leaned to that faction. The part which she had acted in the Revolution had occasioned her incessant regret. Zeal for the Protestant religion, the popular outcry, and the persuasion that the Prince of Wales's birth was an imposture, had, at that eventful period, influenced her conduct. Upon the death of her son, however, her feelings were awakened towards her own family. She wrote to inform James the Second of her calamity. She began to regard her brother's legitimacy with different views from those which, during the irritations between her and her mother-in-law, she had been disposed to entertain.⁵ She privately solicited her father's sanction for her acceptance of the crown in case of the King's death; and, far from being averse to the restoration of her own family, she declared her resolution to make a restitution of the crown, whenever it was in her power to perform what she considered an act of justice.⁶

The decline in William's bodily health, and mental energy, rendered these negotiations by no means unimportant, for the King's mind had been harassed by a series of trying and aggravating, events. His distress and irritation upon the disbanding of his guards, and his exclamation, "If I had a son, by God these guards should not leave me!" betrayed the humiliation and the bitterness of spirit from which the unhappy monarch suffered; and it is well known that he even meditated relinquishing that crown which had cost him his peace of mind. Wasted with vexation, asthmatic, dropsical, His Majesty had recourse to wine

---

3. *Ibid.*
4. Coxe, p. 88.
5. Dalrymple, Appendix.
6. Coxe, from Macpherson's *Hist.*, vol. 2, p. 130.

to recruit his cheerfulness. Even in a state of partial inebriation, William was still the politician. He wished to have it supposed that he intended to settle the succession upon the reputed Prince of Wales, in order that his real design, of entailing it upon the Electress of Hanover, might not transpire prematurely. In one of those parties in which the King relaxed himself, in company with the infamous Lord Wharton, whom he always called "Tom," he said to his lordship, "Tom, I know what you wish for—you wish for a republic."

"And not a bad thing, sir, neither," was the reckless peer's reply.

"No, no," returned the King, "I shall disappoint you there. I shall bring over King James's son upon you."

Lord Wharton, with a low bow, and an affectation of deep reverence, answered, sneeringly, "that is as your Majesty pleases." William was not displeased at the answer thus elicited.[7]

When the succession was, by act of parliament, entailed upon the Princess Sophia of Hanover, a woman of rare endowments, of science, knowledge of the world, and personal accomplishments, it was the office of Lord and Lady Marlborough, by their endeavours, to prevent any opposition on the part of Anne; and they are supposed to have employed their influence, since, independent of their advice, she adopted no measure.[8] The Prince of Denmark took little share in public affairs, and was merely the affable, obliging cipher that nature had originally intended him to appear.

Upon the death of James the Second, and the proclamation of his son, in France, King of England, a storm was suddenly aroused in the British dominions. Both Whigs and Tories at this time were averse to the restoration of the Stuarts. It has been alleged, as a reason for this indifference, that the Tories being in power, and having place, had little more to desire. The Whigs were bound by the principles which actuated them at the Revolution. All parties were indignant that the King of France should presume to name a King of England, without consulting the English people.

The summoning of a new parliament, which entered into all William's views for war, and the conclusion of what is called by historians the Second Alliance, were events which rapidly followed the indignity imposed at St. Germains. Not satisfied with those proceedings, the House of Commons attainted the young Pretender, a boy of twelve years old, and framed a bill, which passed into a law, requiring all per-

---

7. Dalrymple, b. 7, p. 132.
8. Coxe.

sons in public stations to abjure him. A similar act, attainting the exiled Queen, Mary of Modena, was also contemplated; but the peers, high-minded generally as a body, refused to countenance the measure.

William, conscious of his decay, signed this treaty, the last to which he put his name. He appointed the Earl of Marlborough general of the troops in Flanders, and ambassador at the same time, knowing his great abilities both as a general and as a diplomatist, and believing he could best serve his country by placing such a trust in such a man. The final actions of the sovereign were those of a benefactor to his country. The last charter which he signed was the East India Charter, then esteemed, as a political measure, of great importance. The last act of parliament to which he gave his consent, was that fixing the succession in the House of Hanover. The last message which he sent to Parliament was a recommendation of an union between England and Scotland: this was five days before his death.

Broken with premature decay, for he was now only in the fifty-second year of his age, William, whilst planning a war which he calculated to finish with glorious success in four years, received his death-stroke. Some say that he was mounted on a charger once belonging to the unfortunate Sir John Fenwick, whose death was imputed to William as an act of injustice; others, that he was on a young and ill-trained horse, when, by the stumbling of the animal, he was thrown, and dislocated his collar-bone. The King was near Hampton Court at the time of the accident. The bone was set, and might have united without difficulty; but His Majesty had business at Kensington, whither, disregarding pain, he went in his coach. The bandage of the setting was unloosed, but was set again. Fever came on; a cough, fatal to so debilitated a frame, succeeded. The King, retaining his composure to the last, gave his consent, when on his deathbed, to the act of attainder against the Pretender, in compliance, it is said, with the entreaties of the Princess Anne,[9] who was terrified at the anticipated result of his death without the act being completed.

And now William prepared to meet that Creator, whose precepts, as given to us through his Son, he had in many respects studied to obey; though the snares of a political career, and the peculiar situation in which his elevation to the throne had raised him in this country, had presented to him incessant temptations. Since the death of his Queen, the King had been devoted to Lady Orkney, to whom he

---

9. Cunningham, vol. 1, p. 252.
10. Dalrymple.

had made a grant of some lands in Ireland, which, in common with those given to Lord Portland, and other followers, had been revoked by parliament. Yet, whilst unfaithful to Mary during her lifetime, and degrading the pure memory of her character, and her enthusiastic attachment to himself, by putting such a successor in her place in his affections, William cherished the memory of his lost wife. Fastened to his arm was found a ribbon attached to a gold ring, in which was some hair of Queen Mary. Unknown to any of his attendants, the reserved monarch had carried this relic about him, and it was discovered only when the last offices of laying out the body were performed.[10]

On his deathbed, William's affections seemed to be restored to their wonted channel. Lord Portland, whose faithful services had been of late superseded by the attractive qualities of Keppel Lord Albemarle, stood near him. The dying King looked steadfastly at him, endeavoured to speak to him, but was unable. He placed Portland's hands upon his heart, and in that position expired. His last words, uttered with composure, were these, "*Je tire vers ma fin.*" It is remarkable, that upon the post-mortem examination, when almost every important organ of the suffering monarch's emaciated frame was found to be diseased, his head was alone exempted from any trace of disease.[11] Hence his eye, that eagle eye, which his foe, the Duke of Berwick, could not regard at the Battle of Landen without admiration, retained its brilliancy and its searching keenness of expression to the last.[12]

The character of William the Third has been minutely expatiated upon by historians. In comparison with the monarchs of the Stuart line, he rose transcendent; but even without challenging such a parallel, his merits appear of the highest order. His intellectual powers were by nature capacious and sound. His acquirements were admirably adapted for the station which he held. Courageous, prompt, discerning, war was his favourite pursuit. Reserved and taciturn in private life, on public occasions his eloquence was both effective and polished. The last speech that he made in parliament, and which appears to have been impromptu, was one of the ablest harangues ever addressed by a British monarch to his subjects.

The outward deportment of William, like the unsightly binding of a scarce book, concealed his merits from the vulgar eye, whilst, by the reflective, the intrinsic value was more strongly exemplified by contrast. More than irritable, passionate, or, as the language of the

---

11. *Flying Post*, 1702.
12. Dalrymple.

times expresses it, "choleric" to his attendants of the bedchambers his benevolence, his ready forgiveness, his magnanimous appreciation of merit even in those whom he personally disliked, were shown in innumerable passages of his life. These qualities were conspicuously displayed in the restoration of Lord Marlborough to royal confidence, after a detected intercourse with the court of St. Germains. And whilst Lady Marlborough casts aspersions on the noble-minded monarch, of petty import, she is obliged, for consistency's sake, to pass over those later days of his life, when William generously placed a man whom he disliked at the head of military affairs, for the simple, but unfashionable, and, unhappily, not often regal reason, that he thought him best adapted to fill that trust. The unreasonable jealousy which he evinced towards the Princess Anne was, in fact, the great blemish of his social character.

Descended from a noble succession of heroes, the five great Princes of Orange, William, proud of his own country, must, in spite of that natural partiality, be regarded as one of the greatest benefactors that these islands have ever possessed. To him we owe the secure establishment of that faith for which he showed regard, not by forms, for those he somewhat too much despised, but by maintaining that toleration which is its essence. It is melancholy to reflect that William, deceived, disappointed, and latterly disliked by his subjects, was often so depressed as to long for his release. Yet, as his prospects brightened, and when James's death removed a continual source of faction, he declared to his faithful Portland, that "he could have wished to live a little longer."[13]

By the King's death, the weight of affairs in England fell upon Marlborough, who immediately returned to this country. And now, to the dawn of his fortunes, over-clouded as they had sometimes been, succeeded the brightness of day. In his fifty-third year, Marlborough was still vigorous; his activity was unimpaired, his constitution unbroken, except by occasional attacks of ague, when in campaign. His experience of men, his insight into parties, his popular qualities, independent of his public services, had been attained during a long course of vicissitudes; circumstances sufficiently adverse to form a decided and well poised character. At this period, too, the manly comeliness of person which he is said afterwards to have regretted, when gazing at an early picture of himself he exclaimed, "That was a man," still remained, undiminished by age and toil.

---

13. Burnet, vol. 5, p. 69.

"From his birth," says a contemporary writer, "the Graces were appointed to attend and form him; polished in address, and refined in manners as in the gifts of nature; fit to adorn a court, and shine with princes."[14]

The Countess of Marlborough, ten years younger than her distinguished husband, though past the bloom, could scarcely have lost the attractions of her surpassing, and what is more remarkable, unfading beauty of face and form. Perhaps the "scornful and imperious" character of her countenance, described by Horace Walpole, may have assumed its fixed expression about this time, when she discovered the extent of her influence, and was betrayed into a forgetfulness of what was due to her own station, and to majesty. "Her features and her air," says her sarcastic censor, "announced nothing that her temper did not confirm;" and he seems to consider it doubtful which of these two attributes had the greatest influence in "enslaving her heroic lord."[15]

Until an advanced age, Lady Marlborough possessed evident remains of remarkable loveliness; her fair hair, so celebrated, was unchanged by time; her most expressive eyes still lighted up her countenance; her flashes of wit enlivened her natural turn for communicating those reminiscences of former days, which could scarcely have appeared tedious under any circumstances, but which the shrewdness and talent of this extraordinary woman rendered exceedingly diverting. There was one feature in the Duchess of Marlborough's composition which contributed to enhance the charms of her conversation, and which, probably, strengthened the influence which she acquired over the minds of others. This was her fearless plain-speaking. The style of her Vindication shows her candour; the matter of that amusing work, with certain exceptions,[16] establishes her character for truth. Even her worst enemies appear in their replies to have been unable to disprove, or even to deny, most of her statements, but were forced to content themselves with abusive comments.[17] The same honesty and

---
14. Marlborough's *Apotheosis*, p. 11. London, 1714.
15. *Reminiscences*, p. 313.
16. With one exception: in her *Conduct* she seems to imply that the Duke of Marlborough had held no correspondence whatsoever with James the Second, She does not indeed, say so; but disingenuously says, if Lord Marlborough had acted so and so. There was abundant proof of his negotiations with the exiled family.
17. Such is the style of the work, entitled, *The Other Side of the Question*, and also of the *Review of a late Treatise, entitled 'An Account of the Conduct of Sarah Duchess of Marlborough, &c.,' in a Letter addressed to a Person of Distinction*. In this work, which was written by a nobleman, there seems to be more of invective than of fact.

openness, we are told, were manifested in the Duchess's conversation as in her writings.

"This might proceed," observes the editor of a recent publication, "partly from never thinking herself in the wrong, or caring what was thought of her by others."[18]

It might also proceed from that knowledge and that tact, which, during "sixty years of arrogance," as Horace Walpole terms her career, she must have acquired; and which, perhaps, taught her, that needless explanations are, in conversation, as in print, the worst of policy. But, with all her faults, duplicity has never been alleged against the lofty Duchess of Marlborough. It was foreign to the generous warmth of her nature; it was foreign to the audacity, for no milder term can be applied, of her temper. Evasion would scarcely have suited her purpose with the placid, subservient, but also somewhat manoeuvring Anne, who was born not to rule, but to be ruled, and who was daunted by the arrogance and fearless truth of her groom of the stole. Disingenuousness would have destroyed her influence over the just and honourable Marlborough,—an influence which even coldness, conjugal despotism, nay, fiercer passions, could not destroy, but which would have sunk directly, had the foundation of that faulty but lofty character been found defective. It was not Lady Marlborough's beauty, it was not her native, though untutored ability, it was not her wit, which prolonged her influence over her husband; but it was her truth, her contempt of meanness, her abhorrence of flattery, and her genuine fidelity to friends.

She was, as Doctor Johnson has expressed it, "a good hater;" and if that signify "a hater" without the garb of dissimulation—a hater who eschews false alliances, and hangs out true colours—one may be allowed to feel a certain respect for the character, even whilst we condemn the principle of hatred. No one ever accused the Duchess of Marlborough of smiling to betray. She could have torn her foes to pieces, sooner than have accorded to them one reverence which her heart conceded not. Her insolence to the Queen, her contempt of Anne's understanding, and her presumption and arrogance, cannot, however, be defended. Nor can the unfeminine qualities which she displayed, be viewed otherwise than with dislike and disgust.

The Duchess of Marlborough's dismissal from Anne's favour may be said to have commenced, in reality, when that Princess ascended the

---

18. Lord Wharncliffe's edition of *Lady Mary W. Montague's Letters*. Introduction, p. 75.

throne of England. The favourite was now wholly devoted to Whig principles; Anne was always, in her heart, a Tory. Lady Marlborough could ill brook opposition from one whose actions she had for years guided, and who had scarcely dared to move except at her bidding. The Queen had, as a monarch, one great failing, which characterised the house of Stuart: she allowed too great familiarities in those around her, and forbore to rebuke insolence, or even to check presumption.[19] No one was so likely to presume upon this want of dignity as the Countess of Marlborough. Her haughtiness soon grew into down-right contumacy. Even whilst holding the Queen's fan and gloves, or presenting them to Her Majesty, in the capacity of an attendant, she turned away her head with contempt directly afterwards, as if the poor harmless Queen inspired her with disgust.[20] How long Anne bore with such conduct, remains to be seen. For the first ten years of her reign Lady Marlborough, however, ruled paramount.

---

19. *Review of a late Treatise*, &c., p. 53.
20. Horace Walpole's *Reminiscences*.

CHAPTER 11
1702
Efforts of Lady Marlborough

Queen Anne was not tantalised by suspense concerning the result of her predecessor's illness. Particulars were hourly sent by Lord and Lady Jersey to Lady Marlborough, of the King's state, as "his breath grew shorter and shorter;" an attention which, instead of gratifying the Countess, "filled her," as she declares, "with horror."[1] The courtiers, who had been weeping at the bedside of the late monarch, hastened to depart from Kensington, and to remove into the more genial atmosphere of St. James's palace, where they offered their congratulations to the new sovereign in crowds.[2] The Queen was proclaimed in the courtyard of St. James's, on the day of the King's death, March the eighth, 1702, at five o'clock in the afternoon, both Houses of Parliament attending the ceremony."[3]

A solemn mourning was ordered, and the members of the privy council were enjoined to hang their coaches with mourning, and to put their servants in black liveries; the Queen wearing purple—at that time royal mourning. Two days after the King's death, Her Majesty went to the House of Lords, attended by Lady Marlborough, and preceded by the Earl of Marlborough, carrying before her the sword of state. She addressed both Houses in the usual mode, and inspired admiration and confidence by the dignity, self-possession, and graciousness of her manner. "Her speeches were delivered," says Bishop Burnet, "with great weight and authority, and with a softness of voice, and sweetness in the pronunciation, that added much life to all that

---

1. *Conduct*, p. 21.
2. Cunningham, vol. 2, p. 257.
3. *London Gazette*.

she spoke." Yet she offended the partisans of the late King, by saying "that her heart was entirely English;"[4]—which appeared to challenge an invidious comparison with one whose affections, it was well known, had often reverted to the kingdom which he had quitted.[5] The speculations which were set afloat concerning the fate of parties, and the opinions which Her Majesty's political appointments would display, may readily be imagined. By a proclamation issued, however, immediately after her accession, the Queen signified that all persons at present in authority should continue to hold their places, until Her Majesty's further pleasure should be made known.[6]

Notwithstanding the known influence, and the avowed opinions, of Lady Marlborough, the Whigs regarded the accession of Queen Anne as unpropitious. The principles of the adverse party had been instilled into her mind at a very early age, by Compton, Bishop of London. She owed the Tories many obligations; in particular, the settlement of her annuity, which they had secured, in opposition to the wishes of William and Mary. Her mother's family were devoted loyalists, or, rather, when times changed and appellations were changed also, zealous Tories.

The capacity of Queen Anne was limited, her notions were contracted, her prejudices consequently strong.[7] Any opinions imbibed could with difficulty, therefore, be eradicated from a mind which could view only one side of the question; and early prepossessions seldom lose their hold over our feelings, even when our judgement strives to dispel their influence. Easy, and regardless of forms in private, Anne, when seated on her throne, was jealous of her prerogative, retaining that attribute of the Stuarts, whether it were implanted by others, or the result of a disposition naturally tenacious of certain rights. Her heart had never been wholly weaned from her father during his lifetime, nor from those sentiments which James had inculcated both by precept and example; and, in the Whigs, she saw only a party who were anxious to curb the power, and to abridge the independence of the crown, upon a plan equally systematic and dangerous.[8]

Before any political changes were adopted, the funeral of King William took place. After several deliberations in council, it had been

---

4. Cunningham, Boyer, Dalrymple, Somerville.
5. *Flying Post*, or *Postmaster*. March 8, 1702.
6. *Postboy*. March 10.
7. Character of Anne by the Duchess.
8. Somerville's *Queen Anne*.

agreed to perform his obsequies privately. The royal corpse was carried from Kensington in an open chariot, during the night of Sunday, the 12th of April, to the chapel of Henry the Seventh at Westminster. The pall was borne by six Dukes. Prince George was chief mourner, supported by two Dukes, and followed by sixteen of the first Earls in England, as assistants, among whom was the Earl of Marlborough. A long train of carriages closed the procession. Amidst the solemn service, and the swelling anthem, the body of William was interred in the same vault with Charles the Second, and with his late consort, Queen Mary.[9]

On the twenty-third of April the coronation of Queen Anne took place. Her Majesty was carried in a low open chair to Westminster Abbey, from the Hall. The ceremonies were those anciently prescribed, and the Queen made the responses with her usual clear articulation and accurate pronunciation.[10] When the Holy Bible was opened, she vouchsafed to kiss the bishops;[11] and the ceremonials of the day concluded with a banquet, during which Prince George sat by her side. The Queen, who had remained at the Duke of Gloucester's apartments in St. James's till her own rooms were hung with black, now went to Kensington at night, and remained at St. James's during the day.[12] The Countess of Marlborough was, on all occasions, her constant attendant.

The change from royal robes to suits of mourning; from festive halls, and the shouts of the people, to the now deserted apartments of her son, or her own sombre, though stately chambers, would have grated upon a more sensitive disposition than that which Anne possessed. Perhaps the coronation of her father, when the crown tottered upon his head; perhaps the half rebuke of her sister, upon a similar occasion, occurred with bitterness to one who was now nearly the last of her family, with the exception of her maternal uncle, and of her attainted nephew. At the coronation of Mary, Anne, observing the Queen to be heated with the weight of the royal robes, and tired with the solemnity, said to her in a low voice, "Madam, I pity your fatigue."

"A crown, sister," returned Mary, quickly, "is not so heavy as it seems to be, or as you think it;" the words being eagerly caught by the

---

9. Boyer, p. 15.
10. *London Courant,* April 24th, 1702; Flying Post, 1702.
11. *Ibid.* April 23rd.
12. *Daily Courant,* April 15th.

curious attendants around.[13]

Whilst the public were amused with the pageantry of this imposing ceremony, busy cabals occupied the private hours of the Queen, and within her palace, a contemporary writer has not hesitated to affirm, there was a very busy market of all the offices of government. "For," says Cunningham," the Queen's own relations being kept at a distance, all things were managed by the sole authority of one woman, to whom there was no access but by the golden road; and it was to no purpose for the Earl of Rochester to set forth his own duty, affection, and the rights of consanguinity."[14]

This "woman," it needs scarcely to be stated, was the Countess of Marlborough, whose frank avowal of her exertions to form the Queen's household, at this period, in her Conduct, was not necessary to establish that which all the world knew. With respect to the grave charge preferred against her by Mr. Cunningham, the consideration of her imputed corruption must be hereafter discussed.

The elevation of her royal mistress to the throne . brought the Countess, as she observes, "into a new scene of life, and into a sort of consideration with all those whose attention, either from curiosity or ambition, was turned to politics and the court."[15] Hitherto, whilst her personal influence over the Princess had furnished many a topic for the gossip of the day, it had produced no apparent effect upon the affairs of the nation, the Princess herself never having been allowed any means of interference in politics, or power in public appointments. But now the Countess began to be regarded as one who possessed a great extent of patronage,—that curse and temptation, as it often proves; in short, as one, "without whose approbation neither places, pensions, nor honours were conferred by the crown."[16] The intimate friendship with which she was honoured by the Queen favoured this supposition.

Yet the Countess's ascendency over Her Majesty, great as it was, proved not sufficiently strong to overcome those obstinate, though it must be acknowledged, honest prejudices by which the Queen was governed. Queen Anne had, as the Duchess observes, "been taught to look upon all Whigs, not only as republicans who hated the very shadow of legal authority, but as implacable enemies to the Church of

---

13. *Review of a late Treatise*, &c., p. 22.
14. Cunningham, b. 5, p. 259.
15. *Conduct*, p. 121.
16. *Conduct*.

England." Prince George carried this dislike of the popular party even to a greater length; and, having received many indignities from a Whig ministry in the former reign, he threw into the scale against them all his resentments. Even Lord Marlborough and Lord Godolphin, though open to conviction, and having (so says the Duchess) "the real interest of the nation at heart," were, from education and early associations, partially Tories, and of "the persuasion that the high church party were the best friends to the constitution, both of Church and State; nor were they perfectly undeceived," remarks the gifted instrument of the conversion of these great men, "but by experience."[17]

The Countess of Marlborough had, therefore, almost invincible obstacles to encounter, before she could hope to compass that which she avowedly had at heart, the establishment of the Whig party in the royal councils. But to so determined a spirit as hers, impediments based upon the wills and opinions of those whom she was wont to govern, only heightened her ardour in the cause which she espoused. From natural disposition, an enemy to all false pretensions, and to everything that resembled hypocrisy or cant, the clamorous zeal for religion boasted by the Tories was peculiarly disgusting to her frank temper. She detected, through the outcry raised against the Whigs, the workings of self-interest, not the fervour of attachment to the sacred Liturgy, and to the purified ordinances which had been so lately rescued from impending destruction.

The plea set forth for "safety of the church" she regarded merely as a plausible means of working upon weak minds, and blinding others to the selfish motives of personal ambition. For many years a secure looker-on, almost in a private station, Lady Marlborough had probably seen sufficient of the leaders of both parties to be fully aware that men of all political opinions are actuated by mixed motives, and that whilst we witness many transactions which are of "good report," we must not seek for "whatsoever is honest, whatsoever is pure," from the principal actors in a political faction.

It was Lady Marlborough's lot chiefly to observe the higher orders of society, whose immediate interests were affected by the success of those opinions which they maintained, and she could not, from experience, be aware that it is the middling classes who really and earnestly cherish certain notions, in the importance of which to the public good they firmly believe. Public opinion is composed of more ex-

---

17. *Ibid.* p. 125.

tended tributes than those which the Countess of Marlborough took into account. There can be little doubt, from the manifestations which popular feeling continually displayed during the reign of Queen Anne, that the pervading sentiments of the people were in accordance with those of the high church party, whose intolerance and perversion of terms she justly reprobates.

"The *word* church," observes the Duchess, fearless of the calumnies which attached a want of religion to her other failings, "had never a charm for *me*, in the mouths of those who made the most noise with it; for I could not perceive that they gave any other distinguishing proof of their regard for the *thing*, than a frequent use of the *word*, like a spell to enchant weak minds; and a persecuting zeal against Dissenters, and against more real friends of the church, who would not admit that *persecution* was agreeable to its doctrine." And after this strong passage she adds, "And as to state affairs, many of these churchmen seemed to me to have no fixed principles at all, having endeavoured, during the last reign, to undermine that very government which they had contributed to establish."[18]

Such persons as those to whom the Duchess here alludes, have been well described by a later writer, of sound discernment, as exhibiting "in their conversation the idiom of a party;" and suspecting "the sincerity of those whose higher breeding and more correct habits discover a better taste." [19]

Notwithstanding Lady Marlborough's efforts, the Queen continued to be extremely reluctant to show any favour to the party which her favourite espoused. Lord Marlborough and Lord Godolphin, being thought to stand on neutral ground, were, in a degree, claimed by both Whigs and Tories; but it was owing to the zeal and perseverance of Lady Marlborough that any professed Whigs were retained in office. The Earl of Marlborough was, indeed, obliged to be absent for a fortnight, whilst all the cabals called into play, on the forming of a new cabinet, were in activity.[20] By the Queen's command, in his capacity of commander of the English forces, and plenipotentiary, he was sent to the Dutch states, with a letter of condolence to them on the death of William.

---

18. *Conduct*, p. 126.
19. Mrs. Hannah More.
20. *Conduct*.

Whilst at the Hague, the Earl was appointed by the States, general of their forces, with a salary of ten thousand pounds a year;[21] and on the fifth of April he returned to take the chief direction of affairs, and to receive new honours from the hand of his gracious sovereign.

Although reported to have been "more ambitious of gain than of power," the Earl and Countess must have experienced considerable disappointment when the formation of the new cabinet was completed. Lord Somers, who at this time was a deferential votary of the powerful Countess, and Lord Halifax, who came into public life under Lord Godolphin's auspices, were both dismissed the council. In order to comprehend the state of parties, and to understand in which direction the weight of talent and influence was likely to preponderate in those unsettled times, some reference must here be made to the preceding reign; and a short account of the principal actors in the scenes of those factious days may not prove uninteresting.

Lord Somers, whom Horace Walpole describes as "one of those divine men, who, like a chapel in a palace, remain unprofaned, whilst all the rest is tyranny, corruption, and folly," had possessed more influence in the councils of William than any other minister. He was, therefore, on the accession of Anne, one of the most conspicuous marks for the violence of faction. Agreeably to custom, those who could discover little to blame in the elevation of this distinguished statesman, deprecated his origin. The race from which he rose to a pre-eminent sphere, have been described "as the dregs of the people."[22] To his honour, and not to his shame, might the fact redound, supposing the statement to be true; but, unhappily for those who exulted in such a source of humiliation, and attributed the modest demeanour of the Lord High Chancellor to a consciousness of this humble origin, Somers sprang from a family both ancient and respectable.

His ancestors, though not distinguished by the honours of rank, were neither *hewers of wood nor drawers of water*.[23] From the time of the Tudors, one branch of the Somers family had owned and inhabited an ancient house in the northern suburbs of the city of Worcester, which edifice, hallowed by the appellation of the "White Ladies," from its site, that of an ancient monastery, had been spared by foes, and honoured by friends, during all the convulsions of the civil wars.

In "Somers's House," as the respected tenement was called, "Queen

---
21. *Churchill's Annals*, 1702.
22. Swift. *Four Years of Anne*.
23. See Bishop Watson's *Life*.

Elizabeth had been received, and entertained in her progress through the county. The extensive and richly cultured gardens of the old conventual residence had furnished the famous pears which that Queen, in the fullness of her approbation, had added to the city arms, as a testimony both of her satisfaction in eating the fruit, and of her admiration at the good order by which a tree, laden with it, and transplanted from the garden of the "White Ladies" into the market-place, could be preserved from injury.

In Somers's house Charles the Second took refuge before the battle of Worcester, and left there the sacred relics of his garters, waistcoats, and other garments, when he fled to Boscobel. And in this time-honoured mansion, where his mother was placed for security, was born the celebrated John Somers, just at the eventful time of the battle of Worcester, 1651. His birth occurring in this species of sanctuary, and in those times of commotion, was not inserted in any register.

The father of Lord Somers, notwithstanding the protection which his roof had afforded to Charles the Second, commanded a troop of horse in Cromwell's army; but quitted the profession of arms upon the establishment of the Commonwealth; and, enjoying a patrimony not exceeding three hundred pounds a year, took a house in the precincts of the cathedral at Worcester, and commenced practising as an attorney. On his father's pursuit of this calling, honourable in proportion to the principle with which it is exercised, the future greatness of the young John Somers was founded.

The civil wars had thrown into concision some of the finest estates in the county; and the elder Mr. Somers, in his legal capacity, found ample employment in settling disputed rights, and revising dilapidated fortunes. Amongst other families, the Talbots, Earls of Shrewsbury, placed their estates and finances in his hands. The Earl of Shrewsbury, at that time young, gay, accomplished, the godson of Charles the Second, and the pupil of Father Petre, was a Roman Catholic; and had been, from his infancy, the object of the zealous care and attention of those active missionaries, the Jesuits. His spiritual guides and his other tutors had formed a brilliant, and perhaps what may be termed an amiable character, but had not produced a sound statesman, or an irreproachable moralist. From his infancy, the licentiousness of a court, and the darker passions that lurk in the shadows of that bright scene, had been familiar to this young nobleman.

Five years before his acquaintance with Somers commenced, Lord Shrewsbury had lost his father in a duel with the Duke of Buckingham, whose horse was held by the abandoned wife of the murdered nobleman, in the disguise of a page. Lord Shrewsbury had attractive and popular qualities, which rendered him afterwards the darling of a people in whose cause he proffered his fortune and influence, to compass the Revolution.

At the period when his acquaintance with the Somers family began, he was disgusted with the unsatisfactory life of a courtier, notwithstanding the adulation paid to his rank and to his possessions, through the medium of personal flattery, and by the incense offered to his talents. Resolved, also, to rid himself of the numerous priests and other dependents who thronged around him, he retired to his estate in Worcestershire, where much of his property was situated; but his seat at Grafton not being in a fit state to receive him, the young nobleman made the house of his agent, at the White Ladies, his principal abode. And here a strange contrast must have been presented to the scenes, and the society which the young but satiated man of fashion had quitted.

"Somers'-house," as the old mansion was irreverently called by the vulgar, was large enough to contain many separate families; and numerous Blurtons, Foleys, and Cooksey's, with whom the family of Somers had intermarried, had already taken up their abodes in the capacious edifice. These simple, and, as it happened, united and industrious relatives, lived in the most primitive manner that could be devised, somewhat after the fashion, but without the peculiarities, of a Moravian establishment. They spent the mornings in their respective occupations: some attended to the fen on the Somers property, and in cultivating teasels; others were engaged in the clothing trade, in manufacturing woad and madder; others superintended the labours of the cottagers, dependencies twenty in number, after the conventual fashion; and the making of bricks, tiles, and other building materials, which the dilapidated state of the city brought into great request.

When the labours of the day were ended, all the relatives, their children and visitants, repaired to the great hall of the old nunnery, dined together at one common table, the products of their farm and their fishponds furnishing the *viands*, and passed the evening in conversation or merriment, or in discussions more engrossing, on politics and family interests. At Christmas, the board was spread after the ancient fashion; and the collar of brawn, and the huge saltcellar were displayed in the old conventual hall during the whole winter.

In this busy and happy scene, the friendship of Lord Shrewsbury with young Somers took root. Often occasional visitors swelled the number of the inmates; for the old dormitories of the nuns were used by the hospitable father of Lord Somers to supply the deficiency of inns and taverns. Nor is it of slight importance to trace those circumstances which mark the early portion of a great man's life. In the motley society of the "White Ladies," the future Chancellor of England probably learned to know himself and others. His prudence, his pliability in matters of little consequence, his firmness in matters of moment, may all have had exercise in the various emergencies and temptations to which a boy is exposed among a large assemblage of older persons, with whose affairs, and in whose family politics, he must necessarily, sometimes involuntarily, participate.

So ardent was the friendship contracted in these scenes between Lord Shrewsbury and Somers, that the latter, although intended for the bar, delayed his removal to the university until he was twenty-two years of age, in order that he might not sooner be separated from his friend, and from the society at the "White Ladies." So strong was the attachment formed by Lord Somers to the old house where these social days were passed, that one of his first cares, in after times of prosperity, was to repair the venerable edifice, together with the Priory of St. Oswald adjoining.[24]

Nor did the happy community of the "White Ladies" cease to welcome their favourite member, young Somers, at each college vacation, after his removal to Oxford. The Earl of Shrewsbury and his friend made, upon such occasions, that happy home their place of meeting. The foundation of Somers's fortunes was laid by the introduction which his friend afforded him to Lord Shaftesbury, Sir William Temple, and other leaders of the opposition, to the court of Charles the Second: but a far greater benefit was achieved for Lord Shrewsbury himself, in his conversion to a pure faith.

The vacations of the "White Ladies "were not idly, though they might sometimes be unprofitably, spent. The celebrated Richard Baxter acted as the spiritual guide of several members of the Somers family, and at that time resided at Worcester. By the arguments of this pious divine, aided by the conversation of Mr. Somers, who was nine years older than his friend. Lord Shrewsbury was prepared for that conversion to the Protestant faith, which Tillotson afterwards confirmed and commemorated. It might have been well for public morals,

---

24. *Life and Character of John Lord Somers*, by Richard Cooksey, Esq. 1791.

if the pursuits of the two friends had not taken another direction. The famous *Tale of a Tub* is supposed to have had its origin in the leisure of the White Ladies. Shrewsbury and Somers are said to have sketched the characters, and composed the plan of the poem; Lord Shaftesbury, and Sir William Temple treasured up the imperfect outlines, and entrusted them to Swift; Swift manufactured the materials into their well-known form, and gave them to the world.[25]

Like all really popular works of fiction, life itself supplied the characters. Blurton, the uncle of Lord Somers, was portrayed in Martin, the good church-of-England man. The grandfather of Lord Somers was exhibited in Jack the Calvinist, the devoted disciple of the Presbyterian Baxter. Father Peter was drawn from the famous Father Petre. For the publication of this noted satire, Swift, as it is well known, lost the chance of a bishopric, in consequence of Queen Anne's scruples.

The introduction to Russell and Sidney, which Lord Shrewsbury afforded to his friend, confirmed those political principles which Somers in a degree inherited. During the reign of Charles the Second, he was employed in writing state papers, ascribed to Sidney, but certainly the productions of Somers's pen. He wrote the celebrated answer to King Charles's declaration on dissolving the last Parliament. The study of the classics varied the severer toils of law and politics. It was not, however, until he had entered his thirty-seventh year, that Somers drew upon his merits as a lawyer, and a statesman, the distinguished approbation which had hitherto been accorded to him by the learned few. In 1688 he became counsel for the bishops imprisoned by James the Second; and by the great display of ability on that memorable occasion, his future station in his profession, and in the state, was determined.

From that epoch in our country's annals, Somers held on a consistent and a patriotic course, until his death. He rose, says his bitterest foe[26] to "be the head and oracle" of the Whig party. "He hath raised himself by the concurrence of many circumstances," says the same writer, "to the greatest employments of the state, without the least support from birth or fortune; he hath constantly, and with great steadiness, cultivated those principles under which he grew."[27] Although incorrupt in his high station, he was compared to Bacon, but only in the intellectual features of his noble character. As a statesman

---

25. Maddock's *Life of Somers*, p. 34.
26. Swift.
27. *Four Last Years*, p. 7.

he was true to his principles, above the littleness of avarice, inflexible upon points of conscience, benevolent, energetic, just. During his long life he sought every adequate means of benefiting mankind, and he projected schemes to benefit posterity.

The public career of Somers was irreproachable, but not happy. Often deceived in those whom he thought his friends, or the friends of his principles, Lord Somers had suffered the indignity and injustice of an impeachment in the late reign. His glorious refutation of that factious charge achieved for him a reputation which an untried man could scarcely have attained.

It was these trials of fortitude that drew from the early friend of Somers the following observation.

"I wonder," thus wrote the Earl of Shrewsbury from Italy, "that a man can be found in England, who has bread, that will be concerned in public business. Had I a son, I would sooner breed him a cobbler than a courtier, a hangman than a statesman."[28]

Lord Somers had no opportunity of evincing how far his sentiments in this respect agreed with those of the noble Earl. He never married, and his moral character shared in the general contamination of the age.[29] The Duchess of Marlborough, in her opinions of the Whigs, comments severely on his conduct in this respect; even whilst he was seated on the woolsack, he offended the laws of society, and injured his best interests by his example.[30] But her insinuations against his integrity as a chancellor were refuted, by the unblemished probity which all historians have attributed to this eminent and upright, but, as it must unhappily be allowed, not wholly irreproachable man.

Lord Halifax was the other Whig member of the council who was dismissed at the same time with Somers. These noblemen were both, at that time, the personal friends of the Earl and Countess of Marlborough; yet it was impossible, the Countess declares, to introduce Lord Somers into the administration until near the close of Marlborough and Godolphin's influence with the Queen.[31]

Lord Somers, bland and courteous, never offending in word or look, humble, as if unconscious of his great abilities, and yielding to others far inferior to himself in judgement and knowledge, was not enslaved by the talents, the beauty, and the power of Lady Marlbor-

---

28. Cooksey's *Life of Somers.*
29. *Ibid.*
30. *Private Correspondence*, vol. 2, p. 148.
31. *Private Correspondence*, vol. 2, p. 149,

ough; and, even at this time, he was secretly disgusted by her arrogance and love of domination. He submitted to the will of the Queen, as manifested in his dismissal, with a lofty calmness, which gave that act of Her Majesty the semblance of an indignity, disgraceful to her judgement, rather than of a mortification imposed upon Somers.

Nor did the slights of worldly friends, and the taunting opposition of foes, weaken his resistance to those measures of which he disapproved, or abate his ardour to promote schemes of which he augured well, whether proposed by a party who had deserted him, or by adversaries who rejoiced in his adversity. Repressing the impulses of a temper naturally impetuous, he permitted the extensive information which he possessed concerning all the political interests of Europe, his profound knowledge as a lawyer, and his manly eloquence, still to be useful in the service of his country; and his great character stood unsullied by petulance; a mark for envy, which could not sap its noble foundations, although it might by calumny injure and deface its exterior. But whilst Lord Somers thus encountered unmerited contumely, his companion in the loss of office, Lord Halifax, was not so resigned to the loss of an importance on which his vanity rendered him dependent for comfort.

"Mouse Montague,"[32] as Lady Marlborough, writing after their estrangement, contemptuously calls Lord Halifax, was descended from the house of Manchester, but, being a younger brother, his patrimony amounted to fifty pounds a year only. With this, as the Duchess remarks, he "could make no great figure."[33]

His name was given him for a political work, which first brought him into notice; for it was the fashion of the day to attach some appellation to the great men who most attracted public attention. Even the pulpit was sometimes the origin of such appropriations; and the great Godolphin is said to have been mortified and enraged by the addition of "Volpone" to his other designations, affixed to him by a sermon preached by Dr. Sacheverel.

Mr. Montague, endowed with his humble title, soon rose into fame. He became a member of parliament, and attracted the notice of Godolphin. He had abilities which recommended him to the notice of that able minister. His knowledge of finance was accurate; and

---

32. Halifax was called "Mouse Montague," from the circumstance of Lord Dorset's presenting him to William the Third as a Mouse.—*Granger's Biography*,
33. *Private Correspondence*, vol. 2, p. 158.

he displayed minor qualifications which were serviceable, when conjoined with those of others, though they might not have enabled him to stand alone. Montague exercised the arts which please, and possessed the talents which dazzle. It would be presumptuous to say of the man whom Addison extolled, and whom Steele described, (in a dedication be it remembered,) as "the greatest of living poets,"[34] that he had, as Swift said of Lord Sunderland, but an "understanding of the middling size." But he was, as Pope observes, "fed with dedications," though he does not appear, from all accounts, to have been very willing to recompense his flatterers by feeding them in return.

As a politician, he was timid and uncertain, because governed more by a desire for his own interest, than by a fixed principle. His oratory was energetic as well as elegant; but his conduct wanted the vigour which gave expression to his language only. His patronage of literature and of literary men, however it may have been ridiculed, was the most respectable feature in a character which cannot stand the test of examination. His poems, with the exception of two, were written upon public events, in which the views of a politician were mingled with the gallantry of a man of the world. It is not to be expected that a poem on the death of Charles the Second, or an ode on the marriage of the Princess Anne, should display much inspiration.

His lordship's verses on the *Toasting Glasses* of the Kit-Cat Club are allowed by Horace Walpole, with contemptuous brevity, to be "the best of the set." His "knack of making pretty ballads," which Lady Marlborough graciously ascribed to him, elevated as it was by flattery into excellence, was not the only social talent which Lord Halifax possessed. He read aloud admirably; and Lord Godolphin, having a good deal of that business to do, employed him frequently in this way. His manners, notwithstanding that the Duchess of Marlborough compares him, for ill-breeding, to Sir Robert Walpole, were acknowledged to be elegant.

His disposition was social; and, where circumstances did not tend to draw money from his pocket, he was benevolent. He had the merit (ascribed to him by Steele, who sullied the just praise by the subsequent flattery) of having, "by his patronage, produced those arts which before shunned the light, into the service of life."[35] To his exertions, as first commissioner of the Treasury, the stability of paper credit and the improvement of the crown were due. He projected the national

---

34. See Dedication to the fourth volume of *Tatler*.
35. Dedication to the *Tatler*.

library; and, to bring his merits to their climax, he had the honour of sharing an impeachment with Somers, and of defending himself against it with success.

Lady Marlborough encouraged the advances made by Lord Halifax to procure her favour, and courted his regard in return. His predominant weakness was a love of female admiration; and although, as the Duchess, in her old age, and when there was no Lord Halifax to show himself, or to hear her remarks, observed, "he was a frightful figure," yet he "followed several beauties who laughed at him for it."[36] Such were her expressions when parties and politics pleased no longer. In her younger and busier days, the manoeuvring Lady Marlborough humoured the politician and the coxcomb, by "projecting marriages and other allurements."[37]

> "She came," says Cunningham, "one evening to his lordship's country villa, as if by accident, bringing with her performers and instruments to compose a concert, which lasted till late in the night."[38]

The Italian music, then lately introduced, engrossed the fashionable world; and so busied in the acquisition, and with the patronage of this newly-imported taste, were even politicians, that the enemies of the Duke of Marlborough gave out that men of no experience—men frequenting the theatres, squandered the public money, as well as their own, and mismanaged public affairs. Lady Marlborough attended the numerous entertainments with which Halifax, combining profit with pleasure, treated the citizens, with whom he possessed much interest. The ladies all smiled upon the noble poet, who managed his costly galas with skill and effect. But the thrifty politician (careful and covetous, as many persons are in private who passionately love display) ate upon pewter when alone, that his plate might not be injured by too much rubbing. Indeed, according to Lady Marlborough, he did worse; for he sometimes paid the authors whom he patronised, with presents given by others, the merit of which he took to himself.[39]

Lord Halifax had not, at this period of his life, experienced how unsafe it is to lay bare the weaknesses of the heart of man to that dangerous being, a female wit. Self-interested, vain, restless, petulant, and even almost absurd, as he was, we cannot suppose him devoid of some

---

36. *Correspondence*, vol. 2, p. 166.
37. Cunningham, vol. 6, p. 316.
38. *Ibid.*
39. *Correspondence*, vol, 2, p. 154.

good qualities, which secured him the confidence of Godolphin, and the esteem of Somers; yet the well-known and, in their way, almost unequalled lines of Pope will be called to recollection.

Proud as Apollo on his forked hill,
Sat full-blown Buffo, puff'd by every quill;
Fed with soft dedication all day long,
Horace and he went hand in hand in song.[40]

In strong contrast with Halifax, how must the social qualities of Somers have risen in comparison; how refreshing must have been his good sense, which set forth all his great qualifications in order and beauty; how delightful that delicate sense of politeness which sprang in him from a humanity of disposition; which appeared in the least important of his actions; which manifested itself in the kindly expression of the countenance, in the refined manners, in the very tone of his voice. How admirable at once the solidity and the eloquence of a mind which comprehended not only the most abstruse sciences, the most profound and varied knowledge, but which displayed the graceful acquirements of an accomplished gentleman.

Whilst Halifax employed his hours of recreation "to fetch and carry sing-song up and down," Somers, by dividing his time between the public scenes of life, and the retirement of a cheerful, not an unemployed and gloomy and selfish retirement, attained a perfection of taste, an elegance and purity of style, that few men of his profession and station, engrossed as they must necessarily be with dry and recondite researches, have been enabled to acquire. He had, says Swift, "very little taste for conversation;"[41] and, unlike his associate *Buffo*, who

Received of wits an undistinguished race,

consoled himself, in his hours of recreation, "with the company of an illiterate chaplain or favourite servant."—Yet the man who never delivered an opinion of a piece of poetry, a statue, or a picture, without exciting admiration from the just, and happy, and delicate turns of expression which he adopted, must have loved to commune with higher minds than the unsuitable companions whom Swift has assigned to his leisure hours.[42]

Queen Anne retained in his office, as lord high steward, William Duke of Devonshire. This nobleman, "a patriot among the men, a

---

40. Pope's *Epistle to Arbuthnot*.
41. *Four Last Years*, p. 9.
42. *Freeholder*, p. 39. May 4, 1716.

Corydon among the ladies,"[43] had officiated at Her Majesty's coronation, as he had done at that of William and Mary,—where his stately deportment and handsome person, as in costly attire he bore the regal crown, eclipsed the sickly monarch, lowly in stature, behind whom he walked, whilst his daughter bore Queen Mary's train.

Whilst a boy, he had borne the royal train, with three other noble youths, at a similar ceremonial, when Charles the Second ascended the throne. Yet, though descending from a stock devoted to the Stuarts, and though his grandmother, the celebrated Countess of Devonshire, was instrumental in the Restoration, the high-minded peer became, upon conviction, a strenuous supporter of that liberty and of those rights upon which the second James so largely encroached. He voted for the bill of exclusion, and spoke boldly, though always with politeness and temper, upon that famous measure.

At the trial of his friend Lord Russell, when it was almost deemed criminal to be a witness in behalf of the illustrious prisoner, Lord Cavendish, with the Earl of Anglesea, Mr, Howard, Tillotson, and Burnet, gave his testimony to the honour, the prudence, and good life of the distinguished sufferer. When he found that the doom of Russell was inevitable, he sent him a message, entreating to be allowed to change cloaks with him, and to remain in the prison whilst Russell should make his escape. The noble refusal of the generous offer is well known. It was Cavendish's sad office to attend his beloved, and more than ever honoured friend, to the last; to solace the wretched Lady Russell, and bear the last message of affection from the noblest of beings to one who merited all his love.

In the court, and in the senate, Lord Cavendish displayed the gallant qualities which had been manifested in the prison of Lord Russell. Insulted in the precincts of the court by Colonel Culpeper, a creature of King James's, he retaliated by dragging the offending party out of the presence-chamber, and caning him on the head. For this act he was prosecuted and fined 5000*l.* But Cavendish, then Earl of Devonshire, chose rather to go to the King's Bench prison, than to pay a fine which he thought exorbitant. He escaped to Chatsworth, where, in the midst of difficulties occasioned by loans in the former earl's time to the exiled family never repaid, and aggravated by Lord Cavendish's own rash castigation of Culpeper, his energetic mind framed a plan for remodelling the venerable pile in which he had sought security. The

---

43. Horace Walpole.

famous waterworks, the gardens, pictures, statues, and a great portion of the modernised structure, were the result of this nobleman's magnificent taste and profuse expenditure.[44]

His splendour and liberality were guided by an economy as essential to the peer who wishes to retain his independence, as to the peasant. His attention to the meanest of his guests was such, that when he gave an entertainment, he would send for the groom-porter to inquire if he, and all of the same degree, had received due provision. His love of liberty was shown in a favourite saying of his, *that the deer in his park were happier than subjects under a tyrannical king*: or, as he expressed the same sentiments in his own poetry—

O despicable state of all that groan
Under a blind dependency on one!
How far inferior to the herds that range,
With native freedom, o'er the woods and plains![45]

But whilst the noble Cavendish detested that tyranny under the effects of which Russell had perished, and the whole British nation had suffered, in the properties and safety of its subjects, during the reign of James the Second, his well-conditioned mind cherished the elevating sentiments of loyalty, where loyalty was justly due. That bond of social union he prized, as every rightly thinking man must prize it, as an auxiliary to freedom, and a rallying point for the sincere, and the well-intentioned of all political opinions, however opposed on other points.

The character of Lord Cavendish affords an illustration of the truth, that it is perfectly consistent with the lover of liberty, and the advocate of the subject's right, to cherish the most ardent zeal for the maintenance of regal authority, and to feel the strongest personal attachment to the sovereign. Far from being one of those who, in the unsettled state of the government, desired that its disarranged elements might settle into a republic, the Earl of Devonshire, though he signed the association to invite William the Third to England, was the first of the nobility to step forward to protect the person of the Princess Anne, whom he guarded with a loyal and chivalric zeal which has been already described,

This model for English noblemen had received the honour of a dukedom in 1694, the preamble to his patent containing some of

---

44. Collins's *Baronage*, vol. 1 p. 110.
45. In a poem, entitled *An Allusion to the Bishop of Cambray's Supplement to Homer.*

the highest compliments from William and Mary ever offered from a monarch to a subject. He was one of the few who was honoured with an equal respect and confidence by their successor. Unhappily for the Whig party, to whom his influence was consistently given, this peer did not enjoy his restored fortunes, and high favour, many years after the accession of Anne.

His deathbed was instructive, as the last scene of a life which, exhibiting the most generous and heroic qualities, had displayed, nevertheless, sundry irregularities. The love of pleasure and the love of virtue are sometimes strangely conjoined in the same character. Courteous, though commanding; in person at once attractive and stately; accomplished in the ornamental arts—poetry, painting, music; standing on a high eminence, and living, from his youth upwards, in public life;—the errors of the Duke of Devonshire were attributable to the pervading spirit of the times. What we call virtue in private life was not then recognised by the great and fashionable. The Duke, like most other men of his class, had fallen into those received notions which exempt men from the purity, and decorum, which are at once the restraint and the safeguard of woman.

On his deathbed the man of pleasure and of the world felt that he had driven off his repentance too late. Happily, his senses were spared to him. He sent for Dr. Kennet, and entreated that prelate "to pray heartily with him to God that he would accept of his repentance." He declared himself ready to ask pardon of all whom he had offended, and also to forgive others. At every successive visit from his reverend adviser, he reiterated his repentance. His prayers for the "peace of God" were earnest, and, as it seemed, effectual.

After the many agonising struggles of a wounded and chastened mind—after evincing his real piety by acts of justice and of charity, (beautiful planets, which should ever shine upon the deathbed,) peace was given to him. Fortitude and patience were added to that inward conviction of pardon. He fixed the probable hour of his departure, and asked what was the easiest way of dying. His soul departed, as it seemed, in a peaceful slumber. "And thus," says his biographer, "he fell asleep, not merely like an ancient Roman, but rather like a good Christian."[46]

The death of Cavendish raised up a memorable controversy among the clergy, upon the propriety of receiving deathbed repentance, and

---

46. Collins's *Baronage*, vol. 1, p. 118.

of ratifying it with the administration of the sacraments. The question, as was usually the case in those days, was raised by party clamour rather than by religious zeal; and Dr. Kennet, who preached the funeral sermon of the Duke, was branded with opprobrium by the whole body of the clergy, for a contempt of discipline.[47]

Of a very different character was Thomas, created, in 1714, Marquis of Wharton, whose white staff was given by the Queen, before his face, to Sir Edward Seymour,—an affront so marked as to draw down the following threat in private from the offended nobleman:—"That he would soon provide himself with other rods to chastise the new ministers."[48] This able, but unprincipled man, received his dismissal in a manner very different from the dignified demeanour of Somers, on incurring a similar mortification. Wharton was a specimen of those unsound materials of which parties are composed, and of which honest and great men are forced, by political compact, to make use.

It seems singular that a man who scoffed at all religions, and outraged every right feeling, should have been brought up in the most rigid puritanical principles. The mother of Lord Wharton, more especially, was one of the zealous adherents to the Presbyterian faith. But though he deviated from the parental precept, and conformed to the national worship, Wharton had imbibed in his early education a love of constitutional freedom, which not all the seductions of royal favour could efface.[49]

His morals he owed to a different school A favourite companion of Charles the Second, he never, like Marlborough, and Somers, and Cavendish, retrieved the errors of early youth by a sincere and effectual amendment. The consciences of those individuals were wounded by a sense of their transgressions; but his was hardened. His nature was debased by habitual sin; they, "like sheep, were led astray," but their hearts were not corrupted. Purity, holiness, honour, had always charms for these great men, and must always have charms for those who are really great; but, to Lord Wharton, these lights were dim.[50]

"Like Buckingham and Rochester," says one who understood him well, "he comforted all the grave and dull, by throwing

---

47. Dalrymple, b. 10, p. 130.
48. Cunningham, b. 2, p. 259.
49. See Cunningham.
50. His infamous example was renewed in that singular, gifted, and most profligate nobleman, his son, Philip Duke of Wharton. Modern times scarcely furnish a parallel to the character of this peer.

away the brightest profusion of parts on witty fooleries, which may mix graces with a great character, but can never compose one. If Julius Caesar had only rioted with citizens, he had never been the emperor of the world."

The courage of this bad, wild, singular man was not equal to his assurance. Abuse sometimes displays cowardice; it is the cool and temperate who are usually courageous. Lord Wharton, with the levity of a man who really loved nothing but pleasure, and really prized nothing but self-interest, could jest at his own want of heroism. When seized by the guard in St. James's Park for singing the Jacobite air, "The King shall have his Own again," as he has himself recorded in his ballad,

The duke he drew out half his sword,
The guard drew out the rest.

The worst attribute of Philip Duke of Wharton, as a citizen of the world, was his indifference to reputation. Men of pleasure are not generally indifferent to a character for honour and consistency; but Lord Wharton cared merely for ephemeral applause. Attached, in reality, to no party, and having no actual motives but those of expediency, there was not the slightest dependence to be placed upon those visionary things, his opinions, beyond the moment when he was haranguing a popular assembly, or debating in the House of Lords. It is well known that at a later period, in 1723, upon the third reading of a Bill of Pains and Penalties against Atterbury Bishop of Rochester, Lord Wharton accomplished a brilliant display by a most dishonourable artifice.

He went to Chelsea, where the minister resided, and professing his resolution to effect a reconciliation with the court by speaking against the Bishop, requested some suggestions upon the case. Thus enticed, the minister went over the whole argument with his lordship. Wharton returned to town, passed the night in drinking, (his libraries being, as Horace Walpole observes, made taverns,) went to the House of Lords, without going to bed, and made a most eloquent speech in favour of the Bishop, showing all the weak points of the arguments which he had thus surmounted, in the most able and masterly manner. In the opinion entertained of Lord Wharton by the world, William seems to have coincided; for, in spite of Wharton's activity as one of his most powerful partisans, and of His Majesty's endurance, not to say enjoyment, of his coarse and fearless jokes,[51] he advanced Wharton to no place of political importance. By William, Lord Wharton was made

---

51. Horace Walpole's *Reminiscences*.

comptroller of the household, an office far below his ambition, and, as far as ability should be taken into account, his deserts.

Wharton was an associate, but not a friend, of Marlborough and Godolphin. He was, in truth, a brier in their path; a dangerous friend, more dreaded than a foe; a man whose elevation they feared even more than his open enmity. He was an able debater, bold, and therefore likely to be, to a certain extent, powerful; for irresolute characters are governed by those of a decisive and fearless temper. His fluency, however, was devoid of all grace, his manner was coarse, his wit pungent, but always tainted with grossness. His attacks upon others were unsparing and reckless.

The absence of all religion—not merely the sceptical turn of many of those who aimed at being thought wits, but an avowed, and, as it is not difficult, in such a case, to believe, an actual infidelity,—may sufficiently account for the dereliction from all that is honourable and estimable, which Thomas Lord Wharton's political career presented. It also accounts for the marked indignity offered to him by Queen Anne in the mode of his dismissal. Sir Edward Seymour, the leader of the Tories, and the promoter of the impeachment of Somers and Halifax in 1701, was substituted in his place.

The privy seal was given to the Marquis of Normanby, a nobleman of great accomplishments and of personal beauty, who was not the less agreeable to Anne from having been the first who aspired to her hand, before Prince George was fixed upon as her destined husband. Rich, young, attractive. Lord Normanby, then Lord Mulgrave, might doubtless have succeeded in obtaining her consent; but though his addresses were silenced, they were not forgotten by the Queen.[52] The appointment of Lord Nottingham and Sir Charles Hedges to be principal secretaries of state completed the manifestation of the Queen's inclination for the high church party.

---

52. Boyer, p. 14.

CHAPTER 12
1701-2

Dissatisfaction of the Countess of Marlborough

The Countess of Marlborough viewed all these changes with a very dissatisfied mind. "The wrong-headed politicians," as she designated them, who succeeded those "who had been firm to the Revolution," found, in her, a determined, and, what was more to their injury, a persevering enemy. The Countess did not, after the manner of her sex, break out into loud invectives at these ministerial appointments, nor excite the Queen, if that were possible, by violent arguments, to maintain a cause which always becomes dearer to ladies in proportion to the frequency of the attacks made upon it. Sagacious, though resolute, she resolved, from the very beginning of the Queen's reign, "to try whether she could not, by degrees, make impressions on her, more favourable to the Whigs."

The difficulties of her task would have deterred a less ardent character; and the zeal with which she accomplished her purpose argues, in some measure, for the reality and genuineness of her principles; for if, as it was broadly stated, offices were avowedly sold by Lady Marlborough, it could be of little importance to her, supposing that she were governed solely by such base motives as were imputed to her, which party had the ascendency, as long as she herself remained in favour.

"As to private interest," remarks the Duchess, "the Whigs could have done nothing for my advantage more than the Tories. I needed not the assistance of either to ingratiate me with the Queen; she had, both before and since her accession, given the most unquestionable proofs that she considered me, not only as a most faithful servant, but as her dear friend.¹

"It is plain, therefore," continues the Duchess, "that I could have no motive of private interest to bias me in favour of the Whigs; everybody must see that had I consulted that oracle about the choice of a party, it would certainly have directed me to go with them to the stream of my mistress's inclination and prejudice. This would have been the surest way to secure my favour with her." ²

She appears, nevertheless, from one of the Queen's letters, never to have abated in her zeal for the Whig principles, on account of the Queen's often avowed predilections for the Tories, "Your poor, unfortunate, faithful Morley," writes Anne, who, after the death of the Duke of Gloucester, added the last epithet to those terms of affection which she generally used, "would not have you differ in opinion with her in the least thing. And upon my word, my dear Mrs, Freeman," she adds, "you are mightily mistaken in your notion of a Tory. For the character you give of them does not belong to them, but to the church. But I will say no more on this subject, but only beg, for my poor sake, that you would not show more countenance to those you seem to have so much inclination for than for the church party."³

Such was the style in which the Queen of England addressed her subject, about a year after her accession. But it is probable that even at this time Anne began to fear, rather than to love this female keeper of her royal conscience.

The world, at least the court world, all contributed, of course, to intoxicate, by interested adulation, the haughty, rather than vain mind of the groom of the stole and keeper of the privy purse. The Whigs, whom Lady Marlborough declared she regarded as her personal enemies, paid her but little respect, but the Tories were ready to overwhelm her with compliments, upon any little service, paid or unpaid, which she might condescend to perform for one of their party. Lord Rochester, whom the Countess never forgave for having recommended Queen Anne to send her to St. Albans during the disputes between the two royal sisters,⁴ condescended to write her a "very fine

---

1. *Conduct*, p. 130.
2. *Conduct*, p. 181.
3. *Ibid.* p. 129.
4. Boyer, Appendix.

piece," when a vacancy occurred in the Queen's household, and when it was his desire that his daughter,[5] Lady Dalkeith, first cousin to Her Majesty, should be made one of the ladies of the bedchamber.

> "I confess," says the Duchess, "indeed, I was not a little surprised at this application from his lordship. I thank God, I have experience enough of my own temper to be very sure I can forgive any injury, when the person from whom I have received it shows anything like repentance. But could I ever be so unfortunate as to persecute another without cause, as my Lord Rochester did me, I am confident that even want of bread could not induce me to ask a favour of that person; but surely his lordship had something very uncommon in his temper."[6]

The appointment was not given to Lady Dalkeith, on the pretext that the number of ladies fixed by the Queen had been exceeded during the lifetime of the deceased lady whom Lady Dalkeith had wished to succeed; to which was added the declaration, that upon the first vacancy the list was to be reduced to ten, which number the Queen considered sufficient

This, probably, was merely an excuse. The Duchess, indeed, declares that she could have forgiven his lordship's ill-treatment of herself, if she had thought that he sought to promote the Queen's true interest. "But the gibberish of that party," as she calls it, "about non-resistance, and passive obedience, and hereditary right, I could not think it forebode any good to my mistress, whose title rested on a different foundation." She therefore naturally desired to keep Lord Rochester, a high churchman from hereditary principles, and his family, as much from the Queen's presence as she possibly could; whilst she endeavoured by all possible means to work upon the opinions of the well-disposed, but shallow and obstinate Anne.

It is not such minds as those either of the Queen or the favourite, that are open to conviction.

> "I did," says the Duchess, "speak very freely and very frequently to Her Majesty upon the subject of Whig and Tory, according to my conception of their different views and principles."[7]

The Queen had, indeed, assured her that she could not give her a

---

5. Lord Rochester married Henrietta, daughter of Lord Burlington, by whom he had five daughters and one son, who succeeded him in his titles. "He was," says Mackay, "easily wound up to a passion."—Pref. to *Clarendon Papers*, vol. 1, p. 18.
6. *Conduct*, p. 132.
7. *Conduct*.

greater proof of her friendship than in speaking plainly to her on all things; and of this proof the Countess was ever disposed to give Her Majesty the full experience and benefit.

The Queen had not long ascended the throne, before an order in council was issued, to "prohibit the selling of places within Her Majesty's household." But this, it was observed, was not done, until Lady Marlborough had disposed of a considerable number.[8] Indeed, from the testimony of various historians, this practice, on the Countess's part, appears to have been notorious; yet how can her noble professions be made to agree with her alleged shameless corruption?

"If I had power to dispose of places," she writes to Lord Godolphin, "the first rule I would have would be, to have those that were proper for the business; the next, those that deserved upon any occasion; and whenever there was room, without hurting the public, I think one would with pleasure give employments to those who were in so unhappy a condition as to want them."[9]

Upon the disinterestedness or the cupidity of Lady Marlborough's disposition, and respecting the sincerity of her professions, posterity is far more likely to put a fair and just construction than were her jealous and party-inflamed contemporaries.

The conduct of the Queen, in throwing her government chiefly into the hands of the Tories, was attributed to the understanding between Lord Marlborough and that party, that the war with France and the grand alliance should be continued; a measure upon which he founded the basis of his future fortunes.[10] By some writers it was insinuated, that a difference of opinion upon political subjects existed between the Earl and his Countess; and that the Queen's first political changes were promoted by Lord Marlborough in opposition to the Countess, and accomplished for the purpose of being at the head of the grand confederacy: and it was surmised that he fell into the Queen's inclinations to favour the Tories, contrary to the wishes of his Whig consort.[11]

By another partisan of the high church party it has been declared, that when Queen Anne came to the throne, both the Earl and Countess of Marlborough were the "staunchest Tories in the kingdom;" and

---

8. Boyer, p. 33.
9. Essay from the *Quarterly Review*.
10. Burnet
11. *Other Side of the Question*, p. 157.

that the subsequent change of politics was accounted for by jealousy of the Queen's relations. Prince George and Lord Rochester, whose influence was obnoxious to those who would not be contented with a divided rule. "Hence," says this writer, "these two noble personages now mentioned, thought fit to put themselves at the head of the Whig interest, which they knew they could manage without fears of a rival."[12]

Meantime, the administration of the late King's affairs led to much discontent, and gave rise to shameless peculation "This was an age," says a contemporary writer, "when such a spirit of rapacity prevailed, that not only were bad men greedy of gain, but even those that were reputed men of virtue endeavoured to bring all things into confusion, so that they might acquire to themselves preferments, titles, and honours."[13] Godolphin, whose character for probity stood well with all parties, descended so far as to advise the Queen not to pay the late King's debts, or, at least, only so much as he thought proper to allow. He discharged the claims of those who could exercise the greatest political interest; others he delayed; others disallowed; a proceeding dishonourable to the Lord Treasurer, the more especially as the King had left assets enough to satisfy all demands, independent of aid from the Exchequer.

And whilst this ill-advised frugality was disgraceful in the extreme, it was likewise inconsistent with the laws of England, by which every just claimant is entitled to protection.[14] The Prince of Denmark presented the King's equipages and horses to Lord Grantham, the master of the horse. The Queen took the royal ensigns of the Order of the Garter. When the rest of King William's goods and furniture were to be divided, Lord Montague threatened the Countess of Marlborough with a prosecution for his share, which, it is presumed, he suspected her ladyship of appropriating; but the favourite contrived to pacify the angry nobleman, and to effect an union by marriage between her own and Lord Montague's family.[15]

Upon the return of Lord Marlborough from Holland, the Queen announced to both Houses of Parliament her intention of declaring war against France, and this measure being approved, war was proclaimed on the fourth of May.

---

12. *Remarks upon the Conduct*, &c, p. 43.
13. Cunningham, b. 4, p. 125.
14. *Ibid.*
15. *Ibid.*

The succession was now settled, and the Electress Sophia of Hanover was ordered to be prayed for by her Christian name, indicating that her title to the throne was by her own blood. Towards this Princess, eminent for her accomplishments and personal character, Anne evinced throughout her reign far more jealousy than she ever manifested towards the young Pretender, lately proclaimed in France, King of Great Britain. It was reported, immediately after the death of William the Third, that that monarch had left among his papers a scheme for setting aside his sister-in-law from the succession, for bringing in the House of Hanover, and even for imprisoning Anne to effect this purpose. The Tories, in order to influence the elections, talked loudly and confidently of the truth of these reports. Five commissioners, namely, the Dukes of Somerset and Devonshire, the Earls Marlborough, Jersey, and Albemarle, were empowered to examine his late Majesty's papers, in order to prove the truth or falsehood of these rumours. Eventually they were declared by a vote of the House of Commons to be false and scandalous.[16]

The oath of abjuration, notwithstanding a general expectation to the contrary, was taken by both Houses of Parliament, with, however, a mental reservation by many, that the right of the pretended Prince of Wales, solemnly abjured by them, was a legal, and not a divine right, or birthright; nor did they consider their abjuration binding in case of a revolution or a conquest. "This," says Burnet, "was too dark a thing to be inquired after, or seen into, in the state matters were then in." Yet the lurking spirit of disaffection, like a blight, had its unseen but perceptible influence upon all classes of society; more especially upon that which, struggling to hold the reins of empire, was harassed by party clamour. The well-known, and, it must be acknowledged, excusable partiality of the Queen for her own family, kept alive the spirit of Jacobitism in the country. Lady Marlborough fearlessly spoke her sentiments to the Queen on this subject.

"When I saw," she observes, "she had such a partiality to those that I knew to be Jacobites, I asked her one day whether she had a mind to give up her crown; for if it had been her conscience not to wear it, I do solemnly protest I would not have disturbed her, or struggled as I did. But she told me she was not sure the Prince of Wales was her brother, and that it was not practicable for him to come here, without ruin to the religion

---

16. Burnet, vol. 5, p. 88.

and country."[17]

Whilst this struggle for power was carried on between parties at home, Marlborough was negotiating in Holland for a continuance of that alliance which raised his prosperity to its height. The French monarch, on the death of William, had in vain endeavoured to detach the Dutch from the English interest. The personal influence of Marlborough, and his talents as a negotiator, completely frustrated this attempt on the part of Louis; but some time elapsed before he could, with equal success, arrange another matter of dispute. The Queen was extremely desirous that her husband, the Prince of Denmark, should succeed to the command of the united forces, and, in a great measure, supply the place of the late King in Holland.

The Dutch were by no means agreeable to this proposition, which was, in the first instance, made an absolute condition by the Queen. Prince George had the ambition to desire, without the talent to acquire distinction; he was, moreover, a confirmed invalid, and of a very moderate capacity for anything, especially for military operations. The States, therefore, offered to Marlborough the powers which he had negotiated to obtain for Prince George, and that great general deemed it expedient to accept their proposals, and to return to England, to expound all that had passed between him and the States, and to maintain the necessity of promoting a good understanding between them and England.

Lord Rochester, in the council, with Other Tories who were favourable to the French interests, loudly opposed a war which they foresaw would augment the power of Marlborough, and consequently of his lady and her Whig friends. But, notwithstanding these clamours, war was proclaimed on the fourth of May, in London, at the Hague, and Vienna; and Marlborough once more set sail from the English shores, and repaired to Holland. But whilst the measures which he advocated were thus carried into effect. Lord Marlborough had the mortification to perceive a growing coolness between himself and Lord Rochester, an impetuous and well-intentioned man, between whom and Lord Marlborough there had been a friendship of long standing, unshaken by Lady Marlborough's dislikes and bickerings.[18]

In quitting the shores of England, the great general experienced, in the midst of many sources of vexation, how invariably the eminents

---

17. *Narrative* on Mrs. Morley's coming to town. St. Albans, 1709. Coxe, Vol. 1, p. 142.
18. Coxe, p. 153.

and the successful, pay a tax to the rest of mankind for the possession of their envied advantages. Marlborough, hurried from one kingdom to another—harassed by the loss of friends—fortunate, but not happy—would, in certain seasons of depression, have gladly exchanged all his bright prospects and high honours, for the leisure of Holywell, and for the real affection of his idolized wife.

Lady Marlborough accompanied him to Margate, where her husband was detained for some days by contrary winds. At last the wind changed; the vessel was ready to sail; the signal to depart was given. Lord Marlborough, who had been solicitous for war, ardent in the expectation of reaping honours on the plains of Holland, eager to depart, saw the signal which summoned him, with unwonted anguish. He contemplated, perhaps, years of separation from her to whom, in absence, every fond thought was given; who, though past the bloom of youth, was the object of an attachment almost romantic—an attachment, enthusiastic as it was, which elevated the noble and affectionate heart of the great Marlborough.

Since the accession of Anne, his domestic comfort had indeed been impaired by the altered position of his spoiled and arbitrary wife. The event which called her forth into public life, called forth also passions which embittered the intercourse between her and the good, the moderate, the kind-hearted Marlborough. It was in vain that he had endeavoured to control her vehement enmities, or to subdue her eager desire of interference in political affairs. Her busy spirit was not kept in subjection by any of that useful fear which sometimes serves as a restraint, on important occasions, to women who, in the minor concerns of life, can act the tyrant with a resolution worthy of a reasonable cause.

Lady Marlborough was not restrained, by any respect for the understanding of the Queen, from intruding her notions on politics, when unbidden or unwelcome. Her high spirit had been wounded unpardonably, by the appointment of a Tory ministry, in direct opposition to her wishes; and she chose not, even whilst obliged to submit, to permit the Queen to enjoy her sovereign pleasure unmolested. Incessant bickerings, in which Marlborough and Godolphin were obliged to interfere, and to soothe the angry passions of "Queen Sarah," as she was popularly called, had already begun to weaken the ardent friendship of Mrs. Freeman and Mrs. Morley, while they embittered the life of Lord Marlborough in another way.

Both Lord Godolphin and the Duke considered it their duty, in such disputes, to take the Queen's part. Doubtless, as far as fluency, courage, and perseverance were concerned, it was obviously the weaker side; but, in the adjustment of these differences, Lord Marlborough and his wife were often opposed in opinions; and Godolphin and Marlborough must infallibly have been disposed to agree with their subsequent foe, Harley. "I see," said that consummate courtier, "no difference between a mad Whig and a mad Tory."[19]

Matrimonial differences were the result of these rencontres; and the temperate, benevolent Marlborough suffered keenly from the occasional irritability of a wife, to purchase whose affections he would, as it appears from his letters, have made any sacrifice but that of principle.

Notwithstanding all these painful remembrances, the bonds of domestic life, which he was leaving, had abundant charms to rivet the noble heart of the most humane, the most exemplary of heroes. Lord Marlborough, who could face the enemies of his country undaunted, was overwhelmed with grief when he bade his wife and family farewell. He hastened on board the vessel, to conceal the agitation which he could not master. How beautiful, how touching, is the following letter, written by him from on board the vessel, shortly after this parting!

It is impossible to express with what a heavy heart I parted with you when I was at the waterside. I could have given my life to have come back, though I knew my own weakness so much that I durst not, for I should have exposed myself to the company. I did, for a great while, with a perspective glass, look upon the cliffs, in hopes I might have had one sight of you. We are now out of sight of Margate, and I have neither soul nor spirits; but I do at this minute suffer so much, that nothing but being with you can recompense it. If you will be sensible of what I now feel, you will endeavour ever to be easy to me, and then I shall be most happy, for it is, only you that can give me true content.

I pray God to make you and yours happy, and if I could contribute anything to it with the utmost hazard of my life, I should be glad to do it.[20]

What can we say to the woman who could undervalue such af-

---

19. Coxe, Papers, B. M., vol. 41, p. 22.
20. Coxe, p. 158. From *Marlborough Papers*.

fection, and fritter away the happiness, the glory of being Marlborough's wife, in petty intrigues and heart-burnings which marred their matrimonial felicity. Some qualities there must have been, generous and attaching in her character, which attracted, in spite of the vexations raised by her provoking activity and interference—in spite even of temper, that word of mighty import in the catalogue of human woes—the ever-returning affection of her husband towards her. The most gentle, the most irreproachable of wives could scarcely have deserved proofs of tender consideration more touching than the foregoing and following letters; and, probably, to speak seriously, would not have received them. It is a remarkable fact, that the most arrogant women often inspire the greatest devotion in those to whom fate has united them, especially if the partner of that lot be of a gentle and clinging disposition.

"I do assure you," writes the great Marlborough, on occasion of some political broil, "I had much rather the whole world should go wrong than you should be uneasy, for the quiet of my life depends only on your kindness. I beg you to believe that you are dearer to me than all things in the world. My temper may make you and myself sometimes uneasy; but when I am alone, and I find you kind, if you knew the true quiet I have in my mind, you would then be convinced of my being entirely yours, and that it is in no other power in this world to make me happy but yourself."

On another occasion he adds:

'Tis impossible, my dearest soul, to imagine the uneasy thoughts I have every day, in thinking that I have the curse, at my age, of being in a foreign country from you, and, at the same time, with very little prospect of being able to do any considerable service for my country.[21]

And again:—

July 17, 1702—from the Meuse. We have now very hot weather, which I hope will ripen the fruit at St. Albans. When you are there, pray think how happy I should be walking alone with you. No ambition can make me amends for being from you. If it were not impertinent, I should desire you in every letter to give my humble duty to the

---

21. Coxe, Papers, p. 43. .

Queen, for I do serve her in heart and soul. [22]

I am on horseback, or answering letters all day long; for, besides the business of the army, I have letters from the Hague, and all places where Her Majesty has any ministers; so that if it were not for my zeal for her service, I should certainly desert, for you know, of all things, I do not love writing.

At another time he writes to her,:

I am very impatient for the arrival of Devrell, you having given me hopes of a long letter by him; for though we differ sometimes in our opinion, I have nothing here gives me so much pleasure as your letters; and believe me, my dearest soul, that if I had all the applause, and even the whole world given me, I could not be happy if I had not your esteem and love.[23]

---

22. Coxe, vol. 1, p. 159—172.
23. Coxe, MSS. British Museum, vol. 41, folio, p. 11.

Chapter 13

Dangers Which Beset Marlborough

The Countess of Marlborough was now left to steer her course alone, amid the intricacies of politics. Her path was protected by the friendly assistance of Lord Godolphin, who was at once her guide and support, and the constant correspondent to whom Marlborough disclosed his inmost sentiments.

Dangers and difficulties perplexed the hero, even amid his most brilliant success. The campaign of the Meuse had been concluded, Liege taken, and Marlborough was preparing to return to England, when an accident occurred which had nearly closed for ever the splendid career of him on whom the fortunes of England depended. In descending the Meuse, from Maestrecht, in order to go to the Hague, the boat in which he sailed was separated in the night from its companion, manned with sixty men, and Marlborough was left with a guard of twenty-five men only. A French vessel from Gueldre was lurking among the reeds and sedge on the river, as Marlborough's small party became apparent. The adverse party suddenly rushed on the boat, and overpowered the guards.

In this situation, the coolness of Marlborough, and his perfect command of countenance, saved him from discovery. The Dutch deputies on board were furnished with French passports, but Marlborough disdained to solicit one from these functionaries. A man standing near him thrust into his hands a pass which he drew out of his pocket. It happened to be a French passport which had been formerly given to General Churchill, Lord Marlborough's brother, who had quitted the service from ill health. Although aware that it was out of date, and that the slightest inspection might detect the imposition, Marlborough composedly presented it. He was, in consequence, permitted to proceed, whilst his escort were detained. To the man who saved his life, he gave a pension of fifty pounds.[1] Marlborough reached the Hague in safety, where rejoicings of the greatest enthusiasm upon his escape gratified the kind heart which was touched by the homely tribute of the lower orders.

It must have been with no common feelings that the Countess welcomed back her husband, after a risk so imminent. In her *Vindication of her Conduct* she alludes but seldom to Marlborough, and seems to make far less account of his victories and defeats, than of her own successful or frustrated intrigues; and of the sentiments with which she welcomed to his home him whom the multitude compared to Caesar for good fortune, and declared that he was shown to be peculiarly in God's favour, from his unparalleled success,[2] there is, in her writings, no record.

During the Duke's absence, the Tory party had been greatly augmented in strength. After disposing of several important posts, to most of which Tories were preferred, Her Majesty, in July, passed an order in council against the selling of places in her household and family; but this was not issued until, as the enemies of Lady Marlborough observed, abundance of places had been purchased from the favourite.[3]

Elections for a new Parliament were carried on with great warmth, the Tory interest predominating. On the sixth of August, the Queen prorogued the Parliament until the eighth of October; and three weeks afterwards, accompanied by Prince George, she set out by Windsor for Bath, the use of the waters being recommended for the Prince's asthma. It is probable that Lady Marlborough, in her capacity of Groom of the Stole, accompanied, her royal mistress on this occasion; it indeed appears, from several of the letters, that she[4] frequently visited Bath. At Oxford, where the Queen rested one night, she was received with manifestations of loyalty and affection. She honoured the convocation of the university with her presence, and, in reply to an address, assured the magnates of "her favour and protection; and that she should always have a particular regard to this great body, so considerable in itself, and so useful both in Church and State."

After receiving the usual present of a Bible, a common prayer-book, and a pair of gloves. Queen Anne partook of a splendid banquet, at which most of the distinguished members of her government

---

1. Coxe, 192. Note.
2. Cunningham, b. 5, p. 296.
3. Boyer, p. 33.
4. Coxe, MSS., B. M.

were present, many of whom had received the title of Doctor of Law. When these ceremonials were finished, she proceeded on her road to Bath, where she remained until the beginning of October, and where, doubtless, "Queen Sarah" remained with Her Majesty.

And now commenced that course of prosperity which proved so intoxicating to the mind of Lady Marlborough, and which is said to have engendered the vice of cupidity in the otherwise noble nature of Marlborough. It is one of the besetting temptations of a long career of success, that it induces us to set a value upon our exertions, and our merits, which produces the curse of discontent. Nothing can come up to our sense of what we deserve: and the bounties of fortune, like some luscious liquors, create only a thirst for more.

The Queen, in her speeches at the opening of her first Parliament, referred to the successes of her arms under Lord Marlborough, she was answered by an address, congratulating Her Majesty upon that head, and declaring that the Earl had signally "retrieved the ancient honour and glory of the English nation," a phrase which satisfied neither Marlborough nor his captious wife. The Queen went in great state to St, Paul's to return thanks, and received an address of congratulation from the Commons upon the recovery of her asthmatic consort, whose illness had assumed the form of lethargy.[5]

In November Lord Marlborough returned, and immediately received the thanks of the House of Commons for his services. This honour, accepted with the most graceful, or, as some call it, artful humility by Marlborough, was succeeded by a declaration of the Queen in council, that it was her intention to make his Lordship a Duke.

Her determination was expressed in these terms: "I am so satisfied of the eminent services of my Lord of Marlborough to the public and myself, both in the command of the army, and in the entire confidence he has settled between me and the States General, that I intend to make him a Duke." [6]

This new distinction is said to have proceeded entirely from the favour of Her Majesty, unsolicited, and indeed by Lady Marlborough undesired. It is difficult to believe this of so ambitious a woman; yet thus writes Lord Godolphin to her Ladyship on this momentous occasion.

In sending to Lady Marlborough the address of the House of Lords, he says:—

---

5. Boyer, p. 35.
6. State of Europe, 1702.

I am apt to think Mrs. Morley may have something to say to you upon the subject, which perhaps you may not like; but I think it should be endured upon such an occasion, when it is visible to the whole world that it is not on your account.[7]

The Queen followed this prefatory letter with the following gracious and delicate mode of announcing her intentions.

St. James's 22nd October.

I have had this evening the satisfaction of my dear Mrs. Freeman's of yesterday; for which I give you many thanks, and though I think it a long time since I saw you, I do not desire you to come one minute sooner to town than it is easy for you, but will wait with patience for the happy hour; and only beg, when you do come, you would send for a coach, and not make use of a chaise.

Lord Treasurer intends to send you a copy of the address of the House of Lords, which is to be given me tomorrow, and that gives me an opportunity of mentioning a thing which I did not intend to do yet. It is very uneasy to your poor unfortunate, faithful Morley, to think that she has so very little in her power to show you how sensible I am of all Lord Marlborough's kindness, especially when he deserves all that a rich crown could give. But since there is nothing else at this time, I hope you will give me leave, as soon as he comes, to make him a duke. I know my dear Mrs. Freeman does not care for anything of that kind, nor am I satisfied with it, because it does not enough express the value I have for Mrs. Freeman, nor ever can, how passionately I am yours, my dear Mrs. Freeman.[8]

"Ambition," the Duchess of Marlborough observes, "had no share in procuring that new title;"[9] and the following extract from a letter addressed by her, on this occasion, to one of her friends, appears to confirm the declaration of one who was as little addicted to duplicity as any person inhabiting the atmosphere of a court could possibly be.

"I believe," she says, "there are very few in the world who do not think me very much pleased with the increase of honour the Queen gave Lord Marlborough when he commanded the

---

7. Coxe, p. 202.
8. *Marlborough Papers.*
9. *Conduct*, p. 303.

army at her coming to the crown; and perhaps it is so ridiculous, at least what few people will believe, that I would not mention it but to those that I could show the original letters to. If there be any truth in a mortal, it was so uneasy to me, that when I read the letter first upon it, I let it drop out of my hand, and was for some minutes like one that had received the news of the death of one of their dear friends; I was so sorry for anything of that kind, having before all that was of any use.

"I fear you will think what I say upon the subject is affected; and therefore I must repeat again, that it is more uneasy to me for a time than can easily be believed. I do think there is no advantage but in going in at a door; and when a rule is settled, I like as well to follow five hundred as one. And the title of duke in a family where there are many sons is often a great burthen; though at that time I had myself but one, I might have had more, and the next generation a great many. To conclude, a higher title was not my feat; and if I saw you, I could convince you of it."

Lord Godolphin, who knew her reluctance to the proffered honour, wrote to soothe her alarms, and to pacify her on the occasion. At the time that these letters were written, there was not the slightest reason to suppose that they would ever be made public; and the Countess is therefore borne out in her assertion, that the distinction came to her family, not only unsolicited but undesired.[10]

"I give you many thanks," writes the Lord Treasurer, "for the favour of your letter, which I received this evening. I did easily believe Mrs. Morley's letter would make you uneasy, but having her commands not to speak of it, I durst not say any more, than just to prepare you to submit to what I found by her she was convinced was necessary' for the satisfaction of the public. I have waited upon her this evening to let her see how truly uneasy you were, and have begged of her, when she sees you, not to part till she has made you easy again, either by your submitting to please her, or by her condescending to cure your apprehensions."[11]

Lord Marlborough appears to have been far less averse to the favour meditated by his gracious sovereign than his more cautious, and,

---

10. *Conduct*, p. 305.
11. Coxe, p. 204.

in common affairs, more sagacious wife.

Nov. 4th.—

"You know," he observes, writing from the Hague, in reply to some letters in which the subject had been broached, "I am very ill at compliments, but I have a heart full of gratitude; therefore pray say all you can to the Queen for her extraordinary goodness to me. As you have let me have your thoughts as to the dukedom, you shall have mine in short, since I shall have the happiness of being with you so soon."

He proceeded, however, to take counsel upon the occasion from the Pensionary Heinsius, a man of great sagacity, and one of his intimate and partial friends. Heinsius, across the channel, ventured to differ with the female arbiter who ruled Godolphin and Marlborough, and strongly recommended the acceptance of the high honour. He represented that it would give Marlborough greater consideration with the allied princes, and could not create jealousies, since it was bestowed wholly as a reward for the good services of the last campaign. To Marlborough's objection that he should, until he had an estate, make a worse figure as a duke than as he was, the Pensionary replied, that "the Queen's kindness was such, Lord Marlborough need not doubt a fortune; and that whatever was done at this time, for his fortune as well as the title, would be without envy, since all the people were pleased with what he had done."

Heinsius concluded his arguments by representing to the great general that it was not reasonable to expect in any future campaign such signal success as had accompanied the last; and he begged his lordship, for "the good of the common cause, the Queen's service, and his own sake, that he would think this the proper time for being distinguished."

This discussion made considerable impression on the judgement of him whom it chiefly concerned. Lord Marlborough assured the Pensionary that he would acquaint the Lord Treasurer and Lady Marlborough of the matter, and that he should be guided entirely by their decision. "I do beg of you," he adds, addressing his wife, "that you will do me justice that it is not my vanity that makes me think what the Pensioner says is reasonable."[12]

The Queen having, on the second of December, announced her intention of honouring the Earl of Marlborough with a dukedom,

---

12. See *Lord Marlborough's Letter*, fragment. Coxe, p. 206.

enhanced the obligation ' conferred, by sending, in ten days afterwards, a message to the House of Commons, stating that she had added to the distinction a pension of five thousand a year upon the revenue of the post-office, payable during the term of Her Majesty's natural life. She further observed, "that if it had been in her power, she would have granted the same terms in the pension as in the honour, that is, by making it permanent; and that she hoped they would think it so reasonable in this case, as to find some methods of doing it."[13]

This message occasioned warm debates in the House, and an address was returned, importing that the Commons, "to their inexpressible grief," could not comply with Her Majesty's wishes; and that they begged leave to lay before Her Majesty their apprehensions of making a precedent for the alienation of the revenues of the crown, which had been so much reduced by the exorbitant grants of the late reign."

The Queen, notwithstanding sundry complimentary matters from Her Majesty to the Commons, and from the Commons to Her Majesty, was yet unable to accomplish her point. Her justly-prized general and his favoured wife were fruitlessly indignant, at what they considered almost as a desertion of their interests, by their ministerial friends. They, on the other hand, attributed the Duke's efforts to have the grant of five thousand a year made perpetual, to that fondness for money with which this great man has been repeatedly, and, perhaps, not undeservedly, reproached.[14] Sir Christopher Musgrave remarked, "that he disputed not the merit of the Duke of Marlborough's services; but that it must be acknowledged they were well paid;" and the profitable employments which had been already bestowed upon different members of his family were brought into array against his demands.

Whilst these objections to the Duke's claims were boldly advanced in the House of Commons, the public, without the doors of that august assembly, were lavish of satirical remarks, which stung the Duke and Duchess, and even the Queen herself, to the very quick. Amongst other satires that were circulated, a lampoon was handed about, importing that the Queen intended to give one Duke (Marlborough) all the gold which another Duke (Ormond) had brought from Vigo.[15]

---

13. Boyer, p. 87. 14. Cunningham, b. 6, p. 314.
15. The Duke of Ormond had recently, in a very gallant manner, taken Vigo, in conjunction with Sir George Rook. A great booty was taken, but whilst the Spaniards sustained a heavy loss, the English were not comparatively benefited. "A great deal of the treasure taken at Vigo," says Burnet, "was embezzled, and fell into private hands; one of the galleons foundered at sea."—Burnet, vol. 5, p. 115.

Wounded and incensed by these remarks, the Duke entreated the Queen to recall her message, lest he should be the cause of obstructing the public business.[16] The Queen complied with this request; but, on the very day when the Commons presented their remonstrance, generously intimated her intention to the Duchess of Marlborough, of adding to the annuity of five thousand pounds, two thousand pounds out of the privy purse. This kind and prompt mark of affection was thus announced:

> I cannot be satisfied with myself without doing something towards making up what has been so maliciously hindered in the Parliament; and therefore I desire my dear Mrs. Freeman and Mr. Freeman would be so kind as to accept of two thousand pounds a year out of the privy purse, beside the grant of the five. This can draw no envy, for nobody need know it. Not that I would disown what I give to people that deserve, especially where it is impossible to reward the deserts; but you may keep it as a secret or not, as you please. I beg my dear Mrs. Freeman would never any way give me an answer to this; only comply with the desires of your poor, unfortunate, faithful Morley, that loves you most tenderly, and is, with the sincerest passion imaginable, yours."[17]

The proffered bounty was, with a feeling of honour, lofty and praiseworthy, declined. So disinterested a refusal might be considered as setting aside the charge of covetousness against Marlborough, and the imputed, grasping conduct of his wife. But, unhappily for those who would wish to exalt human nature, years afterwards, when the Duchess was out of favour, she had the meanness, by her own acknowledgment, to claim the two thousand pounds a year thus offered, and thus, at the same time, refused; and to press her claim by sending the Queen one of her own letters, in which she enforced the Duchess's acceptance of the grant; and to demand that Her Majesty should allow her to charge the sum, with arrears, from the time of the offer, in the privy purse accounts.

The Queen, though alienated from her favourite, was generous enough to agree to her proposal—the Duchess mean enough to receive the money.[18] The original refusal, therefore, we cannot but sup

---

16. Boyer, p. 37.
17. Coxe, p. 208.
18. *Conduct*, p. 295.

pose, proceeded from the just, though not liberal Marlborough, who disdained to accept, from the Queen's private bounty, a grant which the assembly of the nation had refused. Thus was the affair settled; but Marlborough never forgave the Tories their opposition to his claims. In offering to the Parliament his hearty thanks for their approbation of his services, he made this speech:—"He was overjoyed," he said, "that the House thought he had done service to the public; but that he would hereafter endeavour, as it had always been his wish, that he might be more indebted to his country, than his country to him."[19]

The subsequent rupture between Marlborough and the Tories originated on this occasion. The Duke was indignant, it is said, at being placed merely on a footing with Sir George Rooke, and the Duke of Ormond, who received the thanks of the Houses at the same time with his grace. He was also wounded, and not without reason, at the apparent disposition to undervalue his services which his friends manifested. These sentiments were shared, to their fullest extent, and exasperated with every womanly invective, by her who had continually regretted the early partiality of the Duke to a party whom she abhorred. But it was not long before, in the course of events, the Duchess perceived that her direst foes were not those who openly and vehemently opposed her ambitious views.

Amid the clamours of Whigs and Tories, and during the storm of their hostilities, a middle or moderate party gradually and silently arose, and, fostered by circumstances, attained a powerful ascendency. These "trimmers" as they were contemptuously called, gained accession to their numbers, amongst those who, like the Duke of Marlborough, beheld with regret the extravagances into which both factions were betrayed, in their avidity for preferment.

Robert Harley; afterwards Earl of Oxford, was the leader of this new and powerful schism from the Tory school of politics,—which he appeared, in a great degree, to have latterly deserted.

The political career of this being of ephemeral influence was, indeed, one of artifice. "His humour," says Lord Cowper, "was never to deal clearly, nor openly, but always with reserve, if not dissimulation, or rather simulation, and to love tricks, even, where not necessary, but from an inward satisfaction he took in applauding his own cunning. If any man was ever under the necessity of being a knave, he was."[20]

The great instrument of the proud Sarah's fall, Harley, was well un-

---
19. Cunningham, vol. 6, p. 314. 2
20. *Lord Cowper's Diary*, MS., p. 16.

derstood by his foe, even whilst, yet, he flattered her weaknesses, and temporized with the party whom she espoused. To a plain, familiar, unoffending manner, great application and extensive reading, Harley united an aspiring genius, and, as the Duchess remarks, as much knowledge as anyone living, "of the secret of managing the corruptions of human nature."[21] Educated among dissenters, his moderation, and the support which he gave to the succession of the house of Hanover, had conciliated the Whigs, whose cause he now pretended, with various reservations, to advocate. His election to the office of Speaker had been, nevertheless, regarded by the Tories as a triumph, although it had been carried almost by unanimous consent.

Yet, by dexterous management, Harley contrived, when the high church party became overbearing and obnoxious, to erect in himself that resource, of which the Queen afterwards availed herself, to balance parties. Extolled by Swift "for venturing to restore the forgotten custom of treating his prince with respect," Harley was suspected of some deep design by others, when, at his own table, he expatiated with admiration upon the manner of the late King's death, which he compared to that of the ancient heroes, as if it had been above "the mere condition of mortal men."[22] Yet, in public, he still espoused the interests of the Tories, flattering the Whigs, nevertheless, with assurances that he was satisfied that neither King William, nor his ministers, had any design but for the public good, and condoling with them upon the persecution that they had of late years encountered from the clamours of the adverse party. Thus a foundation was laid for that future eminence which Harley, to the downfall of Marlborough and his lady, enjoyed, but with short duration.[23]

In private life Harley was amiable, and, as far as money was concerned, singularly disinterested, for the times in which he lived. With all the weight of business on his mind, he had the power of enjoying the relaxation of conversation in an easy, light-hearted, and pleasing manner. A patron, as well as a proficient in learning, he was, as Pope relates, "above all pain, all anger, and all pride;" and thus, by that happy combination of qualities, escaped those displays by which the vanity and frequent absurdity of Halifax rendered the character of a patron odious, and avoided the ridicule, which sometimes, with less reason, alighted upon Godolphin.

---

21. *Private Correspondence*, vol. 2, p. 126.
22. Cunningham, b. 6, p. 315.
23. Harley first saw the light in Bowstreet, Covent Garden.

Lord Rochester, the main prop of the Tories, and at present the determined rival of Marlborough, was his ally; but proved, subsequently, the only impediment of Harley's pre-eminent favour with the Queen. By much prudence, by the courtesy of his manners, and the command of his temper, he was peculiarly formed to ingratiate himself at a court. Rochester and Harley were, however, opposed to the favourite and her gallant husband. But, at this period, both personal regard and affectionate gratitude were still in favour of the Duchess's continuance in prosperity and power.

Aware of Her Majesty's inclination, Marlborough and his wife sought every means of gratifying the Queen's earnest wishes, in respect to the elevation of her consort. Prince George, to an equal share of the regal dignity with herself. The desire which Anne cherished for the accomplishment of this end, strongly marks her affectionate disposition and unambitious character. But although the Prince of Denmark might be considered as the least dangerous of men, the measure, when brought forward, was overruled by a jealous parliament, as unconstitutional. Disappointed as she was, Anne sought consolation in the endeavour to obtain for her husband a provision in case of his surviving her; a project in which the Tories warmly concurred.

To the bill which was brought in for granting a pension of one hundred thousand pounds yearly, a clause was annexed, continuing to the Prince, after the Queen's death, the offices which he held during her lifetime; and the most violent opposition was raised by the Peers to this clause, which was contrary to the Act of Settlement. The Whigs were clamorous against it, as deviating from the principles of the Revolution, and the bill passed by one vote only. Marlborough, who was still considered as belonging to the Tory party, argued strenuously in the Queen's behalf, and his efforts were repaid by expressions of affectionate gratitude on the part of Anne.

"I ought," wrote Her Majesty, "to say a great deal to both of you in return, but neither words nor actions can ever express the true sense Mr. Morley and I have of your sincere kindness on this, and on all other occasions; and therefore I will not say any more on this subject, but that, to the last moment, your dear, unfortunate, faithful Morley will be most passionately and tenderly yours." [24]

The Queen, who was devotedly attached to her husband, notwith-

---
24. Coxe, vol. 1, p. 210.

standing the disparity of their age, and other circumstances, never forgave those who opposed this measure. It was true that there was little apparent probability of the Prince's living so long as to feel the loss of station and decline of influence which the Queen's death would entail upon his Royal Highness. He had for years been afflicted with an asthma, which during the winter (1702) endangered his life. Yet Anne evinced, on the subject of a provision for her consort, a zeal which she had never yet shown on any other subject.[25] The great world, whilst it admired her domestic qualities, had not given her credit for the strong conjugal affection which marked and elevated both her own private conduct, and which had adorned the character of the late Queen.

The courts of the Stuarts had not been accustomed to qualities so respectable and so amiable. Hence, when even the sedate and virtuous Anne promoted John Sheffield, Earl of Mulgrave, and afterwards Marquis of Normanby and Duke of Buckinghamshire, to be a privy councillor, her preference to that brave and accomplished nobleman was attributed to an early prepossession; Lord Mulgrave having paid his addresses to her before she was contracted to Prince George,[26] Queen Anne resembled, it may be presumed, most other women, who rarely cease to regard with complacency the man who has once displayed towards them affection or admiration, even when those feelings have not been reciprocal.

If, by a stretch of imagination, anything like romance can be attached to the recollection of this amiable Princess, the early addresses of the young nobleman,—addresses which were prohibited as soon as discovered,[27] though proffered at a time when there was little probability of Anne's becoming Queen of England,—may be deemed romantic. "Anne," says the arch-satirist of her day, "had undoubtedly no turn for gallantry, yet so far resembled her predecessor, Queen Elizabeth, as not to dislike a little homage to her person. The Duke," he adds, "was immediately rewarded, on her accession, for having made love to her before her marriage."[28]

Lord Mulgrave, whom the Queen was thought for such reasons to promote, had been a warm adherent to her father, even whilst he manfully reprobated and ridiculed that monarch's religious faith.[29]

---

25. Burnet, vol. 5, p. 125.
26. Boyer, p. 14.
27. *Ibid.*
28. *Royal and Noble Authors*, p. 436.
29. Burnet, vol. 1, p. 683.

Like Rochester, he influenced the Queen's mind,—it may without scandal be presumed, in some measure through her affections,—to the Tory party. In conformity with the fashion of the day, he affected literature.

"The life of this peer," says Horace Walpole, with his usual pointed and well-bred ill-nature, "takes up fourteen pages and a half in folio in the *General Dictionary*, where it has little pretensions to occupy a couple. The author of the *Dictionary*," he adds, "calls the Duke one of the most beautiful prose writers and greatest poets of this age; which is also," he says, "proved by the finest writers, his contemporaries; certificates that have little weight, where the merit is not proved by the author's own works."

"It is said," adds the malicious Walpole, "that the Duke wrote in hopes of being confounded with his predecessors in the title; but he would have been more easily confounded with the other Buckingham, if he had never written at all."[30]

Notwithstanding the Queen's earnestness on the subject of a provision for the Prince her husband, a protest was signed against that clause which enabled him to keep his employments in the next reign, thus making him an exception to all other foreigners similarly situated. It bore the names of seven peers, whilst those of twenty-eight were affixed to a still stronger protest, objecting to the whole bill. Amongst the noble names which thus appeared, that of Lord Sunderland, who had lately succeeded that celebrated statesman his father, gave the greatest offence to Anne, and distress to the Duke and Duchess of Marlborough. Lord Sunderland had aggravated his offence by speaking against the grant.

His father-in-law was grieved, and surprised at the part which his son-in-law took; but the Duchess was incensed by what she considered as a mark of disrespect, and an act of defiance to her will, by one usually flattering and subservient to his stately mother-in-law.[31] Her daughter, Lady Sunderland, with difficulty effected a reconciliation; for the principles of the Whigs were forgotten in the service of Majesty. This perplexing and irritating conduct on the part of Lord Sunderland was one of a series of political vexations, which Marl-

---

30. *Royal and Noble Authors*, p. 436.
31. See MSS. *Letters from Lord Sunderland*, in which he extols the Duchess's political exertions. Coxe, Papers B. M. Vol. 41, p. 13.

borough and his Duchess experienced at the hands of that able, but violent nobleman.

The Duchess of Marlborough had now wholly embarked on that voyage of politics which ended only with her long and weary life. A taste for the excitement for cabal, like a passion for gaming, grows with indulgence; it is rarely wholly relinquished, but fastens itself upon the character, until every faculty is absorbed in what is popularly termed a spirit of party.

The Duchess, whatever were her private motives, had, it must be allowed, extended and sound views upon such subjects as engaged the powers of her energetic mind. Doubtless the society of the able men whose intimacy she had secured, contributed to enlarge those opinions, which could scarcely have been formed in the courts of Charles the Second and his brother, or improved into principles in the contracted court or common-place society of the virtuous, but prejudiced Anne.

It is difficult to draw a distinction between what may be called real liberality of sentiment, and a pernicious licentiousness of profession in our religious concerns. The principle of toleration was mingled, in the days of William and of Anne, with a dangerous laxity, which required rather the counsels of the preacher, or the correctives of an enlightened press, or the chastening hand of popular education, to prevent its growth, than the questionable efficacy of penal enactments. The Test and Corporation Acts had rendered the Sacrament of the Lord's Supper an essential observance to all those who held offices of trust.

This measure, passed (1673) in the time of Charles the Second, had moderated the bitter feelings towards dissenters, in which the high church party had, until that time, indulged; and the zeal which many dissenters had displayed in the service of the country at the Revolution, had procured them offices under government, to obtain which, they had in many instances not scrupled to receive the Communion. A participation in this ceremonial was, by law, only incumbent once, and it might be followed by an immediate, and regular attendance on the services and sacraments of a dissenting meeting-house. The laxity and dissimulation to which this practice conduced, called for remedy; and the remedy was either to be obtained by remitting the test, thus unscrupulously nullified, or by strengthening the penal enactments.

The question became, as usual, a matter for faction to agitate, rather than for the calm light of reason to settle. The dissenters were countenanced by the Whigs: and were supporters of the war, which they deemed essential to establish the principles of the Revolution. The Tories, in attacking them, attacked, therefore, their adversaries in various ways, and, as it was argued, more from political virulence, than from religious zeal.

Yet, since it was allowed that there were many dissenters who reprobated the practice of thus prefacing the Sacrament by making it the vehicle of a false profession, so it may be presumed that there were also numerous persons amongst the high church party, who viewed such evasions of truth with real indignation, independent of party zeal, and who really desired, in the clamour for reformation, that such scandal to religion, and such temptation to the worst passions of our nature, should be prevented by legislative enactments.

It is agreeable to reflect that more just and delicate notions of religion, and its invariable attendant, integrity, now prevail, and that conduct in these matters, such as was common, and even habitual in the days of which we write, would be reprobated by all thinking people in our own times. Men who aspired to hold public offices were then frequently to be seen receiving the Communion of the Church of England once, and, having complied with the statute, were never known to enter a church of the established form again.

Even Prince George received the sacrament as high admiral, yet maintained his Lutheran chapel, in which, when interest called him not elsewhere, he was a continual attendant and communicant.[32] Nor were those who raised the clamour against such inconsistencies, to use the mildest term, much to be commended for the regularity or sincerity of their religious observances. Sir Edward Seymour, the leading partisan of the church, confessed, when discussing the subject of non-conformity, that it was then seven years since he had received the sacrament, or heard a sermon in the Church of England. It was remarkable that the leading members of the House of Commons, who were the most active against dissenters, were all descended from dissenting families. Amongst these were Harley, and Henry St. John, afterwards Lord Bolingbroke.[33]

The bill for preventing occasional conformity was, however, brought into the House of Commons. Its advocates did not attempt to conceal the existence of party motives, but contended, that since the last reign had been begun with a law in favour of dissenters, it was becoming that the gracious sovereign now on the throne should show,

---

32. Burnet, vol. 5, p. 123.
33. Cunningham, book 5, p. 317.

by some mark, her determined protection of the established church.[34] Whilst in the preamble a spirit of toleration was asserted, the enactments of the bill were severe, though vague, and tended to promote the vices of informers, and to produce a spirit of inquisition into every man's actions. It affixed a heavy fine upon every person holding a public office, after attending any meeting of dissenters, not according to the Liturgy of the Church of England, where more than five persons were present, besides the family. Upon functionaries so offending, while exercising their duties, it affixed a fine of five pounds for every day so employed; and, after attending such meeting, they were incapacitated from holding any office, until after a whole year's conformity to the church;—the great object of the bill being, according to a Whig "historian, to model corporations, and to cast out of them all those who would not vote in elections for the Tories."[35] Such was the opinion of Bishop Burnet. The Duchess of Marlborough gives us a much more highly-coloured delineation of the motives and workings of this famous measure, than even the determined and strenuous prelate.

The Church of England, the Duchess thought, could not be in any immediate danger with such a "*nursing* mother" as the Queen, or, as the Tories called her, the illustrious ornament of the church; and the Tories, in bringing forward this famous measure, "by the heat and agitation with which they over-acted their part, exposed their monopolizing ambition, which ought to have been better concealed under the cloak of zeal for the church."[36] The affection of Her Majesty for the church, the Duchess considered, could not be doubted, since, for its better security, she had chosen "its renowned champions to be of her ministry and council. Nevertheless," she adds, "in the very first new parliament after Her Majesty's accession, it was thought necessary, with all diligence, to provide new strength, new supports for this flourishing church, as if it had been in the most tottering and declining condition."[37] The motives for such conduct were, in the Duchess's estimation, interested and invidious. The bill did not, in her opinion, "aim at excluding the *occasional* conformists only, but all those *constant* conformists, too, who could not relish the high church nonsense of promoting religion by persecution."

---

34. Somerville, chap. 11, p. 27.
35. Burnet, vol. 5, p. 120, 121.
36. Conduct, p. 136.
37. *Conduct*, p. 138.

The measure, if intended, as the Duchess further asserts, to distinguish in Her Majesty's estimation the friends, from the foes of the church, succeeded in producing that effect, as subsequent events fully proved. Those who contemplated by its enactments the immediate prevention of the scandal of non-conformity, were disappointed, for it was not finally successful. It was brought into the Commons and passed; its "hottest" panegyrists being, according to Cunningham, "the clergy, and a crowd of women of the lowest rank, inflamed, as it were, with a zeal for religion." "These women," he observes, "expressed as great an exultation at the supposed victory, as if they had taken more pleasure in such religious triumphs, than in the gratification of even their lusts and their appetites."[38]

The Peers, however, less carried away at this time by religious or political zeal than the Commons, threw out the bill, being of opinion, not only that it was the offspring of party and prejudice, but that it would be impolitic during the time of war to disgust so large a body of Her Majesty's subjects as the Protestant dissenters. They argued, also, that it was not then expedient to set about the reformation of religious controversies.

The decision of the press was against the court, but highly acceptable to the people. Prince George, though himself an occasional conformist, was not ashamed to go to the House and vote for the bill;[39] yet even this singular proof of the Queen's good wishes towards the measure could not save it. The commercial part of the nation were warm in their dislike to its principles and details. Lord Somers, in a celebrated speech, in which he designated the great body of merchants, tradesmen, and mechanics, as "the nation," denounced the measure. Lord Wharton lent the aid of his forcible eloquence to advocate the cause of toleration. His speech was strongly characteristic.

"Men's minds," he argued, "are different, and their sentiments of divine worship, various. It were, indeed, to be wished, but is hardly to be expected, that men were all of one opinion. Many people like variety, as I myself do, provided it be not injurious to the public."

It was not long after these debates, that these two lords, "having," says Cunningham, "over-strained their voices in the heat of debates in

---

38. Cunningham, b. 5, p. 138.
39. *Conduct.*
40. Cunningham, p. 318.

Parliament, fell into dangerous sickness."[40]

Such was the violence with which the discussion was carried on.

The loss of the bill was a great mortification to the Tories; and Lord Rochester, about this time, resigned his appointment as Lord Lieutenant of Ireland, it was said, chiefly from his unwillingness to leave England, lest the church should be betrayed in his absence. But it was with more truth supposed, that jealousy of Lord Godolphin, and vexation at the Queen's not making Rochester her sole director and adviser, had a share in producing his lordship's resignation.

> This, "if true," says the Duchess, "affords a remarkable instance how much self-love and conceit can blind even a man of sense; for such, by his own party at least, he was esteemed to be. I don't wonder he should like power, (it is what most people are fond of,) or that, being related to the Queen, he should expect a particular consideration: this was very natural and very reasonable, if he had behaved himself to her as he ought But when one considers that his relation to her was by such a sort of accident, and that his conduct had been so very extraordinary, it is an amazing thing that he should imagine that he was to domineer over the Queen and everybody else, as he did over his own family."[41]

> "Whether the church was in any danger or *not* before," adds the Duchess, contemptuously, "it could not be questioned by any good churchman but it *now* began to be in some peril, when my Lord Rochester was no longer in place, nor in the council."[42]

The Duchess, during the progress and defeat of the Conformity Bill, endeavoured, but unsuccessfully, to bring the Queen over to her own views of the important subject Yet Anne, on being informed that a great portion of her subjects were greatly offended at the attempt made by this bill to shackle their religious professions, endeavoured, in her speech on the opening of the next Parliament, to dissuade the House from this measure, as it might prove a barrier to union at home, and consequently detrimental to the prosecution of the war abroad.

Marlborough, though still reputed to be a high churchman, seconded the wishes of the people by every effort in his power. His popularity, on that account, rose to a pitch of the greatest favour; and

---

41. *Conduct*, p. 142.
42. *Ibid*, 145.

the money and the trade of the country being in the hands of those who espoused the cause of the Dissenters, Lord Godolphin began also to be convinced of the importance of the Whigs as a body, "and to pay them as much regard as the times and the Queen's prejudices would permit."

The next blow to the Tories was manifested by the removal of Sir Edward Seymour and Lord Jersey from their employments, and by the resignation of Lord Nottingham, who was indignant at the favour shown to the Whigs.

The same party spirit which affected the political world, ran with aggravated fury through- out the whole body of the clergy. Divisions now took place, "to describe which," says Burnet, "new names were found out; and they were distinguished by the name of High Church and Low Church."[43] Those who treated the dissenters with moderation, who expressed approbation of the Revolution, and aversion to the House of Stuart—those who wished well to the present war, and ill to France—were considered by their opponents to favour the presbytery, and to be ill affected to the church.

Amongst such, the Duchess of Marlborough figured conspicuously, and, whilst her day lasted, with powerful effect upon the growth and strength of the party with whom she delighted to be classed.

---

43. Burnet, vol. 5, p. 138.

Chapter 14
1702-3
Death of the Marquis of Blandford

How often does it occur, that in the hurry of life some event interposes to show us the fruitlessness of our cares—to prove to us our position, as powerless instruments in the hand of Providence—to mark the weakness of our wills, and the transient nature of all that we prize, and of all that we have sought to gain, by rising early, and late taking rest, and eating the bread of carefulness!

Whilst the Duchess of Marlborough, by the workings of her powerful mind, swayed the destinies of party, and governed her sovereign, it was decreed that a chastising hand should humble and restrain her; that the blow should be aimed in the tenderest part, calculated, to lower her proudest aspirations, and to touch with poignancy those maternal affections of which even the most worldly are never destitute, but which the worldly taste only in bitterness; for interest and pleasure deaden the daily emotions and gentle pleasures of domestic life, whilst they cannot wholly avert the sting which the dormant affections receive.

The Duchess had borne her husband two sons. Of these, Charles the younger, died at an early age. John, the elder, survived until the age of seventeen, when, in all the promise of future celebrity and excellence, he was taken from his parents, just as their hopes of him, their pride of him, and their love of him, had raised their expectations to the utmost height.

Commanding in person, and strong in intellect,[1] this noble youth united with the high spirit of his mother, the gentleness, and graciousness, and strong principles of his father. His religious habits, his

---
1. *Granger*, vol. 2, p. 41.

frequent attendance on the holy sacrament, his assiduity in his studies, and the regularity of his conduct, proved that, how much soever his parents had been absorbed in the concerns of the world, and in the pursuit of greatness, they had neither neglected the formation of his intellect, nor the far more important yet corresponding culture of his sense of duty, and his best affections.

Well might the bereaved parents afterwards exclaim with Congreve, when death had robbed them of this star which shed a ray of brightness on their path of life,

To mourn thy fall, I'll fly the hated light,
And hide my head in shades of endless night;
For thou were light, and life, and wealth to me;
The sun but thankless shines that shows not thee;
Wert thou not lovely, graceful, good, and young,
The joy of sight, the talk of every tongue?
Did ever branch so sweet a blossom bear.
Or ever early fruit appear so fair?[2]

The original intention of the Duke and Duchess was, that their son should, by the favour of the Queen, fill the place of master of the horse to the young Duke of Gloucester. Upon the death of that young Prince, Lord Blandford was sent to King's College, Cambridge, having been prepared for that seminary of knowledge by his previous education at Eton. At Cambridge he was placed under the tuition of Mr. Hare, afterwards Bishop of Chichester, the chaplain subsequently, and the friend and correspondent, of the Duke and Duchess. Under his guidance, and enjoying the friendship of Horace, afterwards Lord Walpole, the young nobleman added credit to his name, by a regularity which would have become the lowliest as well as the most exalted member of the university. His classical attainments were considerable; the courtesy of his manners accorded with an affectionate and modest nature; and his good sense appreciated the important benefits of that college discipline, from which a feebler or more presuming mind would have revolted.

With all these excellencies—the excellencies which would have adorned him in private life, had he been spared—Lord Blandford cherished the ambition to resemble and to emulate his father, in the brilliant course of a military career.

When scarcely sixteen, he entreated permission to join the cam-

---
2. *Congreve's Works.*

paign in the Netherlands. His request was not gratified; for although Marlborough could not repel a thirst for distinction which so well accorded with his own nature, the mother of the high-spirited youth dreaded for her child the dangers which appear not to have overwhelmed her at any time with apprehensions for his father. Lord Blandford, nevertheless, ardent and resolute, persisted in his desires, and sought to obtain for himself and Horace Walpole commissions in the cavalry, that they might serve at the same time, and in the same regiment.

The parent, who dreaded for her son perils by land, and perils by sea, was doomed to lose him by that fatal complaint, which then, in most instances, baffled medical skill, and proved the scourge of society. The smallpox raged in Cambridge. Lord Godolphin, who was at Newmarket, wrote to the inquiring mother accounts of her son's health, which were calculated to satisfy her maternal anxieties, whilst yet the disease had not attacked the delicate, and, as it seems, prematurely gifted youth. Lord Churchill, the lord treasurer acknowledged, was thin almost to emaciation; but he dwelt more minutely upon the displays of his mental and moral qualities than on his health.

> I repeat to you that I find Lord Churchill very lean. He is very tractable and good-humoured, and without any one ill inclination that I can perceive. And I think he is grown more solid than he was, and has lost that impatience of diverting himself all manner of ways, which he used to have. This is truly just as I find him, and I thought it might not be improper to give you this account, that you might be the better judge whether you would desire to see him now, according to the proposal I made in my letter of yesterday, or stay for that satisfaction until my Lord Marlborough comes over.[3]

This was in August, 1703. In October, Lord Godolphin received the young nobleman as a guest in his house at Newmarket, where, unhappily, the smallpox then raged. But it was vainly hoped, by precautions, to avert the risk of infection.

> "What you write," thus Lord Godolphin addressed the anxious mother, "is extremely just and reasonable; and though the smallpox has been in this town, yet he, going into no house but mine, will, I hope, be more defended from it by air or riding, without any violent exercise, than he could probably be any-

---

3. Coxe, vol. 1, p. 217.

where else."

In a few days afterwards, more particular accounts reached the Duchess, and her maternal pride must have been highly gratified by the encomiums which so consummate a judge of character as Lord Godolphin passed upon her son.

"Your pretty son," as the lord treasurer terms him, "whom I have just now parted from; and I assure you, without flattery or partiality, that he is not only the best natured and most agreeable, but the most free-thinking and reasonable creature that one can imagine for his age. He had twenty pretty questions and requests, but I will not trouble you with the particulars till I have the honour to see you."

The foregoing opinion was the last expressed by this well-judging and warm friend, concerning him upon whom the fondest hopes were placed. How gratifying, yet how mournful! Yet the noble youth was prepared for that better sphere to which he was thus early called, to spare him, in mercy, from the snares and troubles of the world, in which he might otherwise have acted a conspicuous, but probably not a happy part.

The letter was followed by alarming intelligence. The smallpox, in its most malignant form, had attacked the darling of these distinguished parents. The Duchess hastened to Cambridge, and found her son in great danger. She sent to London for additional medical assistance, and the Queen, feeling as a mother bereaved, and acting with her usual consideration, despatched two of her own physicians in one of the royal carriages. The medicines were also sent by express from London. But the cares, the fears, the hopes, the efforts of all those who were interested in the young man, were unavailing.

The fatal disorder ran rapidly its devastating course. Dr. Haines and Dr. Coladon, the court physicians, hastened in vain to aid the expiring youth. The grief of the highest, and the sympathy of the lowest, individuals in Her Majesty's realms, availed not: for his hour was come. How far we are, in such instances, to look to secondary causes, it is difficult to say; but it is easy to suppose that the imperfect knowledge of disease in those unscientific days, the unnatural and irritating mode of treating it which prevailed, even within the memory of man, may have aided that consciousness of the importance of his recovery to his parents, and the painful observance of their grief, in increasing the danger of the amiable and lamented youth.

The Queen took his illness to heart, as if it had been the scene of her own sad deprivation acted over again.

"I writ two words to my dear Mrs. Freeman," she says, addressing the Duchess, "and could not help telling her again that I am truly afflicted for the melancholy account that is come this morning of poor Lord Blandford. I pray God he may do well, and support you. And give me leave once more to beg you, for Christ Jesus' sake, to have a care of your dear precious self; and believe me, with all the passion imaginable, your poor, unfortunate, faithful Morley."

Lord Godolphin, in a calmer, but equally kind, equally friendly strain, thus proffers the valuable consolations of a sympathetic heart. :

"The best use of one's best friends is, to assist and support one another under the most grievous afflictions. This is the greatest trial of your submission and resignation to the Divine Providence that God Almighty could possibly send you, and consequently the greatest opportunity of pleasing Him, by that respect and submission which is always due to his severest trials; and, at the same time, the greatest occasion of letting the whole world see that God Almighty has blessed you with a Christian patience and fortitude, as eminent as the reason and understanding by which you are justly distinguished from the rest of your sex."

The concern of a friend is expressed in the foregoing fragment; the anguish of a father in those passages which follow.

The character of Marlborough, the great, the affectionate, the good, the pious, shines forth in these extracts.

I am so troubled at the sad condition this poor child seems to be in, that I know not what I do. I pray God to give you some comfort in this great affliction. If you think anything under heaven can be done, pray let me know it, or if you think my coming cart be of the least use, let me know it. I beg I may hear as soon as possible, for I have no thought but what is at Cambridge.

I writ to you this morning," he adds, "and was in hopes I should have heard again before this time, for I hope the doctors were with you early this morning. If we must be so unhappy as to lose this poor child, I pray God to enable us both to behave ourselves with that resignation which we ought to do. If this uneasiness which I now lie under should last long, I think I could not live. For God's sake, if there be any hope of recovery, let me know it.[4]

These mournful anticipations were followed by the too probable result. Within a few hours after the unhappy father had written this letter, he set off for Cambridge, where he arrived only in time to see his son expire, on the morning of Saturday, the twentieth of February, 1704.[5]

The condolence of friends and relations, and the sympathy even of foes, followed this event. To the chosen place of Lord Blandford's interment, in King's College Chapel, whose sacred walls had witnessed his early and late piety, beneath whose roof he had been a constant attendant at morning and evening prayers,—the disconsolate parents followed the earthly remains of their lost treasure. An inscription, in elegant Latin, on a monument erected to his memory, perpetuates the recollection of his early promise. Not only of the highest rank by descent, but of the most exalted virtues, the external qualities of one so favoured by fortune, and endowed by nature, corresponded, as the inscription states, with his mental attributes. He possessed, it is said, the stately and manly form, and the surpassing symmetry, which constitute the perfection of manly beauty.[6]

In the quickness of his faculties alone did he resemble his mother. His admirable humility, and sweetness of manners, in the midst of all that rank and affluence could effect to spoil him, were the bright reflection of his glorious father. In purity of conduct, though introduced early to a court life, between the period of his leaving Eton and entering on an academic life at Cambridge, he was more happy than that parent; for men are to be judged by circumstances. A sense of religious duty (the only effectual safeguard) led to a "strict observance of decorum, that rather," says an historian, "seemed innate, than acquired."[7] He retained of the court nothing but its politeness, and desired, in the bright prospects which apparently awaited him, nothing but true honour and distinction, not from his position alone, but from his own strenuous exertions.

His parents were deeply, but differently affected by their calamity. The high spirit of the Duchess was subdued, and the best dispositions

---

4. Coxe, p. 220.
5. *Ibid.* vol. 1, p. 219.
6. Collins's *Baronage*, vol. 1, p. 218.
7. *Ibid.*

of her heart were touched, by this bereavement: but ambition soon regained its ascendency over her soul, and the chastening hand was forgotten in the busy interests of the day, the hour. Marlborough, on the contrary, though quickly summoned to a fresh campaign, carried about with him the yearning tenderness, the mournful, though no longer poignant regrets, which a sensitive mind retains for a beloved and lost object After the first bitter pangs had been assuaged, he set off for the seat of war; but in the heart of enterprise, amid the busiest scenes in which he was engaged, the father recalled all that he had hoped and planned for his lost son. In a letter to Lord Godolphin, written from Cologne, he says:

> I have this day seen a very great procession; and the thoughts how pleased poor Lord Churchill would have been with such a sight, have added very much to my uneasiness. Since it has pleased God to take him. I do wish from my soul I could think less of him. [8]

Alas! how many parents may utter the same natural but fruitless wish!

The Duchess, unfortunately for those who feel an interest in probing the long since tranquilised emotions of her turbulent spirit, imposed upon the Duke a condition, with which, in the true spirit of honour, he complied, (though, as he states himself, with regret,) of burning the letters which she wrote to him. She seems, however, to have written in a kind and consolatory manner, and we may infer from the lively gratitude of her husband, that such was not always her custom. What a picture of real attachment is presented in the following passage of the Duke's answer!

> If you had not positively desired that I would always burn your letters, I should have been very glad to have kept your dear letter of the 9th, it was so very kind, and particularly so upon the subject of our living quietly together, till which happy time comes, I am sure I cannot be contented; and then I do flatter myself I should live with as much satisfaction as I am capable of. I wish I could recall twenty years past, I do assure you, for no other reason but that I might in probability have longer time, and be the better able to convince you how truly sensible I am at this time of your kindness, which is the only real comfort of my life; and whilst you are kind, besides the many blessings it

---

8. MSS. *Correspondence of the Duke of Marlborough*. Coxe, Papers, vol. 65, p. 2.

brings me, I cannot but hope we shall yet have a son, which are my daily prayers.[9]

His earnest solicitude on the subject of her health seems to have been fully shared by the Duchess with respect to him. Marlborough, like many men whose minds are tasked to the utmost of their bodily strength to bear, suffered severely from the headache. How that overwrought frame and intellect at last broke down, it is melancholy to reflect.

I have yours of the eighteenth, by which I find you were uneasy at my having the headache. It was your earnest desire obliges me to let you know when I have those little inconveniences of the headache, which are but too natural to me; but if you will promise to look upon my sicknesses as you used to do, by knowing I am sick one day and well another, I must not be punctual in acquainting you when I am uneasy. I think you are very happy in having dear Lady Mary with you; I should esteem myself so, if she could be sometimes for an hour with me; for the greatest ease I now have is sometimes sitting for an hour in my chair alone, and thinking of the happiness I may yet have, of living quietly with you, which is the greatest I propose to myself in the world.

At the very time of his investing the fortress of Huy, after being distracted by opposing councils compelled to adopt plans which he disapproved, and harassed by fatigues, being often fourteen hours of the day on horseback, and marching sometimes five days together,[10]— it was in the midst of these trials of strength and patience that his heart turned towards home, and he found leisure, in the midst of a camp, to write those beautiful letters, unequalled for simplicity, and in the true expression of a tender and noble nature.

Lord Godolphin had written to his friend the painful intelligence that he thought the Duchess to be much out of health. This information roused all the tenderness and apprehensions of the hero's sensitive mind.

"For God's sake," he writes, "let me know exactly how you are; and if you think my being with you can do you any good, you shall quickly see you are much dearer to me than fame, or whatever the world can say; for should you do otherwise than well, I were the unhappiest man living."

---

9. Coxe, 228.
10. Lediard.

Notwithstanding the offer of this noble sacrifice—noble in one who was not merely carried on by impulse, but who had laid plans of the greatest extent for the aggrandizement of his country—the Duchess, who appears to have been a domestic tyrant, could never be wholly satisfied without incessant expressions of regard and devotion. She could not forbear, even at this distance, adding to his many troubles by her exacting spirit. She scrutinized even the language of affection, with the fastidiousness of a spoiled child, loath to be contented.

From the following and other passages, we are led to conclude that the hopes of having a child to supply the loss of him from whom he had been severed, were, at one time, revived in the Duke's mind. On a former occasion he wrote to his wife thus:—

> What troubles me in all this time is your telling me that you do not look well. Pray let me have, in one of your letters, an account how you do. If it should prove such a sickness as that I might pity you, yet not be sorry for it, it might make me yet have more ambition. But if your sickness be really want of health, it would render me the unhappiest man living.

These hopes were further raised, only, unfortunately, to be frustrated. In all other respects the Duchess of Marlborough, pre-eminently blessed, was destined to that one cankering disappointment—that the children of the son-in-law whom she least loved, became the heirs of those honours so dearly purchased by Marlborough.

> "I have just now," says the Duke, in one of his letters, "received yours of the sixth. What you say to me of yourself gave me so much joy, that if any company had been by when I read the letter, they must have observed a great alteration in me."[11]

Yet, with his usual delicacy and consideration, he writes in a consolatory strain, when it appeared to the Duchess that he thought more of his disappointed hopes, than of the ill health which caused them. He urged upon her the tranquillizing of her busy mind, by quiet, and cessation from business, and by looking to higher sources of comfort than the adulation of society, or the favours of a monarch. The chastening hand was not extended to Marlborough in vain, when he could think and write in terms such as these. After entreating his wife to think as little as possible of worldly business, and to be very regular in her diet, which he trusts, by the aid of a good constitution, may set her right in time, he addresses her in the following beautiful strain:—

---

11. Coxe, vol. 1, p. 228.

Op-heeren, Aug. 2.

I have received yours of the twenty-third, which has given me, as you may easily believe, a good deal of trouble. I beg you will be so kind and just to me, as to believe the truth of my heart, that my greatest concern is for that of your own dear health. It was a great pleasure to me, when I thought we should be blessed with more children; but as all my happiness centres in living quietly with you, I do conjure you, by all the kindness which I have for you, which is as much as man ever had for woman, that you will take the best advice you can for your health, and then follow exactly what shall be prescribed for you; and I do hope that you will be so good as to let me have an exact account of it, and what the physicians' opinions are.

If I were with you, I would endeavour to persuade you to think as little as possible of worldly business, and to be very regular in your diet, which I should hope would set you right in a very little time, for you have naturally a very good constitution. You and I have great reason to bless God for all we have, so that we must not repine at his taking our poor child from us, but bless and praise him for what his goodness leaves us; and I do beseech him, with all my heart and soul, that he would comfort and strengthen both you and me, not only to bear this, but any correction that he should think fit to lay on us.

The use, I think, we should make of his correction is, that our chiefest time should be spent in reconciling ourselves to him, and having in our minds always that we may not have long to live in this world. I do not mean by this that we should live retired from the world, for I am persuaded that by living in the world, one may do much more good than by being out of it; but, at the same time, to live so as that one should cheerfully die when it shall be his pleasure to call for us. I am very sensible of my own frailties; but if I can ever be so happy as to live with you always, and that you comfort me and assist me in these my thoughts, I am then persuaded I should be as happy and contented as it is possible to be in this world; for I know we should both agree, next to our duty to God, to do what we ought for the Queen's service.

Happy would it have been for the Duchess, had these higher principles of conduct guided her future path through life. But while the afflictions which bore down the spirit of her husband sank into a good soil, in the mind of this ambitious and restless woman, schemes for the aggrandizement of her family soon succeeded to the gloom of her son's deathbed, and effaced all the solemn lessons which she had there learned.

CHAPTER 15

Costume and Manners

The manners and spirit of the period of which we treat are so fully exemplified in those periodical publications of the day, which are in the hands of every English reader, that no digression for the purpose of illustrating the mode of social life, with which we are all so familiar, appears necessary.

With the costumes of the fashionable world, the pages of the *Tatler*, *Spectator*, and other works, have rendered us intimately acquainted. It is sufficient to remark, that in this last respect the customs which prevailed in the reign of William were but slightly varied when Steel and Addison handed them down to fame. Formality of manner, and decorum in dress, had already succeeded the negligence and indelicacy of the preceding century. Still there were gross absurdities creeping into vogue.

As we have ever borrowed the most startling extravagances from the French, so we owed to Louis the Fourteenth the long reign of perukes, in the adoption of which we were servile copyists, until good sense drove out those disfiguring encumbrances, and left mankind free to breathe and to move un- trammelled. When Anne reigned, many lived, more especially amongst the sons of the aristocracy, who could scarcely remember to have worn their own locks. Boys were quickly disguised in flowing curls—the higher the rank, the greater the profusion.

Thence they rose to the dignity of a *scratch* for their undress, and to that of the waving flaxen peruke, called by a wag, "the silver fleece." White wigs, frosted with powder, had succeeded the dark curling perukes which were in vogue in the reign of Charles the Second; and the use of powder had become lamentably universal. For this extravagance outraged nature was indebted, also, to that most artificial of human beings, Louis the Fourteenth, whose very statues were laden with enormous wigs; and the monarch himself wore one even in bed.[1]

William the Third seldom varied his dress; but, after the accession of Anne, female extravagance and male absurdity rose to their climax. Whilst the summit of each exquisite courtier was crowned with a flowing peruke, redolent of perfume, and replete with powder, on the which sat a small cocked-hat, his nether proportions were mounted aloft on high heels, affixed to varnished and stiffened boots, or to shoes garnished with large buckles. The costume of the present court dress, with its accompaniments of plain cravats and lace ruffles, completes the picture.

The ladies of the court of Anne were befitting partners for such objects. Their hair was curled and frizzed, and in the early part of the eighteenth century it rose high, surmounted by a sort of veil or lappet, but diminished to a small caul with two lappets, termed a mob. Raised heels continued in vogue to a very late period; whilst hoops, in Anne's time, were in their infancy, commencing in what was then called a "commode," which gently raised and set out the flowing train. In this respect our fair ancestresses resembled our modern ladies; but in one essential point they differed greatly. Modesty of attire, brought into public estimation by the example of their truly respectable Queen, was uniformly studied; and the loose and indelicate style in which Sir Godfrey Kneller and Sir Peter Lely painted the female aristocracy, was to be seen no more.

With some deviations, the commendable practice of being adequately clothed, continued until after the time of Sir Joshua Reynolds, whose portraits bear out the fact, that decency of apparel in *his* days, as it had been in those before him, distinguished a gentlewoman from a female of loose character. Unhappily for the nineteenth century, this distinction is now thoughtlessly abandoned.

Concerning the immorality of our forefathers, many hints must necessarily, in the course of this work, escape, without any intention of enlarging upon so disagreeable a subject. There is little doubt but that the free strictures of the public press, conjoined with the influence and example of the court, served greatly to check the misrule and reckless profligacy which, even in the sober days of William, had been accounted spirited and fashionable by the young nobility and their sycophants. The "Hectors," a species of the *bravo genus*, were the

---

1. Noble, vol. 1, p. 386.

illustrious predecessors of the "Mohawks,"[2] whose inglorious courses have been the subjects of so much admirable satire from Addison,[3] and who have gradually subsided into a description of creature less dangerous, though perhaps equally reprehensible and offensive. The female portion of the community, among the higher ranks, are described by a contemporary writer to have been the slaves of punctilio and ceremony, and to have sat, in all the stateliness of their costume, "silent as statues"[4] in the company of men,—amongst whom alone cultivation of the intellect, in those days, had become general.

No sooner was a settled monarchy established, and the country relieved from the dreaded dangers of a second civil war, than literature revived, and resumed the flourishing aspect, though not the sound and vigorous condition, to which, in the days of Elizabeth, it had happily attained. The impoverished state of a great portion of the country, and the decay of many ancient and once wealthy families, rendered the pursuit of literature essential as a profession to those who preferred walking in the paths of science, or following the footsteps of the Muses, to the perilous duties of a soldier, or to the service of a church torn by contentions, and threatened with hourly destruction.

The profession of letters is supposed to have been at its height of prosperity during the middle and latter part of the reign of Anne. Some unpleasant peculiarities, however, attended its exercise. Since those days, the extension of education, and the general taste for knowledge which has consequently been diffused, have gradually effected a considerable change in the position of literary men. The lettered and the scientific are now able to rise to fame independent of individual patronage, excepting in instances of extreme poverty, by which the exertions are either shackled or turned into different and inferior channels.

In the times of Anne, that approbation of literary merit which is necessary to its existence, and which gradually swells into an universal tribute to genius, originated with the higher orders of society, or, at least, if unparticipated by them, languished and died away. In our own days, on the contrary, it is the testimony of the middle classes to merits which they are now qualified to discern, and the gratification which

---

2. See *Account of a Journey to England*, a scarce tract in the British Museum, written at the command of a nobleman in France. 1700.
3. These have since degenerated into the innocent race of dandies, that "domestic wonder of wonders," as a modern writer terms the species—*Sartor Resartus*, p. 284.
4. See *Letter to England*. B. M.

they manifest in the productions of the lettered world, which lead the way to what is vaguely called popularity. It is not easy to define the causes of this remark- able change in one part of our social economy.

From the exclusive enjoyment of the privileges of education, which were confined to the higher classes, and by them only moderately enjoyed, arose the system of patronage which, for nearly a century, regulated the commonwealth of letters. The benefits conferred proceeded solely from the nobility and richer gentry, amongst whom literature and the arts found that protection which is now derived from the common tribute of mankind. No distinction was accounted greater, among the nobility, than the power, and disposition, to reward literary merit. To be a patron of the learned, to protect, with more effectual aids than mere empty commendations, someone, if not several, of the needy wits who came to the metropolis on speculation, was as essential a line of conduct to any young nobleman who aspired to fashionable distinction, as it is now to belong to a certain order of society, or to possess the attributes, without which gentlemen, in every age, must sooner or later sink in the estimation of their own class.

There were few of the stately halls and pleasure saloons of the noblemen of that time, in which some learned dependent was not to be seen, sharing the festivities, and enhancing the social pleasures of the liberal patron, whom he failed not to repay in sonorous verse, or with dedications in prose, of lofty phraseology. The old system of remunerating dedications by sums of money, unhesitatingly offered and unblushingly received, prevailed even until the close of the eighteenth century. More solid advantages were also derived to the fortunate *literati* by patronage.

The celebrated St. Evremond took his seat at Devonshire-house, pensioned by its high-minded and noble owner, and experienced such liberality in England, that he declined returning to France, even when not only permitted, but encouraged to dwell in his native country. Dryden had his Buckingham and his Ormonde, *ducal* patrons with whom he lived on terms of familiarity; and Congreve had friends no less elevated in rank, the Dukes of Marlborough and of Newcastle. Halifax, as we have seen, was "fed with dedications," by Steele and others. Gay had his Queensberry, in whose stately abode he was absolutely domesticated. Innumerable other instances might be adduced.

The notorious fact, that whilst the middling and lower classes were generally indifferent to literature, the gay and the great mingled some attentions to it with all their daily frivolities and nightly revelries, may be accounted for, in the beginning of the last century, by the distinctions of Cavalier and Roundhead being not as yet wholly obsolete: the spirit, though not the form, of these distinctions remained. Before the civil wars, and as long as the Stuarts ruled, taste, fancy, wit, the culture of letters, and the patronage of the arts, were cherished by the highly-born and the well-bred, the more that they were avoided by the Puritans, as temptations to forget the grand business of life.

The young nobleman who had not some small amount of poetical fame, amplified into extraordinary fecundity of genius by the gratitude of poorer and wittier men, seemed to the world scarcely to have fulfilled his destiny, as a man born to all the luxuries of praise and fame. The commotions of the second James's reign, and the indifference of his grave successor to the interests of learning, checked, but did not annihilate the notion, that to nobility some exhibition of literary taste, and an extensive appreciation of it in others, were essential attributes.

The effect of this prevailing fashion of patronage on the one side, and of dependence on the other, was not to destroy our literature, assuredly, for never were its shoots so abundant, nor its blossoms so fair, as in the famed Augustan age; but whilst it called forth imaginative minds, and rendered the pursuit of letters a profession worthy of the name, in so far as emoluments might be procured, it debased the moral character of men in proportion as it rendered their intellectual powers marketable to the rich and the powerful.

Adulation became a trade; and when such base commodity was found to be in request, slander was soon perceived to be no less profitable to him who sped the arrow of calumny which flieth by night, or the pestilence of destruction by day. Indelicacy, and its consequence, immorality, being likewise acceptable, in an age when a father could jest with his son on the success of that son's *amours*,[5] the taste of the lofty and luxurious patron was even consulted by writers whose nobleness of thought and elevation of fancy might have led the world to expect better fruits from the growth of their own untrammelled inclinations.

Hence that mixture of "dissolute licentiousness and abject adulation," of which Johnson too justly accuses Dryden; but from which our older poets, the pure and exalted Milton, and his inimitable predecessors, "Shakspeare, Cowley, Spenser, were nobly exempt. The merriment, and the adulation of Dryden were, as Johnson also remarks, "artificial and constrained, the effects of study and meditation,—his

---
5. Lord Chesterfield.

trade, rather than his pleasure;" and the same may, with reverence, be observed of the prince of flatterers, the great, the little, the powerful, the weak, the satirical, the fawning Alexander Pope.

The system of patronage called into being another class of writers, who also "traded in corruption." These were the political pamphleteers of the day, a paid regiment, in which, to the disgrace of the sex, a female author, unparalleled in any day for the power of invention, or rather of perversion, received no slight encouragement in her gross and horrible attacks upon personal character, from the most eminent in rank and in intellect among the party by whom her services were hired.

Mrs. de la Rivière Manley, or Rivella as she was figuratively called, the pupil, in her early days, of the infamous Madame Mazarin, and the confidante of the scarcely less infamous Duchess of Cleveland, was the disseminator, if not the originator, of those calumnies which party spirit chose to affix to the characters of the Duke and Duchess of Marlborough, and of the latter in conjunction with Lord Godolphin. Her own history, translated from the French, and supposed in the narrative to be communicated by Louis Duc d'Aumont, ambassador in England, in 1712, to his friend General Tidcomb, whilst taking the air in Somerset-house garden, is said, by its dreadful details, sufficiently to prepare those who are condemned to read it, for the subsequent works of this wretched woman.

Of these, the most popular were her '*Atalantis*, the *History of Prince Mirabel's (*Marlborough's*) Infancy, Rise, and Disgrace, collected from the Memoirs of a Courtier lately deceased*," and the *Secret History of Queen Zarah and the Zarazians*,"[6] first published and inserted among the State Tracts by Dean Swift, in 1715.[7] This patronage on the part of Swift, which scarcely excites our wonder in the clergyman who could re-model and publish the *Tale of a Tub*, ceased only with the life of the abandoned Rivella, which closed at an advanced age, in 1724.

Dr. James Drake, the author of *The Memorial of the Church of England*, was a man of liberal education and of considerable attainments, which, unhappily for him, were applied to serve political rancour, instead of being confined to the medical profession, of which he was a member. Dr. Drake was a native of Cambridge, a Master of Arts in that university, and fellow both of the College of Physicians and of

---

6. On the copy of this work, (1712,) in the British Museum, are written these words, "*Splendidi Mendex*."
7. See Tract in British Museum.

the Royal Society. Yet he found it more profitable, notwithstanding the patronage of Sir Thomas Millington, to devote his talents to the service of booksellers, who quickly appreciated his powers of invective and ridicule. It was disappointment on not being made one of the commissioners of the sick and wounded, which induced Drake, after successive publications, to publish the *Memorial*, in conjunction with Mr. Foley, the member for Ipswich.

In this production, after referring to the death of King William, Drake comments upon the "numerous, corrupt, and licentious party throughout the nation, from which the House of Commons was sometimes not free," who might "entertain hopes, from the advantage of being at the helm, and the assistance of their rabble, to have put into practice their own schemes, and to have given us a new model of government of their own projection," and "to have mounted their own beast, the rabble, and driven the sober part of the nation like cattle before them."

That this was no conjecture was proved, the author stated, by the conduct of the party to the Queen, towards whom, "not contented with showing her a constant neglect and slight themselves, they also instructed their whole party to treat her with disrespect and slight. They were busy to traduce her with false and scandalous aspersions; and so far they carried the affront, as to make her at one time almost the common subject of the tittle-tattle of every coffee-house and drawing-room, which they promoted with as much zeal, application, and venom, as if a bill of exclusion had been then on the anvil, and these were the introductory ceremonies." [8]

Lord Godolphin, and certain other of the ministry, were so much scandalized at these comments, that they represented to Queen Anne that the publication was an insult to her honour, and prevailed upon Her Majesty to address both Houses upon the subject, in the Parliament which met October 27th, 1705. Accordingly, after a long debate, "it was voted that the church was not in danger," and Her Majesty was entreated to punish the authors of the *Memorial*.

The printer was accordingly taken into custody, and, being examined before one of the secretaries of state, deposed that the manuscript of the *Memorial* was brought to him by a lady in a mask, accompanied by another lady barefaced, who, together, stipulated to have two hundred and fifty copies printed, which were delivered to four por-

---

8. *Biographia Britannica*, art Drake.

ters sent by the parties who brought the *Memorial*. But although the lady without a mask and three of the porters were found. Dr. Drake remained undiscovered; and the indignant ministry were obliged to convict him upon another publication.

Drake was the editor of a newspaper, entitled *The Mercurius Politicus*, for which he was prosecuted in the Queen's Bench in the ensuing year, but acquitted upon a flaw in the information, the word nor being inserted in the written information, and, in the libel given in evidence, the word not. Eventually the prosecution killed Drake, for the anxieties attending it, and the ill-usage of some of his party, brought on a fever of which he died, bitterly exclaiming against the severity of his enemies. Thus speedily were extinguished an energetic spirit, and abilities adapted to higher purposes than those to which they were applied. Besides displaying in his writings great command of language, Dr. Drake possessed a well-stored and philosophic mind. Amid historical, political, and even dramatic works, he published a *New System of Anatomy*, which, met with deserved praise and success.[9]

It would require a work of some extent to describe the innumerable productions of the day in which the Duke and Duchess of Marlborough, under fictitious names, were alternately defamed and defended. The authors of these productions came forth like bats and owls, in the twilight and in darkness, when the political day of the great Colossus, as the Duke was called, and of "Queen Sarah," was overcast by the shades of night. They were for the most part answered, and they cannot, on the whole, be said to have affixed any stain upon the memory of the great hero, or on the more faulty conduct of the imperious favourite, whom they assaulted generally in the grossest manner, and with invective rather than facts.[10]

Attacks so violent as these soon pass out of remembrance, con-

---

9. *Biographia Britannica*. He wrote the *Sham Lawyer, or Lucky Extravagant*, which he declares on the title-page to have been "damnably acted" at Drury Lane.
10. It is not likely that many people will now take the trouble to read the answers to the Duchess s *Vindication*. The principal of these are, *Remarks on the Conduct of a certain Duchess, in a Letter from a Member of Parliament to a young Nobleman. 1742. The Other Side of the Question, in a Letter to her Grace, by a Woman of Quality. 1742.* The pamphlets for and against the Duke are numerous, and of various titles. *Oliver's Pocket Looking Glass, 1711, new-framed and cleaned, to give a clear view of the Great Modern Colossus. No Queen, or no General. 1712. Rufinus, or the Favourite; a Poem. Our Ancestors as well as We, or Ancient Precedents for Modern Facts*; with others of less imposing titles. *The Story of the St. Alb—ns Ghost, or the Apparition of Mother Haggy. 1712*: a coarse, disgusting attempt to satirize the Duke and Duchess and their family.

sumed in their own heat; for it is only the wary and well-directed operations of a cautious hand that wound, and injure, and endure. Already had the Duke, and Duchess, and their party a powerful, though latent foe, who, in the retirement of an Irish parsonage, divided his days between the gentler arts of deluding the affections, and alternately beguiling and breaking the hearts, of weak, but fondly disinterested women; and of advancing the cause of the church,—if those efforts could be called advancement, which disseminated immorality, whilst they advocated the constitution of the hierarchy.

Jonathan Swift, by all accounts the least loveable, and yet the most dangerous, of mankind, was at this time nominally a Whig, but a disappointed Whig, in his inert and chrysalis state, awaiting only the necessary change to become a Tory. Brought up in dependence, and his deportment as a "fine gentleman spoiled," as he declared, by a subservience half affectionate, half abject, towards his great patron, Sir William Temple,[11] the arbitrary, sarcastic, and selfish spirit of this most able, but most unhappy man, grew under the check of adversity, which cannot soften all natures. He was a tyrant,—from the domestic cruelty of forcing a guest to eat asparagus in King William's way,[12] to the monstrous ingratitude, indelicacy, and perfidy of influencing his supposed wife, the beautiful, the devoted Stella, to bear the imputed ignominy of being his mistress.

He was a time-server, as selfish men may be expected to become; and a calumniator, from the same narrow principles of self-advancement. Swift, at this period, was living in the unrestrained enjoyment of the attachment with which he had inspired the unhappy Stella, then scarcely twenty years of age, in all the bloom of that beauty of form and face which were destined to fade beneath the pressure of suspense, expectation, disappointment, and despair. Already had the moral profligate, if we may so call him, secured his Stella from the addresses of a respectable clergyman, who had applied to Swift in the capacity of the lady's guardian, acting in which office Swift had demanded such unreasonable terms of settlement, that the honest lover was unable to accede to them.[13]

This love of evasion, this mixture of moderation with passion, of prudence with grasping desires, marked the political, as well as the personal character of Swift. Generally speaking, the high churchmen

---

11. See Swift's *Journal to Stella.*
12. That is, stalks and all.—Quoted in Scott's *Life of Dean Swift.*
13. Scott, p. 73.

of those days were Tories, and the low churchmen Whigs. It is not easy to say why, except for the purposes of party, this should be the case; nor can we reasonably justify a suspicion that an ardent promoter of the principles of the Revolution, like Swift, could not be equally sincere in his ultra notions of liberty, and in his vehement advocacy of the high church cause. His subsequent abandonment of the Whig party confirms the uncomfortable and foreboding feelings with which we behold him, in one poem extolling the constancy of Archbishop Sancroft, who refused the oaths to William and Mary,[14] and, in another, on the burning of Whitehall,[15] declaring that nothing could purify that ancient palace, after the residence of the Stuarts. Speaking of James the Second—

He's gone—the rank infection still remains;
Which to repel requires eternal pains:
No force to cleanse it can a river draw,
Nor Hercules could do't, nor great Nassau.

It was not difficult to predict that Swift would be one of the first to lend his too powerful aid to darken the portraits of the Whigs, when any future cloud should throw a gloom over those services and talents which he once magnified and extolled.

The advocate of Somers, and of Halifax, Oxford, and Portland, in 1701, Swift had now become the friend of Addison, Steele, Arbuthnot, and other noted men, whom he met at Button's coffee-house, and to whom, not knowing his rare talents, nor hearing him at first even utter a syllable, they gave the name of "the mad parson." The appearance of the *Tale of a Tub*, in 1704, published in spite of his intimacy with the little knot of friends, called "Addison's senate," in order to benefit the interests of the high church party, by exposing the errors and corruptions of Popery, concentrated the goodwill of the Tory chiefs, who could not be blind to the powerful assistance of one who could aid them with the engine of ridicule.

But, in giving to the world this production, Swift proved himself to be, like many unprincipled men, near-sighted, and destroyed all hopes of that high preferment to which he aspired. Although the *Tale of a Tub* has since been claimed, but with no certainty, as the original idea of Somers,[16] and although it was, at the time of its publication, imputed to a pedantic and simple cousin of Swift, the real author was tolerably

---
14. *Ibid.*, p. 76.
15. *Ibid.*, p. 46.
16. See *Maddock's Life of Somers*; and also Cooksey's, p. 21.

well surmised, and eventually ascertained.[17]

The real lovers of religion, and the sincere adherents of the Church of England, were shocked and disgusted by this celebrated satire, and Queen Anne could never be prevailed upon to bestow on the author the preferment which he panted to obtain, by fair, or, if these were inexpedient, by any means.

If other statements are to be credited, one who held a high place in Her Majesty's confidence was the original framer of the bold composition.

Whether this conjecture be true or not, there is abundant reason to conclude that Swift enriched the original design by the effusions of his surpassing wit, to which he sacrificed the all-important considerations of character. It was not long before he gave proofs, that if he were not the sole author of the *Tale of a Tub*, he was fully capable of being so, by his Letter on the *Relaxation of the Sacramental Text*, which he also endeavoured, but vainly, to conceal.[18] But it was at a later period that Swift began that series of attacks upon the Duke and Duchess of Marlborough, and on their party, in his papers in the *Examiner*, a periodical paper set on foot by himself. Dr. Atterbury, St. John, Prior, Dr. Frend, and other Tory writers, after the administration had passed from the hands of Godolphin and Marlborough into those of Harley and his party.

To this powerful production, sustained with an apparent calmness and exactness of statement, which gave indescribable effect to its bitter remarks and searching analyses, the Duchess of Marlborough was indebted for much of her unpopularity, and Harley for a considerable proportion of his influence over the public mind.[19] The portion of the papers for which Swift was solely responsible, are acknowledged to be greatly superior to the subsequent essays. Swift himself prophesied the inferiority.

Upon the publication of number forty-four, which was the last he wrote, he intimated to his friends that the rest would be "trash for the future;" and the subsequent papers were, he says, "written by some under-spur leathers in the city, and were designed merely as proper returns to those Grubstreet invectives which were thrown out against

---

17. Swift, indeed, at the very moment that he was revising a new edition of the poem, wrote to his bookseller, hinting that he thought that his little parson cousin was at the bottom of the Tub.
18. Scott's *Life*.
19. See notes by Hawkesworth. Swift's *Works*.

the (Tory) administration by the authors of the *Medley* and the *Englishman*, and some other abusive detracting papers of the like stamp."

The result fully bore out this prediction; and the *Examiner*, of all the attacks which were made upon the Marlborough party and their friends, the most obnoxious to them, and beneficial to their enemies, soon sank in reputation, and altogether ceased. But its disparaging effects upon those whom it assailed were long experienced; and the party which this celebrated publication attacked, never recovered the popularity and stability which it first undermined.

Appendix

LETTER FROM MISTRESS WITTEWRONGE, DAUGHTER-IN-LAW OF SIR JOHN WITTEWRONGE, BART. OF ROTHAMSTED PARK, HERTS, TO THE DUCHESS OF MARLBOROUGH, REFERRING TO MRS. JENNINGS.

Sir John Wittewronge came to England from Ghent, in consequence of the persecutions of the Protestants in Flanders. One of his family was maid of honour to Queen Anne, probably through the interest of the Duchess, who appears from the letter to have been a friend of the family.

> May it please your grace, when your grace was last at St. Albans, I endeavoured to have the honour of making my duty in person, but word was brought me by the servant I sent, that your grace's stay there was soe short, that company was not expected; and not knowing when I may hope to have any opportunity of speaking, humbly crave pardon, that I presume to express myself in this manner, which I thought could not be well omitted without a seeming neglect, both of my duty and interest, since your grace will please to remember that it was told me I should be in a capacity in London ere it were long, which I took as a gracious intimation that some favour was intended for my husband, who, I am sure, will deserve it, and has no hopes from any other hand. I must own my affection to the memory of your noble mother, who honoured me with her love, and bestowed upon me many costly favours, which may seem an odd argument in my behalf to hope for more from your grace; but it is godlike to conferr new mercies on them who have been the objects of former ones without any merit,

especially upon such as are truly thankful for what they have received. I begg at least forgiveness, and shall ever remain
Your grace's most dutyfull
Thankful Servant,
Mary Wittewronge.
For her grace the Duchess of Marlborough.
(Endorsed in the handwriting of Mr. Wittewronge)
My wife to Duchess Marlb.

Extract from An Account of the Conduct of the Duchess of Marlborough. 1742.

From the Queen to Her Sister the Princess Anne.

Kensington, Friday, the 5th of Feb.

Having something to say to you which I know will not be very pleasing, I chuse rather to write it first, being unwilling to surprise you, although I think what I am going to tell you should not, if you gave yourself the time to think, that never anybody was suffered to live at court in my Lord Marlborough's circumstances. I need not repeat the cause he has given the King to do what he has done, nor his unwillingness at all times to come to such extremities, though people do deserve it

I hope you do me the justice to believe it is as much against my will that I now tell you, that after this it is very unfit Lady Marlborough should stay with you, since that gives her husband so just a pretence of being where he ought not

I think I might have expected you should have spoke to me of it. And the King and I, both believing it, made us stay thus long. But seeing you was so far from it that you brought Lady Marlborough hither last night, makes us resolve to put it off no longer, but tell you she must not stay; and that I have all the reasons imaginable to look upon your bringing her as the strangest thing that ever was done. Nor could all my kindness for you (which is ever ready to turn all you do the best way, at any other time,) have hindered me from showing you that moment, but I considered your condition, and that made me master myself so far as not to take notice of it then

But now I must tell you it was very unkind in a sister, would have been very uncivil in an equal, and I need not say I have more to claim: which though my kindness would make me never exact, yet when I see the use you would make of it, I must tell you I know what is due to me, and expect to have it from you. 'Tis upon that account I tell you plainly. Lady Marlborough must not continue with you in the circumstances her lord is.

I know this will be uneasy to you, and I am sorry for it; and it is very much so to me to say all this to you, for I have all the real kindness imaginable for you; and as I ever have, so will always do my part to live with you as sisters ought. That is, not only like so near relations, but like friends. And, as such, I did think to write to you. For I would have made myself believe your kindness for her made you at first forget that you should have for the King and me; and resolved to put you in mind of it myself neither of us being willing to come to harsher ways.

But the sight of Lady Marlborough having changed my thoughts, does naturally alter my stile. And since by that I see how little you seem to consider what even in common civility you owe us, I have told you plainly; but withall assure you, that let me have never so much reason to talk anything ill of you, my kindness is so great, that I can pass over most things, and live with you as becomes me. And I desire to do so merely from that motive; for I do love you as my sister, and nothing but yourself can make me do otherwise; and that is the reason I chuse to write this rather than tell it you, that you may overcome your first thoughts; and when you have well considered, you will find, that though the thing be hard, (which I again assure you I am sorry for,) yet it is not unreasonable, but what has ever been practised, and what you yourself would do, were you in my place.

I will end this with once more desiring you to consider the matter impartially, and take time for it. I do not desire an answer presently, because I would not have you give a rash one. I shall come to your drawing-room tomorrow before you play, because you know why I cannot make one; at some other time we shall reason the business calmly; which I will willingly do, or anything else that may show it shall never be my fault if we do not live kindly together; nor will I ever be other by choice but your truly loving and affectionate sister,

M. R.

The Princess Anne's Answer to the Foregoing Letter.

Your Majesty was in the right to think your letter would be very surprising to me. For you must needs be sensible of the kindness I have for my Lady Marlborough, to know that a command from you to part with her' must be the greatest mortification in the world to me; and, indeed, of such a nature, that I might well have hoped your kindness to me would have always prevented. I am satisfied she cannot have been guilty of any fault to you; and it would be extremely to her advantage if I could here repeat every word that ever she had said to me of you in her whole life. I confess it is no small addition to my trouble to find the want of your Majesty's kindness to me upon this occasion, since I am sure I have always endeavoured to deserve it by all the actions of my life.

Your care of my present condition is extremely obliging, and if you would be pleased to add to it so far as upon my account to recall your severe command, (as I must beg leave to call it, in a matter so tender to me, and so little reasonable, as I think, to be imposed upon me, that you would scarcely require it from the meanest of your subjects,) I should ever acknowledge it as a very agreeable mark of your kindness to me.

And I must as freely own, that as I think this proceeding can be for no other intent than to give me a very sensible mortification, so there is no misery that I cannot readily resolve to suffer, rather than the thoughts of parting with her. If, after all this that I have said, I must still find myself so unhappy as to be farther pressed in this matter, yet your Majesty may be assured, that as my past actions have given the greatest testimony of my respect both for the King and you, so it shall always be my endeavour, wherever I am, to preserve it carefully for the time to come, as becomes

Your Majesty's
Very affectionate Sister and Servant,
Anne.

From the Cockpit, Feb. 6th, 1692.

From the Princess Anne to the Queen.

I am very sorry to find that all I have said myself, and my Lord Rochester for me, has not had effect enough to keep your Majesty from persisting in a resolution which you are satisfied must be so great a mortification to me, as, to avoid it, I shall be obliged to retire, and deprive myself of the satisfaction of living where I might have frequent opportunities of assuring you of that duty and respect which I always have been and shall be desirous to pay you on all occasions.

My only consolation in this extremity is, that not having done anything in all my life to deserve your unkindness, I hope I shall not be long under the necessity of absenting myself from you; the thought of which is so uneasy to me, that I find myself too much indisposed to give your Majesty any farther trouble at this time.

February 8, 1692.

Two Letters of kindness from the Princess of Denmark to Lady Marlborough.

The Princess Anne to Lady Marlborough.

To Lady Marlborough.—I had last night a very civil answer from the Bishop of Worcester, whom I sent to speak with, but have heard nothing more of him since, so I dare not venture to go to London today for fear of missing him. If he comes in any time tomorrow, I will not fail of being with my dear Mrs. Freeman about five or six o'clock, unless you are to go to the Tower. And if you do, pray be so kind as to let me know time enough to stop my journey. For I would not go to London, and miss the satisfaction of seeing you. I could not forbear writing, though I had nothing more to say, but that it is impossible ever to express the kindness I have for dear Mrs. Freeman.

To Lady Marlborough from the Princess Anne.

To Lady Marlborough.—Sir Benjamin telling me you were not come to town at three o'clock, makes me in pain to know how your son does, and I can't help inquiring after him and dear Mrs. Freeman. The Bishop of Worcester was with me this morning before I was dressed. I gave him my letter to the Queen, and he has promised to send it, and seemed to undertake it very willingly; though, by all the discourse I had with him, (of which I will give you a particular account when I see you,) I find him very partial to her. The last time he was here, I told him you had several times desired you might go from me, and I repeated the same thing again to him. For you may easily imagine I would not neglect doing you right upon all occasions. But I beg it again for Christ Jesus's sake, that you would never name it any more to me. For be assured, if you should ever do so cruel a thing as to leave me, from that moment I should never enjoy one quiet hour. And should you do it without asking my consent, (which if ever I give you may I never see the face of heaven,) I will shut myself up, and never see the world more, but live where I may be forgotten by human kind.

THE DUCHESS OF MARLBOROUGH TO THE QUEEN.[1]

This letter proves that, so early as the year 1707, the good understanding between the Queen and her favourite was undermined.

August 7, 1707.

Lord Marlborough has written to me to put your Majesty in mind of Count Wrateslaw's picture, and in the same letter desires me to ask for one that he sent Lord Treasurer, which came from Hanover, which I have seen, and which I know you would not have me trouble you with; and I have been so often discouraged in things of this nature that I believe nobody in the world but myself would attempt it; but I know Mrs. Morley's intentions are good, and to let her run on in so many mistakes that must of necessity draw her into great misfortunes at last, is just as if one should see a friend's house set on fire, and let them be burnt in their bed without endeavouring to wake them, only because they had taken laudanum, and had desired not to be disturbed.

This is the very case of poor dear Mrs. Morley; nothing seems agreeable to her but what comes from the artifices of one that has always been reported to have a great talent that way. I heartily wish she may discover her true friends before she suffers for the want of that knowledge, but as to the business of calling for the Princess Sophia over, I don't think that will be so easily prevented as she (perhaps) may flatter herself it will, though I

---
1. Coxe MSS.

can't think there can be many, at least, that know how ridiculous a creature she is, that can in their hearts be for her. But we are a divided nation; some Jacobites that cover themselves with the name of Tory, and yet are against the crown. And whoever comes into the project of that sort must do it in hopes of confusion.

Others there are that are so ignorant that they really believe the calling over any of the House of Hanover will secure the succession, and the Protestant religion. And some of those gentlemen that do know better, and that have so many years supported the true interest against the malice of all the inventions of the enemies to this government, I suppose will grow easy, and be pretty indifferent at least in what they think may be of no ill consequence, further than in displeasing the court, not only in this of the Princess Sophia, but in anything else that may happen; and as Mrs. Morley orders her affairs, she can't expect much strength to oppose anything where she is most concerned.

Finding Mrs. Morley has little time to sparer unless it be to speak to those that are more agreeable, or that say what she likes on these subjects, I have taken the liberty to write an answer to this, which you will say is sincere, and can be no great trouble only to sign it with Morley.

Extract from the Duchess's Letter to Mr. Hutchinson, (This passage relates to the Duchess accepting two thousand pounds out of the privy purse: a sum which she had formerly refused from the Queen. Taken from the Coxe Manuscripts, vol. 43)

But to return to my own case. When the Queen had turned me out of my places, the next thing I had to do was to make up my accounts for the robes and privy purse, with all the care and exactness I could. But in the mean time, while some of my friends persuaded me to let the Queen be asked whether she would not allow me to take out of the privy purse the two thousand pounds a year which she had so often pressed me to accept, since the reason of my refusing it now ceased, when she turned me out of my places, I must confess it went much against me to desire anything of her; but when I considered how great a sum of money I had saved her by the management of my offices, the real service I had done her in many respects, and the dear hours of my life I had spent upon her for many years together, without either asking or having anything of her, (except those few trifles I mentioned before,) after she came to the crown, which any one would think was the proper time for her to have rewarded her old servants, I thought I should not be in her debt though she should give me what I had so often refused, and therefore that I might very well suffer myself to be governed by my friends in letting her be asked about this matter; and accordingly I consented that a copy of one of her own letters, in which she pressed me so much to take that money out of the privy purse, should be shown to her, and that the person who carried it should tell her that I desired to know, before I made up my accounts, whether she still was willing that I should take the money out of the privy purse according as she had desired me in that letter.

When this was proposed to her, she blushed and appeared to be very uneasy, and not disposed to allow of my putting that money into my accounts; but for want of good counsel or instructions to defend herself in refusing that which she had been so very earnest with me to accept before, she consented that I should do it Then I sent in my accounts with that yearly sum charged in them from the time she had offered it to me. But I still used this further caution, of writing at the bottom of the accounts, before I charged the last sum, a copy of the letter I mentioned before, that when she signed them, she might at the same time attest her own letter, and the offer she had made me of her own accord, and pressed me to take in this manner—

> *Pray make no more words about it, and either own or conceal it, as you like best; since I think the richest crown could never repay the services I have received from you.*

After this the Queen kept my accounts almost a fortnight by her, in which time I don't doubt but they were well examined by Abigal and Mr. Harley; but there was no fault which they could pretend to find with them, and they were sent back to me, without the least objection being made against them, signed by the Queen's own hand, who had writ under them that she allowed of them, and was satisfyed they were right; so that the new ministers had nothing left them in this matter but to whisper about the town some scandalous storys of it, and to employ

such of their agents as the *Examiner* in propagating them.
I don't pretend to give you any particular account of these, or any other abusive storys that were industriously raised of me, but leave you to judge of them by the matters of fact which I have now given you a relation of, and which I have told in so full a manner as I think will give you a clear notion of my whole behaviour in all the concerns I had with the Queen, and particularly with respect to everything in which she seemed to show any uneasiness towards me.

Extract from a Letter written by the Duchess of Marlborough, vindicating herself from the charge of selling places; and touching also upon other matters.—Taken from the Coxe Manuscripts, vol. 44, p. 2.

And upon the whole, I solemnly swear, as I hope for happiness here or hereafter, that besides the case of the pages to the Princess, which I have told you of, I never did receive the value of one shilling in money, jewells, or any such thing, either directly or indirectly, for the disposing of any employment, or doing any favour during my whole life, nor from any person whatsoever, upon any such account; and that if there is any man or woman upon earth that can give the least proof to the contrary, I am contented for the future to be looked upon both by friends and enemies, as one of the vilest of women, worse than Abigal herself when I consider her as instrumental in doing the greatest mischief that a nation can suffer; the reducing it from the most flourishing to at least a dangerous condition; and as acting the most ungratefully and injuriously to a person to whom she owes her very bread.
I may be thought, perhaps, in this to put my own vindication upon too ticklish a bottom, when it is considered how far the malice of men will go, in these times especially, in maintaining the greatest falsity against others, when they can serve their own purposes by it But as everybody ought to look upon all general reflections, where no proof is offered at, to be only mere aspersions; so I depend upon it that I shall be able to convict any man, to his own shame, that shall dare to produce any particular instance against me, of my having taken anything for the disposal of any employment I am sensible my enemies have not wanted inclination to have done this long ago, if there had been any room for it; and it is no small vindication of me,

that their own impudence, as great as it is in this respect, has not carried them so far as to offer at any proof against me of this nature.

There is another public vindication of me which I think I ought to take notice of, and that is, that soon after the Queen came to the crown, I was the cause of having the strictest orders made against taking of money for the disposing of places that were ever known at the court; which, how consistent it was with having any designs of my own of making money that way, I leave any one to judge. In the green cloth I found means of making it necessary, for every one that came into any employment there, to make an oath, in the strictest terms that could be, that he did not pay anything for it. And though I could not so easily procure any such effectual means to prevent the same practice with respect to the dispensing of other employments, yet I often pressed the Queen to do all that was possible in it; and upon this there was an order of council made, which everybody knows of about it. All this, I hope, is sufficient to clear me from anything cast upon me with respect to the disposal of employments.

Extract from a work called Sylva, or the Wood, published in 1788; describing the limited education of the Duchess, and the manner in which she delivered the Vindication of her Conduct, so often referred to in this Volume, to Mr, Hooke.[2]

The "old Sarah," as she was then called, published, in 1742, an *Account of her Conduct* under Queen Anne; which *account,* by the way, affords an excellent insight into the manoeuvres of a court, and would greatly confirm the idea given of it in the two preceding numbers. She was assisted herein, by Mr. Hooke, the historian, to whom, though oppressed with the infirmities of age, and almost bed-rid, she would continue speaking for six hours together. She delivered to him her account without any notes, in the most lively, as well as the most connected manner; and though the correction of the language is left to Hooke, yet the whole is plainly animated with her spirit; and as some philosophers have said of Saul with regard to body, she was *tota in toto, et tota in qualibet parte.* She was of a strong understanding and uncommon sagacity, which I premise to justify my wonder at the strange neglect of education among the females; for her woman would have

---

2. See chapter 9.

written as well, and perhaps better.

Here follow, merely as curiosities, two letters from her own handwriting, directed "For Doctor Clarke, att his haus near St. James' Church," without alteration of either grammar or orthography; that is *verbatim et liberatim,* as Mrs. Bellamy upon a like occasion expresses.

An Inventory of the Jewels belonging to the Duke and Duchess of Marlborough.—Copied from the Coxe Manuscripts, vol. 48.

	Weight.		Value.		
	Car.	Gr.	£	s.	d.
In the Duke of Marlborough's George, eleven jewels	0	95			
A brilliant of the first water, and very lively weight, in a ring; the gift of the Emperor . .	10	1¼	900	0	0
A brilliant drawing to the crown, and a fowle on one side; the gift of the king of Prussia, in a coulant to a cross	13	0¼	1,500	0	0
In her grace the Duchess of Marlborough's earrings, the two brilliants under . .	-	-	900	0	0
A fine spread brilliant, the bottom very deep, drawing upon the blue	6	2¾	450	0	0
A high-crowned brilliant, good water, and perfect cleane	7	0½	450	0	0
A clear lively stone, well spread, but a little drawing, (in the cross)	5	2¼	300	0	0
A fine stone of good water, perfectly cleane, but thin, (the middle stone of a button for a loope) .	2	3¼	150	0	0
A spread stone, but drawing to the crown, (in a collet for a little cross)	3	1¾	150	0	0
A good water, and a fine lively cleane brilliant, (in the cross)	4	1¾	130	0	0
A fine lively cleane stone, but drawing in the water, (in the cross)	4	2¼	130	0	0
The middle stone of a button for a loope, very white, extremely spread, and cleane and lively .	2	0¾	100	0	0
A very fine stone, in all perfection of colour and cleaness, (in the cross)	2	1¾	60	0	0
A cleane stone, a little drawing, (in the cross) .	2	2¼	60	0	0
A brilliant of the first water, and almost perfectly cleane, (in a ring)	5	0	210	0	0
One fassett diamond drawing	2	3¼	100	0	0
The other fassett drawing yellowish. The two middle stones of the button . . .	2	0¼	80	0	0
Forty-four fassetts in the loopes . . .	7	2	45	0	0
Sixteen fassetts in the buttons above . .	9	0	72	0	0
Two high fassett diamonds through the four points in buttons, each set round with eleven brilliants, all valued at . .			220	0	0

Forty-four fassett diamonds in the two loopes . . .	35	0	0
Twenty-two fassett diamonds in a buckle . . .	60	0	0
Two loopes with forty brilliants in them . . .	-	-	-
Twenty-four brilliants round the two brilliant buttons . .	-	-	-
Twelve buttons of the same sort	355	0	0
Twelve loopes that go with them	135	0	0
Two buttons of another fashion, with seven diamonds, each of them about the bigness of the middle stone . . .	130	0	0
Two loopes, with thirteen diamonds in each, and one large diamond at the bottom of each loope	210	0	0
Four buttons, with nine diamonds in each, of another fashion and smaller	50	0	0
Four loopes, with ten diamonds in each loope . . .	25	0	0
A fine large rose diamond, perfect cleane, set for a coulant .	360	0	
Five fossett diamonds in a cross	220	0	0
A pair of ruby earrings set with brilliants about them, and a cross and coulant set with diamonds, and a pearle necklace to it, with rubies mixt with them, all at . . .	90	0	0
A blue enamelled cross set with diamonds . . .	20	0	0
A pair of shoe-buckles set with fossett diamonds . . .	20	0	0
A large brilliant in a ring, in which is his grace the Duke of Marlborough's picture	800	0	0
Two rose diamonds cut through the pints, very high, cleane and lively	170	0	0
Two middle drops to earrings	160	0	0
Four side drops to ditto	70	0	0
A yellow rose diamond, set in a ring which his grace wears .	150	0	0
A large brilliant ring; the gift of the Emperor . .	1,500	0	0
A large rose diamond set in a ring; the gift of the King of Poland	1,500	0	0

Endorsed in the Duchess's handwriting with these words:

All the brilliants and other small diamonds, except those described in this book, were bought with the Duchess's own money, as likewise all the pearles of every sort The two best pendant drops cost of Mr. Dolbin 500*l*., and were once valued at 2,200*l*.

Dated December the 30th, 1718, from a book of Sarah Duchess of Marlborough's,—Additional Catalogue.

A large pearl necklace, containing thirty-nine pearls; the two end pearls are what are called pendant pearls.

Two very large pendant pearls that cost five hundred pounds, but are valued at more than double the price, set in earrings with two brilliant diamonds.

Two hundred and eighty-four pearls in a string, for a bracelet.

Three strings in a necklace, with a brilliant hook. Near four hundred pearls in three; and the hook contains sixteen diamonds.

One hundred and forty-seven pearls in a bracelet, with the Duke of Marlborough's picture.

Nine old pearls.

A pair of pendants, with eight false French pearls, set about with brilliants.

A pair of ruby earrings, with six drops, set round with diamonds.

A ruby cross, set round with diamonds.

In the necklace twenty-six fossett diamonds; all the rubies false but the middle one and those in the cross.

Five large diamonds in a cross; one very large one for the middle collet, one large one to buckle it behind, with two little ones: in all nine.

A brilliant buckle for a girdle, with sixteen diamonds.

A brilliant buckle for the Duke of Marlborough's picture, with eight diamonds and a drop.

Such another buckle for four pictures of my daughters.

The Duke of Marlborough's picture in a ring.

A large buckle for a girdle of fossets.

A buckle for a girdle of lesser fossets.

Four diamond buckles and loops, to put on the neck of a manteau.

Six diamond buckles and loops for manteau sleeves: there is in the loops for the sleeves one hundred and twenty-four diamonds, some brilliants, and some fossetts.

Fifteen loops set for stays, and eight buttons.

One very fine ring fossett set transparent

Six pendant drops set in a sprig, fossett stones all.

Six very fine brilliant drops in a pair of pendants, and two very fine fossetts for the earrings of those pendants.

A very large brilliant ring set transparent
Two pins with four fossett diamonds.
Sixteen collets set with cristalls and hair; sixty little brilliants set in collets to go between the cristalls.
A buckle for one of the bracelets with eight little brilliants and a drop.
Ten brilliant buckles for stays, and two taggs (one lost)
Eight little square buckles for a waistcoat, fossett, and ten taggs.
Seven little white brilliants, unset
A little yellow diamond for the hook of a necklace.
Madame d'Escalache's picture in a locket
Thirty-six brilliant collets, pretty large, for a necklace.
Seventeen of those diamonds generally used for the boddice.
A little bracelet with gold crosses.
A little locket of cristall with my Lord Godolphin's hair.
A pair of earrings with four pretty large brilliant diamonds.
Two little diamond hooks to set drops upon.
Fourty-four small diamonds set in fossetts.
Thirteen more of the same sort
Two small fossett drops with two little diamonds, for earrings.
Two diamond knotts with false blue stones, for earrings.
A large amethyst ring.
A small Turkey ring.
Two French pearls with diamond tops.
A pair of diamond knotts with false green earrings.
A pair of diamond knotts with eight false green stones.
A ring with my mother's hair, and four brilliant diamonds.
A gold snuff-box, with two of the Duke of Marlborough's pictures in it
A gold snuff-box, with the Duchess of Portsmouth's picture in it
A pair of shoe-buckles.
Lady Anne Egerton's and Lady Dye's diamonds, that are in use, are not in this account
Mr. Gibson valued the best pearl necklace by weight that was bought of the Duchess of Beaufort at six hundred and eight pounds, and said he would give so much for it to sell it again, in October, 1715; and besides that, there were five pearls added to it, bought of the Duchess of Montague.
A little diamond hook to a garnet necklace.[3]

---

3. This curious list proves the exact habits of the Duchess.

An Account of what the Grant of Marlborough House has cost the Duke and Duchess of Marlborough.[4]

Paid to Sir Richard Beeling, upon a pretended debt of Queen Dowager's, two thousand pounds.

Building the house, and making the garden, very near fifty thousand pounds.

That article seems almost incredible, but it is not really so extravagant as it appears, because it is the strongest and best house that ever was built; and if it were worth the trouble to look into old accounts when they signify nothing, I could prove what I have said by the payments out of the accounts. As to what has been paid for two grants in Queen Anne's time, there being a mistake in one of them which occasioned another, and the renewal in King George the First's time; likewise the fine and payments upon account of the four little houses to make the way, must have cost a good deal. But it is not worth the trouble of summing up the particulars.

The yearly rents I pay to the crown are five shillings; and thirteen pounds fifteen shillings for Marlborough-house; and thirteen pounds fifteen shillings for the four little houses. The land-tax for Marlborough-house is sixty pounds a year; for the four little houses I don't know what it is. The *Examiner* magnified the vast profit I had by this grant from the crown, which it never cost one shilling. Likewise a great value was set upon the advantage of the lodges in Windsor Park. None of the expense of building either was done by the crown; and it cost the Duchess of Marlborough a great sum of money to make those two lodges what they are, who lost an arrear due from King George the First, the allowance for keeping the Park.

After that, His present Majesty, by letters patent under the privy seal, bearing date the twenty-ninth day of June, in the second year of his reign, was pleased to grant to the ranger of the Great Park at Windsor an allowance of five hundred pounds a year in consideration of the charge of supplying hay for feed of the deer, and paying under-keepers, and gate-keepers, and other subordinate officers doing duty or service there, their wages; and to authorise and direct the payment of the said fee, salary, or allowance, at the receipt of the Exchequer, quarterly, out of his treasure applicable to the uses of his civil government

This salary was stopt by another order at Christmas, 1736, since

---
4. Coxe MSS., vol. 43, p. 158. Also copied from the Duchess's own writing.

which time the Duchess of Marlborough has been at the whole charge of all the payments in His Majesty's Park; notwithstanding that by her grant she has as strong a right to it as anybody can have from the crown. And though Queen Anne gave her this grant, at King George's coming to the crown she paid the usual fees as if it had been given her then, and which 'tis plain, by what has passed since, could not be taken from her. But she did not think it worth making a dispute about that There is likewise in the order to recall the payment, from the crown, that Mr. Bridgman should not continue his payment for an allowance he had for keeping one of the King's gardens in the Park.

That is a thing I don't pretend to have a right to have, for it is not in my grant; nor do I know more of it than that my Lord Ranelagh, when he reduced the prices of the gardeners to the crown, I suppose to please some former ranger before I had it, obliged the gardeners to pay a hundred pounds a year to the gardener that kept that garden in the Great Park. And likewise they paid an allowance out of theirs for keeping the garden that comes into the Little Park; and some allowance for some fruit-trees planted in that park. But I don't know the particulars of the last exactly, because I have computed that this grant of Marlborough-house, which the crown never paid one shilling for, besides the constant rent of the crown, and taxes, at fifteen hundred pounds a year. Now money is at three *per cent*

This statement terminates thus abruptly.

ALSO FROM LEONAUR
AVAILABLE IN SOFTCOVER OR HARDCOVER WITH DUST JACKET

THE RELUCTANT REBEL by William G. Stevenson—A young Kentuckian's experiences in the Confederate Infantry & Cavalry during the American Civil War..

BOOTS AND SADDLES by Elizabeth B. Custer—The experiences of General Custer's Wife on the Western Plains.

FANNIE BEERS' CIVIL WAR by Fannie A. Beers—A Confederate Lady's Experiences of Nursing During the Campaigns & Battles of the American Civil War.

LADY SALE'S AFGHANISTAN by Florentia Sale—An Indomitable Victorian Lady's Account of the Retreat from Kabul During the First Afghan War.

THE TWO WARS OF MRS DUBERLY by Frances Isabella Duberly—An Intrepid Victorian Lady's Experience of the Crimea and Indian Mutiny.

THE REBELLIOUS DUCHESS by Paul F. S. Dermoncourt—The Adventures of the Duchess of Berri and Her Attempt to Overthrow French Monarchy.

LADIES OF WATERLOO by Charlotte A. Eaton, Magdalene de Lancey & Juana Smith—The Experiences of Three Women During the Campaign of 1815: Waterloo Days by Charlotte A. Eaton, A Week at Waterloo by Magdalene de Lancey & Juana's Story by Juana Smith.

TWO YEARS BEFORE THE MAST by Richard Henry Dana. Jr.—The account of one young man's experiences serving on board a sailing brig—the Penelope—bound for California, between the years 1834-36.

A SAILOR OF KING GEORGE by Frederick Hoffman—From Midshipman to Captain—Recollections of War at Sea in the Napoleonic Age 1793-1815.

LORDS OF THE SEA by A. T. Mahan—Great Captains of the Royal Navy During the Age of Sail.

COGGESHALL'S VOYAGES: VOLUME 1 by George Coggeshall—The Recollections of an American Schooner Captain.

COGGESHALL'S VOYAGES: VOLUME 2 by George Coggeshall—The Recollections of an American Schooner Captain.

TWILIGHT OF EMPIRE by Sir Thomas Ussher & Sir George Cockburn—Two accounts of Napoleon's Journeys in Exile to Elba and St. Helena: Narrative of Events by Sir Thomas Ussher & Napoleon's Last Voyage: Extract of a diary by Sir George Cockburn.

AVAILABLE ONLINE AT **www.leonaur.com**
AND FROM ALL GOOD BOOK STORES

ALSO FROM LEONAUR
AVAILABLE IN SOFTCOVER OR HARDCOVER WITH DUST JACKET

ESCAPE FROM THE FRENCH by Edward Boys—A Young Royal Navy Midshipman's Adventures During the Napoleonic War.

THE VOYAGE OF H.M.S. PANDORA by Edward Edwards R. N. & George Hamilton, edited by Basil Thomson—In Pursuit of the Mutineers of the Bounty in the South Seas—1790-1791.

MEDUSA by J. B. Henry Savigny and Alexander Correard and Charlotte-Adélaïde Dard —Narrative of a Voyage to Senegal in 1816 & The Sufferings of the Picard Family After the Shipwreck of the Medusa.

THE SEA WAR OF 1812 VOLUME 1 by A. T. Mahan—A History of the Maritime Conflict.

THE SEA WAR OF 1812 VOLUME 2 by A. T. Mahan—A History of the Maritime Conflict.

WETHERELL OF H. M. S. HUSSAR by John Wetherell—The Recollections of an Ordinary Seaman of the Royal Navy During the Napoleonic Wars.

THE NAVAL BRIGADE IN NATAL by C. R. N. Burne—With the Guns of H. M. S. Terrible & H. M. S. Tartar during the Boer War 1899-1900.

THE VOYAGE OF H. M. S. BOUNTY by William Bligh—The True Story of an 18th Century Voyage of Exploration and Mutiny.

SHIPWRECK! by William Gilly—The Royal Navy's Disasters at Sea 1793-1849.

KING'S CUTTERS AND SMUGGLERS: 1700-1855 by E. Keble Chatterton—A unique period of maritime history-from the beginning of the eighteenth to the middle of the nineteenth century when British seamen risked all to smuggle valuable goods from wool to tea and spirits from and to the Continent.

CONFEDERATE BLOCKADE RUNNER by John Wilkinson—The Personal Recollections of an Officer of the Confederate Navy.

NAVAL BATTLES OF THE NAPOLEONIC WARS by W. H. Fitchett—Cape St. Vincent, the Nile, Cadiz, Copenhagen, Trafalgar & Others.

PRISONERS OF THE RED DESERT by R. S. Gwatkin-Williams—The Adventures of the Crew of the Tara During the First World War.

U-BOAT WAR 1914-1918 by James B. Connolly/Karl von Schenk—Two Contrasting Accounts from Both Sides of the Conflict at Sea During the Great War.

AVAILABLE ONLINE AT **www.leonaur.com**
AND FROM ALL GOOD BOOK STORES

www.ingramcontent.com/pod-product-compliance
Lightning Source LLC
Chambersburg PA
CBHW031622160426
43196CB00006B/247